Guide to
BREEAM

STUART BARLOW

RIBA Publishing

© Stuart Barlow, 2011

Published by RIBA Publishing, 15 Bonhill Street, London EC2P 2EA

ISBN 978 1 85946 425 0

Stock code 76424

The right of Stuart Barlow to be identified as the Author of this Work has been asserted in accordance with the Copyright, Design and Patents Act 1988.

The trade mark "BREEAM" is owned by the Building Research Establishment Limited and is registered in the United Kingdom, the European Community and may be pending or registered in other countries. *Guide to BREEAM* is an independent publication and neither it nor RIBA Enterprises Ltd is endorsed, sponsored, affiliated with or otherwise authorized by BRE Global Ltd, the Building Research Establishment Ltd, or their affiliated companies.

The symbols on the cover are copyright 3DReid and have been used with their kind permission.

British Library Cataloguing in Publications Data
A catalogue record for this book is available from the British Library.

Commissioning Editor: James Thompson
Project Editor: Alex Lazarou
Designed and typeset by Alex Lazarou
Printed and bound by Hobbs the Printers, Hampshire

While every effort has been made to check the accuracy and quality of the information given in this publication, neither the Author nor the Publisher accept any responsibility for the subsequent use of this information, for any errors or omissions that it may contain, or for any misunderstandings arising from it.

RIBA Publishing is part of RIBA Enterprises Ltd.
www.ribaenterprises.com

Contents

Introduction

This independent guide provides property industry professionals, whether architects, consultants, contractors or clients, and those who fund developments, with an overview of the sometimes confusing BREEAM 2011 process. It explains the scoring system, reveals 'quick wins' and clarifies the standard of evidence needed, articulating the rationale for and cost of BREEAM along the way. In short, it focuses on the practical aspects of achieving a respectable rating rather than just promoting the benefits of green building.

Chapter 1 explains why BREEAM Assessments are on the increase, how they are structured and what types of building can be assessed. Although still not mandatory, decent ratings are increasingly being required by planning authorities, funding agencies or by clients who invest in corporate social responsibility. Knowing how to get the most out of BREEAM will obviously enhance the chances of winning work from these sources.

Chapter 2 explains the background to the Assessment process. What needs to be considered before starting? What evidence should be provided to the Assessor? Who does what, and when? In particular, the chapter explains the underlying principles of the scoring system, revealing how Categories are weighted, and the concepts of minimum standards and Innovation credits. Finally, and importantly, it shows when different Issues need to be considered to maximise the final score, and how works carried out by landlords and tenants can impact on the Assessment.

Chapter 3 is structured from the design team's point of view and focuses on those credits which might be considered easier to achieve – the so-called 'quick wins'. Organised Issue by Issue, the guidance identifies three key classes of quick win: smart site selection, design and specification; requiring contractors to adopt environmentally friendly methods; and strategic commissioning of specialist consultants. The information is laid out in a consistent format covering every aspect of the process – prerequisite conditions, lists of required evidence pre- and post-completion, building-type variations, and so on.

Chapter 4 deals with the Issues which are not covered in the previous chapter and which, for one reason or another, are more difficult to capitalise on. These reasons include design complexity or expense, specific building-type requirements, and the need to undertake unusual or specialised design activities or services. Again, the information here is laid out in the consistent and accessible format adopted in Chapter 3.

Finally, Chapter 5 looks at the cost of BREEAM. It explores the benefit of targeting good scores – especially the Excellent rating – and the comparative costs of different credits.

Note that this guide specifically addresses the BREEAM 2011 Scheme for newly constructed buildings. There are other schemes, all of which fall outside the scope of this guide. These include:

- BREEAM In-Use, used to assess and improve the environmental performance of existing commercial, industrial, retail and institutional buildings
- BREEAM Communities, used to assist planners and developers to improve, measure and independently certify the sustainability of development proposals at the planning stage
- BREEAM Domestic Refurbishment scheme, being developed for use in assessing the sustainable refurbishment of existing housing developments
- The Code for Sustainable Homes, used to assess new housing
- EcoHomes 2006, currently used to assess the refurbishment of homes in England and all housing developments in Scotland
- ECOHomesXB, used by housing landlords to assess and monitor the environmental performance of their existing housing stock.

chapter one

Background to BREEAM

1.1 Introduction

Over its 20 years of existence, the Building Research Establishment's Environment Assessment Method (BREEAM) has aimed to provide:

- a credible, independently assessed sustainability label for buildings
- recognition of a building's sustainability credentials
- a driver to stimulate demand for sustainable buildings
- assistance to clients and designers in mitigating life-cycle impacts of buildings.

The auditing process undertaken by independent Assessors certainly meets BREEAM's first ambition. BREEAM-rated buildings (from the 2008 Scheme onwards) are now listed on the *Green-BookLive* website[1] and, with the introduction of the annual BREEAM Awards, BREEAM has begun to make its mark as a vehicle for recognising sustainability credentials in buildings. The Building Research Establishment (BRE) has always promoted BREEAM as a driver for change, and the sustainability performance standards required to achieve BREEAM ratings have certainly risen over the years. Whether it has been solely responsible for stimulating the demand for more sustainable buildings over recent years is debatable, but certainly each successive launch of a BREEAM Scheme has driven up the standards of assessed buildings. BREEAM is increasingly used to audit levels of sustainability performance, both by those who commission buildings and those who regulate their construction. The need to undertake a BREEAM Assessment at the post-construction stage, introduced as part of the BREEAM 2008 Scheme, has extended the auditing process to cover more of the stages of a building's life cycle. The extended influence of BREEAM on the ongoing operation of buildings is a recent development and is yet to be fully quantified.

As with all audit systems, BREEAM is not perfect, but it does offer a verifiable and independent assessment of the sustainability performance of building design and construction. The requirement for a BREEAM Assessment at the post-construction stage, before the final BREEAM certificate can be issued, has overcome the problem of Assessments being carried out only at the design stage. Yet the requirements of any audit system are, to some extent, arbitrary and BREEAM is no exception. For example, contaminated sites that are treated score better than uncontaminated sites, which therefore do not require treatment, regardless of location. Such anomalies seem illogical to many clients.

The aim of this Guide is to provide those who commission, design and construct buildings with an overview of the 2011 version of the BREEAM UK New Construction Scheme (BREEAM 2011). BREEAM 2011 has responded to the changing context of legislation and new standards by:

- accommodating the revised methodology used to calculate compliance in the 2010 version of *Part L2A: Conservation of Fuel and Power in New Buildings other than Dwellings* of the Building Regulations. The requirement to achieve a 25 per cent aggregate reduction in carbon emissions meant that it was no longer possible to use a single benchmark scale based on an Energy Performance Certificate Carbon Index Rating. Continuing this approach might have resulted in some buildings which just comply with the Building Regulations scoring better in a BREEAM Assessment than buildings with lower carbon emissions
- aligning BREEAM's methodologies with the emerging raft of European construction sustainability standards which will operate at the framework, building and product levels. BS EN 15643: *Part 1 Sustainability of Construction Works – Sustainability Assessment of Buildings: General Framework* has already been published. It establishes a framework of principles, objectives and requirements for the sustainability assessment of buildings. More standards will be published throughout 2011 and 2012 to establish frameworks for the environmental, social and economic assessment of buildings, core rules for the environmental assessment of construction products and calculation methods for the environmental assessment of buildings
- aligning BREEAM with international standards such as the United Nations Environment Programme Sustainable Buildings and Climate Initiative's *Common Carbon Metric for Measuring Energy Use and Reporting Greenhouse Gas Emissions from Building Operations*
- satisfying the requirements of BRE's own recently launched *Code for Sustainable Environment*, which requires an integrated approach to design, management, evaluation and certification of environmental, social and economic impacts of buildings
- responding to industry feedback through BRE's own survey and the consultation undertaken by the UK Green Building Council to provide *market-focused but science-led* procedures.

BRE wants BREEAM to be the barometer of sustainable construction within the UK by measuring, evaluating and recording a building's performance during construction and operational life-cycle stages against best practice sustainability benchmarks. In addition to the current list of BREEAM-certified buildings, BRE intends to make data relating to metrics, such as carbon emissions, water consumption, waste generated and indoor air quality, available to the public in the future, which could prove very useful to designers and clients.

1.2 Why undertake a BREEAM Assessment?

There are a number of reasons for carrying out a BREEAM Assessment to audit the sustainability performance of a building. For example, it might:

- be a requirement of the client organisation, to help them to demonstrate that they are meeting their corporate social responsibility objectives
- be a prerequisite for receiving public or private development funding
- demonstrate an acceptable level of sustainability performance to regulatory approval bodies, such as planning authorities
- provide a marketable, sustainable asset.

The private sector property landlord and developer, British Land, is an example of a client organisation using BREEAM to assess and report on progress towards achieving its corporate social responsibility objectives.[2] British Land requires its major office developments to achieve a BREEAM Excellent rating and landlord areas of major retail developments to aim to achieve BREEAM Very Good.[3] Land Securities, another private sector client organisation, also requires its new major office and retail shopping centre developments to achieve BREEAM Very Good.[4] Similarly, the retailer Marks and Spencer set a target of BREEAM Excellent for the fitting out of their new stores and warehouses.[5]

Just as the Homes and Communities Agency requires housing to achieve a minimum *Code for Sustainable Homes* performance standard in order to receive public funding, in 2005 the then Department for Education and Skills made it a condition of any grant of capital funding that schools be designed and constructed to achieve a BREEAM Very Good rating. This applied to all new major school buildings and refurbishment of existing schools over a certain capital value.[6]

In 2007, a BRE study found that over 200 local authorities intended to use or were considering using BREEAM to set a sustainability performance standard of BREEAM Very Good for non-residential developments, within their Local Development Frameworks, core polices or supplementary planning documents.[7] Examples of this can be seen in:

- Manchester City Council's 'Guide to Development in Manchester – Supplementary Planning Document and Planning Guidance' which encourages developments to achieve BREEAM Very Good.[8]
- South Gloucestershire Council's 'Design Checklist Supplementary Planning Document', which requires developments to achieve BREEAM Very Good.[9]
- Ashford Borough Council's 'Local Development Framework Sustainable Design and Construction SPD', which requires all major developments to achieve various BREEAM ratings depending on location.[10]
- More recently, in 2010, the new Welsh Assembly Government's *Planning Policy Wales: Edition 3* (July 2010) required all non-residential planning applications for buildings over 1,000 m^2 or for sites of 1 hectare or more to achieve BREEAM Very Good standard, and the mandatory credits for Excellent in relation to the reduction of CO_2 emissions.[11]

While slow in coming, there is now growing evidence that sustainable buildings are already, and will increasingly become, more marketable than those which are not sustainable. A survey in 2007 showed that while 30 per cent of property investors and agents felt that sustainability issues affected property yields at that time, 60 per cent felt they would do so in the future. Subsequent research in 2008, by CB Richard Ellis, found that in Central London *energy efficiency* was an essential requirement for 58 per cent of tenants and *green attributes* an essential requirement for 50 per cent of tenants. More specifically, recent research into the London property market shows clear positive impacts relating to the use of BREEAM. It found that offices designed and constructed to meet the performance standards required for BREEAM Excellent are attracting a 22–27 per cent premium on their rents.[12]

1.3 The BREEAM Assessment process

The typical process of undertaking a BREEAM Assessment comprises a number of key stages. Figure 1.1 sets these against a typical building design and procurement timeline to show when key decisions have to be made by the client and the design team. These key stages are:

- deciding to carry out a BREEAM Assessment
- appointing a BREEAM Assessor
- appointing an Accredited Professional (AP)
- carrying out the pre-assessment
- registering the project
- carrying out the design stage assessment
- undertaking the post-construction stage assessment.

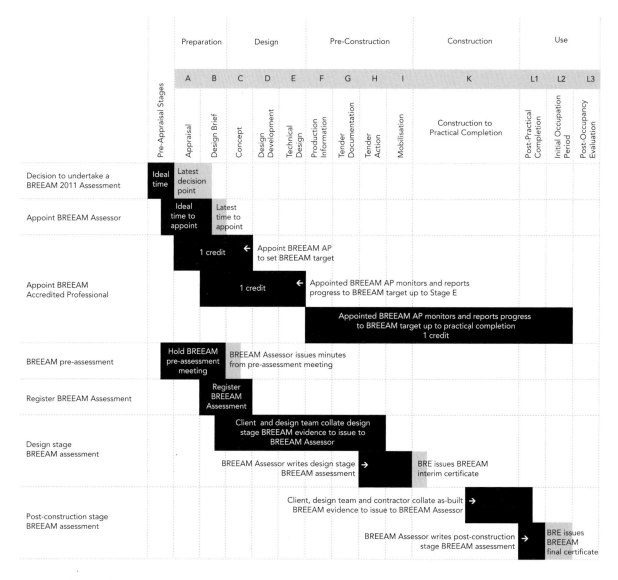

FIGURE 1.1: BREEAM timeline

Deciding to carry out a BREEAM Assessment

On any project the client is ultimately responsible for deciding whether or not to undertake a BREEAM Assessment. As already described, there are a number of drivers that influence this decision. The earlier the decision is taken, the easier it will be to achieve the required standard without affecting either the client's aspirations or the design solution (as described in Chapter 2). Ideally, the decision should have been taken before any appraisal work begins (that is, before RIBA Stage A as indicated on Figure 1.1) and certainly before the client's brief is started. There will also be less impact on costs (as explained in Chapter 5).

Appointing a BREEAM Assessor

Once the decision is made, the client will have to appoint an Assessor, qualified for the Scheme appropriate for the proposed building, and who works for a licensed organisation (whether as a sole trader or for a larger company). All Assessors are registered under the BRE Global Competent Persons Scheme and must have completed a training course (each Scheme requires separate training), passed the BREEAM examination and undertaken a test Assessment. Assessors are also audited by BRE to ensure they achieve a satisfactory standard. Details of all licensed organisations, their Assessors and the Schemes that they are qualified to undertake are available through BRE's *GreenBookLive* website.[13]

The Assessor should be appointed as early as possible, ideally before any appraisal work (RIBA Stage A as indicated on Figure 1.1) and never after the completion of the Design Brief (RIBA Stage B as indicated on Figure 1.1). This will allow the Assessor to advise the design team on what is required to achieve the required rating. It should be remembered, however, that the Assessor is there to audit information provided by the design team and client; it is not their job to generate the information.

Appointing a BREEAM Accredited Professional (AP)

A BREEAM AP is a consultant with specialist skills in sustainability and environmental design and a high level of competence in the Assessment process. Their role goes beyond that of an Assessor by providing expert advice, on a more regular basis than an Assessor, on the Issues that need to be addressed to achieve a particular rating. Appointing a BREEAM AP is worth up to **three credits** in the Assessment, depending on when and for how long the BREEAM AP is appointed, as indicated on Figure 1.1 (see Chapter 2 for details). This service will involve an additional fee for the client. A list of BREEAM APs can also be found on BRE's *GreenBookLive* website.[14]

The pre-assessment

This is the most important stage of the BREEAM process and should, ideally, be done before undertaking any feasibility work (as indicated on Figure 1.1) and certainly before the design brief is completed. The pre-assessment is carried out during a meeting in which the Assessor explains the process to the client and the design team. The client and the design team also agree a target rating with the Assessor. This meeting provides an opportunity to understand which BREEAM Issues and associated credits will have to be considered to achieve the target. The Assessor uses the BREEAM pre-assessment estimator tool to calculate the likely score and rating at the meeting. This stage is critical. It helps to identify the challenging performance requirements for the various Issues, allowing the design team to plan their design strategies accordingly. It also reveals which Issue credits simply cannot be achieved, allowing the design team and the Assessor to agree alternative Issue credits to be targeted to compensate for their loss.

The Assessor will issue minutes of this meeting, and usually a report, to the client and design team confirming the agreed rating and what evidence will be required to achieve the Issue credits targeted. This allows the client and the design team to programme the collation of the required evidence in time for the Assessor to complete the Assessment.

Registering the project

This is a simple online process which the Assessor undertakes using the BREEAM extranet website for Assessors. The following information is required:

- details of the client and Assessor
- address of the proposed building
- the Scheme to be used for the Assessment
- whether the project is new build, refurbishment, part new build and part refurbishment or a fit-out of an existing building
- the number of buildings being assessed – this can be important when a single assessment is proposed to cover a number of similar buildings on a site
- the net floor area of the building
- a brief description of the building and its services.

In some Schemes it is possible to assess a number of separate but similar buildings or units on the same site to provide a single rating for the whole site. To do this, however, the buildings must fulfil the same function and be completed to a similar specification. Credits will be awarded based on the worst performing building on the site.

The design stage assessment

Armed with the information that the client and design team agreed to provide at the pre-assessment meeting, the Assessor can then write the Design Stage Assessment Report. This is ideally completed just before construction starts on site or shortly afterwards. The Assessor audits the design intent in the design team's drawings, specifications and tender documentation. He or she also tests the client's commitment to meeting the requirements to achieve the criteria of the various Issues. Finally, he or she determines whether the evidence provided complies and awards the appropriate number of credits, thus determining the Interim BREEAM score. The Design Stage Assessment Report is usually issued to the client and design team as a draft in the first instance, typically including requests for missing information that is preventing the design from achieving a particular credit or credits. Once the client or the design team has provided the missing information, the Assessor can re-evaluate the Assessment and the final Design Stage Assessment Report will be completed. This will confirm the interim BREEAM score and rating, and will be submitted to BRE. Following quality assurance checks, BRE will issue the Interim BREEAM Certificate to the Assessor, who will pass it on to the client and the design team.

The post-construction stage assessment

At the end of the construction phase, the Assessor must audit the evidence of the building's as-constructed condition against the performance standards achieved in the Design Stage Assessment Report and the requirements for post-construction evidence. This will involve the Assessor visiting the site and completing a site inspection report, with photographs, to verify that the required standards have been achieved, and meeting with the principal contractor, design team and client to review the as-constructed information. This audit forms the basis of the Post-Construction Stage Assessment Report in which the Assessor will determine a final score and is carried out after practical completion.

It is possible to undertake a post-construction assessment without a Design Stage Assessment Report by simply auditing information provided at the post-construction stage against the criteria of all of the BREEAM Issues. This is an extremely bad idea and should not be contemplated unless unavoidable. It will be very difficult, however good the intentions, to achieve a high BREEAM rating because the award of certain credits requires activities or decisions, in relation to certain Issues, to be undertaken or made at the right time within the design process. These deadlines are unlikely to be met if an Assessment is left to this late stage in the process.

Occasionally, the as-constructed information supplied is inadequate and the Assessor is unable to award credits that had been provisionally awarded in the Design Stage Assessment Report. The Assessor will usually issue requests for any missing information in a draft Post-Construction Stage Assessment Report before finalising it. On receipt of any missing information, the Assessor will amend the Post-Construction Stage Assessment Report if appropriate, confirm the final score and rating and then submit it to BRE for quality assurance checks. BRE will then issue the final BREEAM Certificate to the Assessor, who passes it to the client and the design team.

1.4 The structure of a BREEAM Assessment

While BREEAM 2011 covers many different non-domestic building types, they are all assessed in essentially the same way. BREEAM 2011 consists of nine BREEAM *Categories* (plus an *Innovation* Category) divided into 48 *Issues*. The categories are:

- **Management**, which deals with sustainable procurement, responsible construction practices, construction site impacts, stakeholder participation (including consultation with relevant parties, accessible design, building user information and post-occupancy evaluation), life-cycle costing and service-life planning
- **Health and Wellbeing**, which deals with those aspects of a design that impact on the health or wellbeing of building occupants, including visual and thermal comfort, indoor air and water quality, acoustic performance, and providing low-risk, safe and secure access to and use of buildings
- **Energy**, which deals with the reduction of carbon emissions, including the use of energy-efficient building services, plant and equipment, low- or zero-carbon energy-generating technologies, and the ability to monitor energy use by sub-metering
- **Transport**, which deals with access to adjacent public transport networks and local amenities, along with the provision of information on travel options to building occupants, the provision of cyclist facilities and the limitation of car parking
- **Water**, which deals with opportunities for reducing water consumption through the use of efficient sanitary ware, the reuse and recycling of water, the provision of leak detection and prevention of leaks, monitoring controls and the provision of water-efficient equipment
- **Materials**, which considers the embodied life-cycle environmental impacts of materials, the use of responsibly sourced materials and the robustness of the building fabric
- **Waste**, which deals with reducing construction waste, the possible use of recycled

aggregates, the provision of space to encourage operational recycling and encouraging the specification of finishes by the building's occupants

- **Land Use and Ecology**, which considers the environmental impact of site selection including its ecological value and the protection of existing ecological features, mitigating the impact on and enhancing the ecological value of a site and limiting any long-term impacts on a site's biodiversity
- **Pollution**, which deals with the impacts of refrigerants and nitrous oxide emissions, the impacts of surface water run-off from a site and the impact of light and noise pollution on neighbours
- **Innovation** – the BREEAM 2008 Scheme introduced additional credits that could be awarded in recognition of achieving either exemplary levels of performance (above best practice performance currently recognised by BREEAM) in certain Issues or for incorporating innovative sustainability solutions within a building's design. This can help to boost a building's BREEAM performance (see Chapter 2 for a detailed explanation).

The Assessor has to consider whether the evidence provided by the client, design team and contractor demonstrates that a building's design and as-constructed condition complies with the performance criteria given for each of the Issues, in each of the above Categories in order to determine how many credits can be awarded in relation to each Issue. The Assessor will employ a number of proprietary assessment tools and calculators for use with BREEAM 2011 to do this.

BREEAM is structured to allow what BRE calls a 'balanced score card' approach to the assessment of a building's performance against Issues. This allows non-compliance in one Issue to be offset against another. Of course, certain Issues are so fundamental to achieving minimum performance standards that they cannot be offset in this way (see Chapter 2 for more detail).

Table 1.1 shows which Issues, and the number of credits available, could be applied to the different building types. This can vary between specific Assessments to reflect what facilities might be present with a particular building. It can be seen that each of the Categories, with the exception of one, has a similar number of Issues against which each project's performance will be assessed. The exception is the Energy Category, which contains nine Issues. This reflects the importance of energy consumption in buildings and the resultant carbon emissions.

Issues can have different values, measured in credits, ranging from one to, in one instance, 15. Of the 60 per cent of Issues in any Assessment that are awarded either one or two credits, around half are awarded one credit and the other half, two credits. A total of 19 per cent have between three and four credits, and another 17 per cent between five and six credits. Only two Issues can score more than six credits. One is in the Management Category, *Man01: Sustainable procurement*, which has eight credits available; the other is *Ene01: Reduction of CO_2 emissions*, in the Energy Category, where up to 15 credits are available.

Before the 2011 edition, each Scheme had its own separate manual containing specific assessment criteria relating to that building type. This meant that there were between 90 and 100 separate Issues (plus Innovation Issues) across all of the Schemes. BREEAM 2011 has consolidated these into a single BREEAM manual with just 48 Issues. This has been achieved partly by merging around 55 Issues from BREEAM 2008 into 17 Issues in the 2011 edition. Even so, the 2011 edition still includes different assessment criteria specific to the different building types. Some Issues only

TABLE 1.1: BREEAM 2011 – Categories and Issues, credits and schemes

	Commercial buildings		Non-housing buildings							
	Offices	Retail	Industrial	Educational (schools)	Educational (higher education)	Healthcare	Prisons	Courts	Multi-residential buildings	Other buildings
Management Category			12% weighting towards BREEAM score							
Man01: Sustainable procurement	8	8	8	8	8	8	8	8	8	8
Man02: Responsible construction practices	2	2	2	2	2	2	2	2	2	2
Man03: Construction site impacts	5	5	5	5	5	5	5	5	5	5
Man04: Stakeholder participation	4	4	4	4	4	4	4	4	4	4
Man05: Life-cycle cost and service life planning	3	3	3	3	3	3	3	3	3	3
Total credits available in Management Category	22	22	22	22	22	22	22	22	22	22
Weighted % score of 1 credit in Management Category	0.55	0.55	0.55	0.55	0.55	0.55	0.55	0.55	0.55	0.55
Health and Wellbeing Category			15% weighting towards BREEAM score							
Hea01: Visual comfort	3	4	3	3	4	5	3	3	3	3
Hea02: Indoor air quality	4	4	4	6	6	6	4	4	4	6
Hea03: Thermal comfort	2	2	2	2	2	2	2	2	2	2
Hea04: Water quality	1	1	1	1	1	1	1	1	1	1
Hea05: Acoustic performance	2	2	2	3	2	2	2	2	4	2
Hea06: Safety and security	2	2	2	2	2	2	2	2	2	2
Total credits available in Health and Wellbeing Category	14	15	14	17	17	18	14	14	16	16
Weighted % score of 1 credit in Health and Wellbeing Category	1.07	1.00	1.07	0.88	0.88	0.83	1.07	1.07	0.94	0.94
Energy Category			19% weighting towards BREEAM score							
Ene01: Reduction of CO_2 emissions	15	15	15	15	15	15	15	15	15	15
Ene02: Energy monitoring	2	2	2	2	2	2	1	1	1	2
Ene03: External lighting	1	1	1	1	1	1	1	1	1	1
Ene04: Low- and zero-carbon technologies	5	5	5	5	5	5	5	5	5	5
Ene05: Energy-efficient cold storage	0	2	2	0	2	2	0	0	0	2
Ene06: Energy-efficient transportation systems	2	2	2	2	2	2	2	2	2	2
Ene07: Energy-efficient laboratory systems	0	0	0	1	5	0	0	0	0	5
Ene08: Energy-efficient equipment	2	2	2	2	2	2	2	2	2	2
Ene09: Drying space	0	0	0	0	0	0	0	0	1	0
Total credits available in Energy Category	27	29	29	28	34	29	26	26	27	34
Weighted % score of 1 credit in Energy Category	0.70	0.66	0.66	0.68	0.56	0.66	0.73	0.73	0.70	0.56

Table 1.1 continued overleaf

TABLE 1.1 *continued*

	Commercial buildings	Non-housing buildings								
	Offices	Retail	Industrial	Educational (schools)	Educational (higher education)	Healthcare	Prisons	Courts	Multi-residential buildings	Other buildings
Transport Category	8% weighting towards BREEAM score									
Tra01: Public transport accessibility	3	5	3	3	5	5	2	5	3	5
Tra02: Proximity to amenities	1	1	1	1	1	1	0	1	2	1
Tra03: Cyclist facilities	2	2	2	2	2	2	1	2	1	2
Tra04: Maximum car parking capacity	2	0	2	0	2	1	0	0	2	2
Tra05: Travel plan	1	1	1	1	1	1	1	1	1	1
Total credits available in Transport Category	9	9	9	7	11	10	4	9	9	11
Weighted % score of 1 credit in Transport Category	0.89	0.89	0.89	1.14	0.73	0.80	2.00	0.89	0.89	0.73
Water Category	6% weighting towards BREEAM score									
Wat01: Water consumption	5	5	5	5	5	5	5	5	5	5
Wat02: Water monitoring	1	1	1	1	1	1	1	1	1	1
Wat03: Water leak detection and prevention	2	2	2	2	2	2	2	2	2	2
Wat04: Water-efficient equipment	1	1	1	1	1	1	1	1	1	1
Total credits available in Water Category	9	9	9	9	9	9	9	9	9	9
Weighted % score of 1 credit in Water Category	0.67	0.67	0.67	0.67	0.67	0.67	0.67	0.67	0.67	0.67
Materials Category	12.5% weighting towards BREEAM score									
Mat01: Life-cycle impacts	5	5	2	6	6	6	4	6	6	6
Mat02: Hard landscaping and boundary protection	1	1	1	1	1	1	1	1	1	1
Mat03: Responsible sourcing of materials	3	3	3	3	3	3	3	3	3	3
Mat04: Insulation	2	2	2	2	2	2	2	2	2	2
Mat05: Designing for robustness	1	1	1	1	1	1	1	1	1	1
Total credits available in Materials Category	12	12	9	13	13	13	11	13	13	13
Weighted % score of 1 credit in Materials Category	1.04	1.04	1.39	0.96	0.96	0.96	1.14	0.96	0.96	0.96
Waste Category	7.5% weighting towards BREEAM score									
Wst01: Construction waste management	4	4	4	4	4	4	4	4	4	4
Wst02: Recycled aggregates	1	1	1	1	1	1	1	1	1	1
Wst03: Operational waste	1	1	1	1	1	1	1	1	1	1
Wst04: Speculative floor and ceiling finishes	1	0	0	0	0	0	0	0	0	0
Total credits available in Waste Category	7	6	6	6	6	6	6	6	6	6
Weighted % score of 1 credit in Waste Category	1.07	1.25	1.25	1.25	1.25	1.25	1.25	1.25	1.25	1.25

	Commercial buildings		Non-housing buildings							
	Offices	Retail	Industrial	Educational (schools)	Educational (higher education)	Healthcare	Prisons	Courts	Multi-residential buildings	Other buildings
Land Use and Ecology Category	10% weighting towards BREEAM score									
LE01: Site selection	2	2	2	2	2	2	2	2	2	2
LE02: Ecological value of site and protection of ecological features	1	1	1	1	1	1	1	1	1	1
LE03: Mitigating ecological impact	2	2	2	2	2	2	2	2	2	2
LE04: Enhancing site ecology	3	3	3	3	3	3	2	3	3	3
LE05: Long-term impact on biodiversity	2	2	2	2	2	2	3	2	2	2
Total credits available in Land Use and Ecology Category	10	10	10	10	10	10	10	10	10	10
Weighted % score of 1 credit in Land Use and Ecology Category	1.00	1.00	1.00	1.00	1.00	1.00	1.00	1.00	1.00	1.00
Pollution Category	10% weighting towards BREEAM score									
Pol01: Impact of refrigerants	3	3	3	3	3	3	3	3	3	3
Pol02: NO$_x$ emissions	3	3	2	3	3	3	3	3	3	3
Pol03: Surface water run-off	5	5	5	5	5	5	5	5	5	5
Pol04: Reduction of night time light pollution	1	1	1	1	1	1	1	1	1	1
Pol05: Noise attenuation	1	1	1	1	1	1	1	1	1	1
Total credits available in Pollution Category	13	13	12	13	13	13	13	13	13	13
Weighted % score of 1 credit in Pollution Category	0.77	0.77	0.83	0.77	0.77	0.77	0.77	0.77	0.77	0.77
Innovation credits										
Total credits available in Innovation Category	10	10	10	10	10	10	10	10	10	10
Weighted % score of 1 Innovation credit	1.00	1.00	1.00	1.00	1.00	1.00	1.00	1.00	1.00	1.00

apply to certain building types or buildings that contain certain functions or equipment, such as lifts or escalators. This reflects different functions, stakeholder and end-user requirements of the various building types covered. The hope is that this will make the process clearer, more flexible and more consistent, especially when assessing mixed-use buildings.

Once credits have been awarded for each Issue in a Category, they are totalled and given a weighting to establish a Category score expressed as a percentage. The Category scores are then totalled to calculate the final score. BRE believes that weighting each Category's score differently helps to define and rank the relative importance of each Category's environmental impact. The weightings used are the result of consultation with industry stakeholders combined with input from a panel of experts to gain a consensus. The weightings for each Category are shown in Table 1.1 (see Chapter 2 for further details on the impact of weighting on credits). An additional 1 per cent can also be added to the final percentage score for each Innovation Category credit awarded. However, the maximum number of Innovation Category credits that can be awarded in any Assessment is ten, so there is the potential to add up to 10 per cent to the final score. The procedure for awarding Innovation Category credits is detailed in Chapter 2.

Once the final score is calculated, a rating can be determined. The range of ratings that can be given and the scores required are:

- **Unclassified** for a score of less than 30 per cent
- **Pass** for a score that is equal to or more than 30 per cent, but less than 45 per cent
- **Good** for a score that is equal to or more than 45 per cent, but less than 55 per cent
- **Very Good** for a score that is equal to or more than 55 per cent, but less than 70 per cent
- **Excellent** for a score that is equal to or more than 70 per cent, but less than 85 per cent
- **Outstanding** for a score that is equal to or more than 85 per cent for exemplar buildings.

One of the significant changes introduced by BREEAM 2011 is the requirement for buildings that achieve either a BREEAM Excellent or Outstanding rating to undergo a BREEAM In-Use Assessment[15] to certify their ongoing performance. This Assessment must take place within three years of completion if the buildings are to maintain their rating. The theory is that this will encourage the continued high performance of the buildings achieving these ratings, even after they are occupied. BRE hopes this will provide evidence to clients and tenants of the business benefits of sustainable buildings. If an In-Use Assessment is not undertaken, or not certified, then the building's rating will be downgraded from Excellent and Outstanding to Very Good and Excellent respectively. This is published on the *GreenBookLive's* list of certified schemes and a new BREEAM Certificate will be issued to the client.

Exemplar buildings that achieve a BREEAM 2011 Outstanding rating will also be required to provide either a case study of the assessed building, or information to allow BRE Global to write one. The case study will then be published on the BREEAM and *GreenBookLive* websites. Clients will have to commit to providing this information in the Post-Construction Stage Assessment Report when it is submitted to BRE if an Outstanding rating is to be achieved. If the client fails to supply the information then the building's 2011 Outstanding rating will be downgraded to Excellent.

1.5 BREEAM Schemes

BREEAM 2011 sets out a way to assess the *environmental life-cycle impacts* of a range of newly constructed non-domestic building types within four key sectors:

- **commercial buildings** – offices (including offices with research and development areas), retail (such as individual shops, shopping centres, retail parks, restaurants) and industrial buildings (warehouses, process/manufacturing units and vehicle service buildings)
- **public (non-housing) buildings** – educational establishments (including pre-school, primary and secondary schools, sixth-form colleges, further education/vocational colleges and higher education institutions), healthcare buildings (such as hospitals, health centres/clinics, GP surgeries), prisons and courts
- **multi-residential buildings** – student halls of residence, sheltered accommodation, residential care homes, key worker accommodation and military barracks
- **other buildings** – other residential buildings (hotels, hostels, guest houses, secured training centres, etc., which cannot be assessed using the Code for Sustainable Homes), non-residential institutional buildings (including art galleries, museums, libraries, community centres, places of worship), assembly and leisure buildings (cinemas, theatres, concert halls, conference/exhibition halls, indoor/outdoor sports/fitness facilities) as well as any other building types, such as transport hubs, research and development facilities and crèches.

Further guidance on the types of healthcare, educational and multi-residential buildings covered by BREEAM 2011 is given in the appendices to the online *BREEAM Technical Manual*.[16] The buildings listed under the commercial buildings, public (non-housing) buildings and multi-residential sectors are classed as 'standard type buildings', which previously had their own BREEAM manuals. The Other Buildings sector covers what are classed as 'non-standard building types' that were previously covered by the Bespoke Scheme. They now fall under BREEAM 2011 and there is no longer a need for separately tailored assessment criteria. In mixed-use buildings that contain both standard type uses and non-standard uses, the building will be registered as a non-standard building type.

1.6 Schemes not covered in this Guide

As BREEAM Data Centres was only launched in 2010, BRE has decided that the 2010 version of the Scheme will remain in place for the time being and so falls outside the scope of this Guide. BRE has also developed tailored assessment criteria for specific uses, such as for visitor centres for the Forestry Commission and fire stations for the UK Fire Service, which are also outside the scope of this Guide.

Unlike previous Schemes, BREEAM 2011 only applies to new standalone buildings or new extensions to existing buildings in the UK. Refurbishment and fit-out projects will continue to be assessed with the appropriate 2008 Scheme while BRE develop a new Refurbishment Scheme, which they intend to launch in 2012.

It might be possible, however, to assess major refurbishment projects using BREEAM 2011 if agreed with BRE. BRE defines 'major refurbishment projects' as projects where a building's envelope and structure are fundamentally remodelled or adapted and new services (such as lighting, heating, ventilation and cooling) are provided. It is expected that most of a building's sub- and superstructure will be reused in a major refurbishment project, in addition to the retention and renovation of the façade. If only individual elements of a building's envelope, structure or services are being remodelled or replaced, BRE will not class the work as a major refurbishment project. It is important to obtain advice from an Assessor as early as possible regarding the most appropriate Scheme. If there is any doubt, the Assessor can clarify the position with BRE. As BREEAM 2011 only applies to new buildings within the UK, BRE has developed a number of BREEAM Schemes that can be used in other countries. These include:

- **BREEAM Europe commercial**, which has been developed to recognise different construction standards and practices in the European region. It covers office, retail and industrial buildings
- **BREEAM Gulf**, which was launched in 2009 to deal specifically with environmental issues of the Gulf region
- **BREEAM International Bespoke**, which can be used for either single or multi-building schemes anywhere in the world.

Further details of these Schemes can be found on the BREEAM website.[17] The Netherlands[18] and Spain[19] have also chosen to base their sustainable building assessments on the BREEAM methodology. BREEAM schemes are also being developed for use in Norway and Sweden. These schemes are all beyond the scope of this Guide.

1.7 Other rating systems

BRE has to compete in the international market with a range of other sustainability audit systems. BREEAM's principal international competitor is the United States Green Building Council's *Leadership in Energy and Environmental Design* (LEED) green building certification scheme which was launched in 1998.[20] Although it originates in the USA, it is used by a number of international corporations across the world, including some in the UK. It has separate rating systems for new construction (including major renovations), the operation and maintenance of existing buildings, commercial interior fit-out works, schools, retail, health care, homes and 'neighbourhood development'.

One of the key differences between LEED and BREEAM is the method of assessment. BREEAM uses licensed Assessors to audit the evidence provided by the client and design team in order to determine compliance. The Assessors submit their Assessment to BRE, which issues the BREEAM Certificate. Evidence for LEED assessments is normally collated by the design team, although a LEED Accredited Professional can be used to assist in this task, and then submitted to the US Green Building Council which assesses it before issuing the LEED Certificate. While certain industry critics praise LEED for its greater transparency, claiming that it promotes innovation, others feel that BREEAM offers both a better scientific basis and a broader remit because it covers the social aspects of sustainability. There has also been some criticism of LEED's consensus-based approach, which some say is overly responsive to manufacturers' needs.[21]

The Australian Green Building Council operates the Green Star rating scheme[22] for evaluation of the environmental design and construction of building in Australia. This has been in operation for approximately six years and has been adopted for use in New Zealand and South Africa.

A number of other environmental rating schemes have been launched around the world, providing country-specific assessment procedures such as:

- Green Building Index – Malaysian Green Building Council[23]
- Green Mark – Singapore's Building and Construction Authority[24]
- Estidama – Abu Dhabi Urban Planning Council[25]
- Comprehensive Assessment System for Built Environment Efficiency (CASBEE) – Japan[26]
- Sustainable Building Certificate – German Sustainable Building Council.[27]

None of these rating schemes is covered in this Guide.

References

1   Web link to *GreenBookLive* – BREEAM Certified Buildings – 2008 Onwards:
    www.greenbooklive.com/search/scheme.jsp?id=202

2   For British Land update for 'Winter 2010' see:
    www.britishland.com/index.asp?pageid=501

3   For British Land social corporate responsibility policies for 2010/2011 see:
    www.britishland.com/index.asp?pageid=501

4   For Land Securities 'Environmental policy, objectives and targets' see:
    www.landsecurities.com/responsibility/sustainability/environmental-policy-objectives-targets

5   Marks and Spencer 'How We Do Business Report: 2010' see:
    http://corporate.marksandspencer.com/documents/publications/2010/How_We_Do_Business_Report_2010

6   See: http://tna.europarchive.org/20081022170523/http://www.teachernet.gov.uk/management/
    resourcesfinanceandbuilding/schoolbuildings/sustainability/breeam/

7   Josephine Prior and Claire Williams (2008) *Sustainability Through Planning: Local Authority Use of BREEAM, EcoHomes and the Code for Sustainable Homes*, HIS BRE Press, Watford, UK.

8   Manchester City Council, 'Environmental Design: Clause 4.7' in *Guide to Development in Manchester – Supplementary Planning Document and Planning Guidance*', see:
    www.manchester.gov.uk/site/scripts/download_info.php?downloadID=644&fileID=1424

9   South Gloucestershire Council, *Design Checklist Supplementary Planning Document: Part 3*, page 10 see:
    www.southglos.gov.uk/NR/rdonlyres/E26D9144-C40F-45ED-ACA3-1F2812C925DA/0/PTE070520.pdf

10   Ashford Borough Council; Local Development Framework; Sustainable Design and Construction SPD (2009), available at: www.ashford.gov.uk/pdf/SustainableDesign&ConstructionSPD.pdf

11   See Policy 4.11.4, Chapter 4 in *Planning for Sustainability of the Planning Policy Wales*, 3rd edition (July 2010) at:
    http://wales.gov.uk/docs/desh/publications/100720planningppwchapter4en.pdf

12   Andrea Chegut, Piet Eichholtz and Nils Kok (Maastricht University) (July 2011) *The Value of Green Buildings: New Evidence from the United Kingdom*. Available at: www.sirp.se/l/getfile.ashx?cid=280784&cc=3&refid=34

13   For details of BREEAM licensed organisations and Assessors, see:
    www.greenbooklive.com/search/scheme.jsp?id=214

14   For a list of APs, see: www.greenbooklive.com/search/scheme.jsp?id=172

15   For details of the BREEAM In-Use Scheme, see: www.breeam.org/page.jsp?id=373

16   To view the BREEAM online Technical Manual, go to: www.breeam.org/podpage.jsp?id=414

17 For BREEAM International Schemes, see: www.breeam.org/podpage.jsp?id=54

18 See Dutch Green Building Council for details of BREEAM – NL, at: www.dgbc.nl/wat_is_dgbc/dgbc_english

19 News article: 'BRE Global and ITG sign letter of intent for BREEAM in Spain', see:
    www.breeam.org/newsdetails.jsp?id=574

20 For LEED scheme website see: www.usgbc.org/DisplayPage.aspx?CMSPageID=222

21 Inbuilt Ltd, 'BREEAM versus LEED: White Paper' (2010), available from:
    www.inbuilt.co.uk/media/406565/breeamvsleed.pdf

22 For Australian Green Building Council's Green Star Rating scheme, see: www.gbca.org.au/green-star/

23 For Malaysian's Green Building Council's Green Mark scheme, see: www.greenbuildingindex.org/index.html

24 For Green Mark scheme by the Building and Construction Authority in Singapore, see:
    www.bca.gov.sg/greenmark/green_mark_buildings.html

25 For Abu Dhabi Urban Planning Council's Estidama, see: www.estidama.org/

26 For Japan's 'Comprehensive Assessment System for Built Environment Efficiency', see:
    www.ibec.or.jp/CASBEE/english/index.htm

27 For Germany's Sustainable Building Council's 'Sustainable Building Certificate', see:
    www.dgnb.de/_en/certification-system/DGNB_Certificate/DGNB_Certificate.php

chapter two

The Assessment process: an overview

Before starting an Assessment and considering what is needed to demonstrate that the performance standards of the various Issues are being met so that credits may be awarded, it is important to understand a number of aspects of the BREEAM process. The areas that will affect the score and, consequently, your ability to attain your target rating are:

- the evidence that the client and design team need to provide for the Assessor to award credits
- the fact that not all credits have the same value when they are totalled to generate the final score
- the fact that certain BREEAM ratings cannot be achieved even if the final score is greater than the required threshold, without minimum performance standards in certain Issues being achieved
- the fact that the score can be topped up with *Innovation credits* which reward innovative practice or exemplary performance in relation to certain Issues
- when various Issues need to be considered, which members of the design team are usually responsible for ensuring the evidence is provided and the client's role in the process
- how a shell-only design and procurement approach can impact on the process.

2.1 Providing evidence to an Assessor

As explained in Chapter 1, the BREEAM Assessment process is described in detail in a single Technical Manual, available to view online.[1] Essentially, the Assessor audits the evidence provided by the design team, client and contractor against the assessment criteria for each of the Issues to determine how many credits can be awarded in relation to the building being assessed.

Although BRE decided to publish a single manual to simplify the process, different building types have different good and best practice performance benchmarks. In this context, it is important to understand the structure of the Issues. In the 2011 edition, each Issue is identified by its reference number and title (e.g. *Man01: Sustainable procurement*). The manual also sets out the number of credits that can be awarded, whether they are building-type dependent and if any minimum standards apply in relation to various target ratings. There is a brief description of what each BREEAM Issue aims to achieve and its *assessment criteria*. This is followed by *compliance notes* which help in interpreting the assessment criteria and explain how to assess compliance in specific situations or in relation to particular building types.

The number of credits that can be awarded for building-type dependent Issues varies according to the building being assessed. Table 2.1 shows the 13 Issues affected. In addition there are often building-specific assessment criteria that must be achieved for an Issue credit to be awarded. For example:

- *Man04: Stakeholder participation* aims to deliver accessible, functional and inclusive buildings in consultation with current and future users and stakeholders. In addition to the general assessment criteria there are separate and specific assessment criteria for education, healthcare, law courts and major transport node buildings
- *Ene08: Energy-efficient equipment* aims to encourage the procurement of energy-efficient equipment to optimise operational energy savings and includes specific assessment criteria for healthcare buildings.

Not all of the 48 Issues will necessarily be included in an Assessment if the building being assessed does not contain certain elements. Examples of this include:

- *Ene05: Energy-efficient cold storage*, if the building contains no commercial or industrial-sized refrigeration and storage systems
- *Ene06: Energy-efficient transportation systems*, if the building contains no lifts, escalators or moving walkways.

The Issues to be included in an Assessment are normally agreed with the Assessor at the pre-assessment meeting, as described in Chapter 1. The rating targeted and achievable Issue performance standards should also be agreed at this meeting. Making these decisions at an early stage avoids the design team undertaking unnecessary work gathering information for Issue credits that cannot be awarded for reasons beyond their control.

The design team, client and contractor must provide the Assessor with evidence to show that their building meets the criteria laid down for each Issue. To assist in this, each Issue has a *schedule of evidence* table which outlines the types of information and documents that have to be provided for both the design stage and post-construction stage assessments to assess compliance and award credits. If these are not provided then the Assessor will have no means of verifying compliance and will be unable to award any available credits. The range of information and documents that might be needed to demonstrate compliance with Issues' *assessment criteria* is discussed in more detail in Chapters 3 and 4.

At the end of each Issue description in the 2011 *Technical Manual*,[1] additional information is provided to assist those who have to demonstrate compliance with the Assessment criteria. BRE's stated policy is only to request evidence that would normally arise in the course of the design and procurement of a new building. Although in practice many clients, design teams and contractors find themselves undertaking time-consuming and potentially costly work to gather the missing information. The necessary evidence should, however, not exceed that required for a best practice design process.

Crucially, all the performance standards relating to the Issues targeted must be addressed prior to the design stage assessment. It is always prudent to aim to score more than the minimum for the target rating agreed since Issue credits awarded at the design stage might not be awarded at the post-construction stage as a result of:

TABLE 2.1: BREEAM 2011 – building-type dependent Issues

	Commercial buildings		Non-housing buildings							
	Offices	Retail	Industrial	Educational (schools)	Educational (higher education)	Healthcare	Prisons	Courts	Multi-residential buildings	Other buildings
Management Category	No building-type dependent Issues in this Category									
Health and Wellbeing Category										
Hea01: Visual comfort	3	4	3	3	4	5	3	3	3	3
Hea02: Indoor air quality	4	4	4	6	6	6	4	4	4	6
Hea05: Acoustic performance	2	2	2	3	2	2	2	2	4	2
Energy Category										
Ene02: Energy monitoring	2	2	2	2	2	2	1	1	1	2
Ene07: Energy-efficient laboratory systems	0	0	0	1	5	0	0	0	0	5
Transport Category										
Tra01: Public transport accessibility	3	5	3	3	5	5	2	5	3	5
Tra02: Proximity to amenities	1	1	1	1	1	1	0	1	2	1
Tra03: Cyclist facilities	2	2	2	2	2	2	1	2	1	2
Tra04: Maximum car parking capacity	2	0	2	0	2	1	0	0	2	2
Water Category	No building-type dependent Issues in this Category									
Materials Category										
Mat01: Life-cycle impacts	5	5	2	6	6	6	4	6	6	6
Waste Category										
Wst04: Speculative floor and ceiling finishes	1	0	0	0	0	0	0	0	0	0
Land Use and Ecology Category										
LE04: Enhancing site ecology	3	3	3	3	3	3	2	3	3	3
LE05: Long-term impact on biodiversity	2	2	2	2	2	2	3	2	2	2
Pollution Category	No building-type dependent Issues in this Category									
Innovation credits	No building-type dependent Issues in this Category									

- value engineering
- reducing building costs
- responses to resolve construction stage queries
- principal contractors and subcontractors not being fully aware of required performance standards for awarding credits.

2.2 Weighting of Issue credits

As explained in Chapter 1, not all the credits in an Assessment are worth the same in the final score because they are weighted. Each Category has a different number of potential credits within it and, after the credits within a Category are awarded and totalled, they are given a weighting before being added to the aggregated final score. The awarded value of an additional credit in one category can be worth more to the final score than a credit in another category (see Table 2.2 for examples).

The number of credits available in a particular Category can also vary from Scheme to Scheme. So the value to the final score of awarding a single credit within a particular Category will vary depending on the building type being assessed. To understand this more clearly, the percentage value of a single credit for each Category, in relation to a typical assessment for each building type, is indicated in Table 2.2.

Discounting Innovation credits, the weighted percentage value of a single credit is only the same across all building types in the Management, Water, and Land Use and Ecology Categories. The weighted percentage value of a single credit in the Waste and Pollution Categories is nearly the same for all with the exception of one or two building types. There is a greater variation in the weighted percentage value of a single credit in the Health and Wellbeing, Energy, Transport and Material Categories.

Table 2.2 indicates that the most valuable 2011 credits are in the Waste Category, where each credit is worth around 1.25 per cent for most building types. Each additional credit within the Materials and Land Use and Ecology Categories adds around one per cent to a final score, similar to an Innovation Category credit. Credits within the Health and Wellbeing and Transport Categories are worth around 1.0 and 0.9 per cent respectively, while credits in the Energy, Water and Pollution Categories are only worth between 0.6 and 0.8 per cent.

Although a single *Ene01: Reduction of CO$_2$ emissions* credit may appear to be one of the least valuable, overall the Issue contributes over 10 per cent to a final score if all the available credits are awarded.

As the number of Issues has been reduced and reallocated into different Categories in comparison to BREEAM 2008, this has changed the relative importance of credits in some Categories. Figure 2.1 provides a comparison between the BREEAM 2008 and BREEAM 2011 Offices Schemes. The value of credits within the Health and Wellbeing, Materials, Waste and Land Use and Ecology Categories has remained the same, as has the value of Innovation credits. While the value of credits within the Transport Category has increased, the value of credits in the remaining Categories has decreased. A single credit within the Management Category was worth 1.2 per cent to the final score in BREEAM 2008, but it is only worth 0.55 per cent in BREEAM 2011. A Management

TABLE 2.2: BREEAM 2011 – weighted percentage score of single credit in each Category

	Commercial buildings		Non-housing buildings							
	Offices	Retail	Industrial	Educational (schools)	Educational (higher education)	Healthcare	Prisons	Courts	Multi-residential buildings	Other buildings
Management Category	12% weighting towards BREEAM score									
Weighted % score of 1 credit in Management Category	0.55	0.55	0.55	0.55	0.55	0.55	0.55	0.55	0.55	0.55
Health and Wellbeing Category	15% weighting towards BREEAM score									
Weighted % score of 1 credit in Health and Wellbeing Category	1.07	1.00	1.07	0.88	0.88	0.83	1.07	1.07	0.94	0.94
Energy Category	19% weighting towards BREEAM score									
Weighted % score of 1 credit in Energy Category	0.70	0.66	0.66	0.68	0.56	0.63	0.73	0.73	0.70	0.56
Transport Category	8% weighting towards BREEAM score									
Weighted % score of 1 credit in Transport Category	0.89	0.89	0.89	1.14	0.73	0.80	2.00	0.89	0.89	0.73
Water Category	6% weighting towards BREEAM score									
Weighted % score of 1 credit in Water Category	0.67	0.67	0.67	0.67	0.67	0.67	0.67	0.67	0.67	0.67
Materials Category	12.5% weighting towards BREEAM score									
Weighted % score of 1 credit in Materials Category	1.04	1.04	1.39	0.96	0.96	0.96	1.14	0.96	0.96	0.96
Waste Category	7.5% weighting towards BREEAM score									
Weighted % score of 1 credit in Waste Category	1.07	1.25	1.25	1.25	1.25	1.25	1.25	1.25	1.25	1.25
Land Use and Ecology Category	10% weighting towards BREEAM score									
Weighted % score of 1 credit in Land Use and Ecology Category	1.00	1.00	1.00	1.00	1.00	1.00	1.00	1.00	1.00	1.00
Pollution Category	10% weighting towards BREEAM score									
Weighted % score of 1 credit in Pollution Category	0.77	0.77	0.83	0.77	0.77	0.77	0.77	0.77	0.77	0.77
Innovation credits										
Weighted % score of 1 Innovation credit	1.00	1.00	1.00	1.00	1.00	1.00	1.00	1.00	1.00	1.00

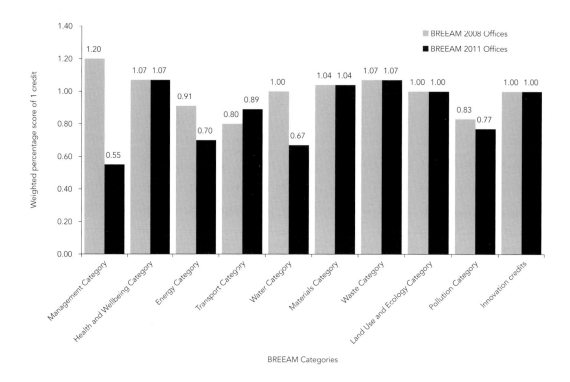

FIGURE 2.1: Comparison of BREEAM 2008 and BREEAM 2011 Offices Schemes

Category credit has gone from being the most valuable to the least valuable contributor to a final score. Yet if all the credits are awarded in *Man01: Sustainable procurement*, that Issue alone will contribute 4.4 per cent to the final score. In other words, it is still important to target the credits available from Issues in the Management Category despite their apparently reduced value.

2.3 Minimum performance standards

In addition to achieving the minimum score for a particular rating, as outlined in Chapter 1, BREEAM 2011 minimum performance standards must also be achieved in a number of Issues. This ensures that certain fundamental environmental issues are not overlooked. In some Issues this means having to achieve a certain number of credits, while in others only the performance standard set out in a particular assessment criterion has to be achieved. These requirements are highlighted in Chapters 3 and 4.

As you would expect, the number of Issues in which these minimum performance standards have to be achieved increases from what is required for a simple Pass rating up to the Outstanding rating (Figure 2.2). The four Issues in which minimum performance standards have to be achieved even for a basic Pass rating are:

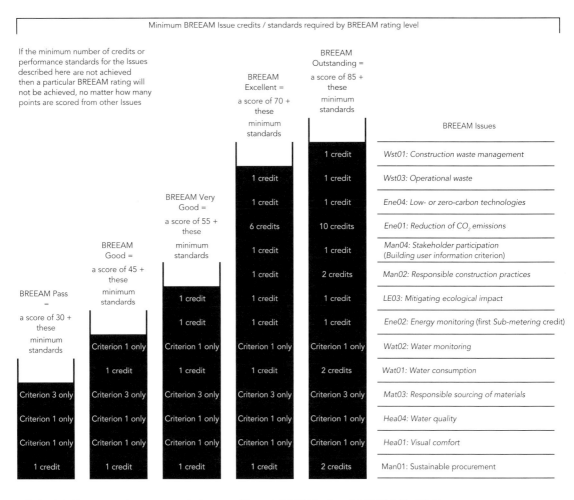

Minimum BREEAM Issue credits / standards required by BREEAM rating level					

BREEAM Outstanding = a score of 85 + these minimum standards

BREEAM Excellent = a score of 70 + these minimum standards

BREEAM Very Good = a score of 55 + these minimum standards

BREEAM Good = a score of 45 + these minimum standards

BREEAM Pass = a score of 30 + these minimum standards

If the minimum number of credits or performance standards for the Issues described here are not achieved then a particular BREEAM rating will not be achieved, no matter how many points are scored from other Issues

BREEAM Pass	BREEAM Good	BREEAM Very Good	BREEAM Excellent	BREEAM Outstanding	BREEAM Issues
				1 credit	Wst01: Construction waste management
			1 credit	1 credit	Wst03: Operational waste
			1 credit	1 credit	Ene04: Low- or zero-carbon technologies
			6 credits	10 credits	Ene01: Reduction of CO_2 emissions
			1 credit	1 credit	Man04: Stakeholder participation (*Building user information* criterion)
			1 credit	2 credits	Man02: Responsible construction practices
		1 credit	1 credit	1 credit	LE03: Mitigating ecological impact
		1 credit	1 credit	1 credit	Ene02: Energy monitoring (first *Sub-metering* credit)
Criterion 1 only	Criterion 1 only	Criterion 1 only	Criterion 1 only	Criterion 1 only	Wat02: Water monitoring
	1 credit	1 credit	1 credit	2 credits	Wat01: Water consumption
Criterion 3 only	Criterion 3 only	Criterion 3 only	Criterion 3 only	Criterion 3 only	Mat03: Responsible sourcing of materials
Criterion 1 only	Criterion 1 only	Criterion 1 only	Criterion 1 only	Criterion 1 only	Hea04: Water quality
Criterion 1 only	Criterion 1 only	Criterion 1 only	Criterion 1 only	Criterion 1 only	Hea01: Visual comfort
1 credit	1 credit	1 credit	1 credit	2 credits	Man01: Sustainable procurement

FIGURE 2.2: Minimum performance standards required for each BREEAM rating, © BRE Global Ltd 2011

- *Man01: Sustainable procurement* – **one credit** from eight available, for example:
  - appoint a project team member/specialist commissioning manager to monitor and programme the commissioning of a building's services and
  - ensure that building services are commissioned to BSRIA and CIBSE guidance
- *Hea01: Visual comfort* – Assessment criterion 1 has to be achieved:
  - all fluorescent and compact fluorescent lamps have to be fitted with high-frequency ballasts
- *Hea04: Water quality* – Assessment criterion 1 has to be achieved:
  - all water systems to comply with the Health and Safety Executive's (HSE's) *Legionnaires' disease – The Control of Legionella Bacteria in Water Systems: Approved Code of Practice and Guidance* (2000)
- *Mat03: Responsible sourcing of materials* – Assessment criterion 3 must be achieved:
  - all timber to be sourced in accordance with the UK Government's Timber Procurement Policy.

To achieve a Good rating, you must to also meet the following two Issues' minimum performance standards (as well as those to achieve a Pass).

- *Wat01: Water consumption* – **one credit** from five available:
  - reduce water consumption by 12.5 per cent
  - specify water-efficient sanitary ware
- *Wat02: Water monitoring* – *Assessment criterion 1* has to be achieved:
  - provide pulsed water meters to mains water supply to all buildings/units on site.

To achieve a Very Good rating the minimum performance standards of two further Issues must be met:

- *Ene02: Energy monitoring* – **one credit** from first sub-metering credit
  - provide sub-meters (with pulsed outputs) or a Building Energy Management System (BEMS) to monitor major energy-consuming services
- *LE03: Mitigating ecological impact* – **one credit** from the two available:
  - ensure that there is minimal change to the ecological value of the site, as explained in Chapter 3.

None of the minimum performance standards required to achieve a Very Good rating should cause great difficulty in most designs. The possible exception is to achieve the one credit in *LE03: Mitigating ecological impact*, which might prove tricky and entail careful consideration on certain sites.

To achieve a BREEAM Excellent rating, however, requires the minimum performance standards for a further five Issues to be met. The requirements of the following four should be met with relative ease:

- *Man02: Responsible construction practices* – **one credit** from two available:
  - require the principal contractor to participate in the Considerate Constructors Scheme[2] and
  - achieve an Assessment score of between 24 and 31.5.
- *Man04: Stakeholder participation* (building user information criterion) – **one credit** from one available:
  - provide a Building User Guide to help the building's occupant/non-technical facility managers to operate it efficiently.
- *Ene02: Low- or zero-carbon technologies* – **one credit** from five available:
  - instruct an energy specialist to undertake a feasibility study to establish the most appropriate local (on-site or near site) low- or zero-carbon energy sources and one of the recommended technologies installed.
- *Wst03: Operational waste* – **one credit** from one available:
  - include dedicated space(s) for segregation/storage of operational recyclable waste.

The minimum performance standard of the fifth Issue will certainly need more consideration:

- *Ene01: Reduction of CO_2 emissions* – **six credits** from 15 available:
  - building design has to achieve the equivalent of a 25 per cent improvement on its compliant Target Emissions Rate (TER) calculated for the 2010 version of the Building Regulations *Part L2A: Conservation of fuel and power in new buildings other than dwellings*.

For an Outstanding rating, two things are required. First, the minimum performance standard must be met in one additional Issue:

- *Wst01: Construction waste management* – **one credit** from four available
- produce a Site Waste Management Plan
    - require the principal contractor to limit the level of non-hazardous construction waste to equal to or less than 13.3 m³ or 11.1 tonnes per 100 m² (gross internal floor area).

Second, for an Outstanding rating the minimum performance standards for four Issues must be improved as follows:

- *Man01: Sustainable procurement* – **two credits** from eight available, so additionally:
    - require the principal contractor to carry out a thermographic survey of the completed building fabric.
- *Man02: Responsible construction practices* – **two credits** from two available:
    - require the principal contractor to participate in the Considerate Constructors Scheme[2] and
    - achieve an Assessment score of between 32 and 35.5.
- *Ene01: Reduction in CO$_2$ emissions* – **ten credits** from 15 available
    - equivalent to a 40 per cent improvement on a building's compliant TER calculated for the 2010 version of the Building Regulations *Part L2A: Conservation of fuel and power in new buildings other than dwellings*.
- *Wat01: Water consumption* – **two credits** from the total of five available:
    - reduce water consumption by 25 per cent.

2.4 Topping up a score with Innovation credits

As explained in Chapter 1, it is possible to top up a building's score with additional Innovation credits, which can add up to an additional 10 per cent. There are two ways in which Innovation credits can be awarded.

The first is by meeting the *exemplary level performance standards* for the BREEAM Issues, as indicated in Table 2.3. Achieving exemplary level performance standard means that a building's performance in relation to a particular Issue has gone beyond that required by the standard BREEAM best practice assessment criteria. These credits will generally only be awarded to innovative design solutions. For instance, BRE's benchmark statistics suggest only the top 5 per cent of construction projects currently achieve the exemplary level performance standard for *Wst01: Construction waste management*, indicating the degree of difficulty. The Innovation credit from *Man02: Responsible construction practices*, however, is more easily achieved if working with consensus contractors.

The second way to achieve Innovation credits is to make an application to BRE Global, through the BREEAM Assessor, to have a particular building feature, system or process recognised as being innovative. You must be able to demonstrate that the proposal will improve the sustainability performance of a building's design, operation, maintenance or demolition. The application will have to include:

TABLE 2.3: Issues with exemplary level performance standards, © BRE Global Ltd 2011

Issue	Innovation credits available	Performance standard required for Innovation credit
Man01: Sustainable procurement	1	Building's facility manager committed, for the first three years of the building's occupation to undertake, at quarterly intervals: • to collect occupant satisfaction, energy- and water-consumption data and issue to BRE for publishing annually • to check data against the building's expected performance and make necessary adjustments • to set targets to reduce building's energy and water consumption and monitor progress towards meeting them • to feed back lessons learned to client and design team for future use
Man02: Responsible construction practices	1	Main contractor participates in, for example, Considerate Constructors Scheme and achieves an assessment score of 36 or more
Hea01: Visual comfort	1	Improve daylight factor performance standard in relation to the daylighting criteria to between 3 and 5%, depending on building type
Ene01: Reduction of CO_2 emissions	5	Building is assessed to be carbon negative – a building that is a net exporter of zero-carbon energy
	1	The building's $EPR_{NC} \geq 0.9$ and has zero net carbon emissions from the energy required for space heating/cooling/water heating/ventilation/lighting and **10%** of the building's regulated energy is generated from carbon neutral on-site/near-site or accredited external energy sources and is used to meet demand of unregulated systems/processes
	2	The building's $EPR_{NC} \geq 0.9$ and has zero net carbon emissions from the energy required for space heating/cooling/water heating/ventilation/lighting and **20%** of the building's regulated energy is generated from carbon neutral on-site/near-site or accredited external energy sources and is used to meet demand of unregulated systems/processes
	3	The building's $EPR_{NC} \geq 0.9$ and has zero net carbon emissions from the energy required for space heating/cooling/water heating/ventilation/lighting and **50%** of the building's regulated energy is generated from carbon neutral on-site/near-site or accredited external energy sources and is used to meet demand of unregulated systems/processes
	4	The building's $EPR_{NC} \geq 0.9$ and has zero net carbon emissions from the energy required for space heating/cooling/water heating/ventilation/lighting and **80%** of the building's regulated energy is generated from carbon neutral on-site/near-site or accredited external energy sources and is used to meet demand of unregulated systems/processes
Ene04: Low- and zero-carbon technologies	1	Where a local low- or zero-carbon technology has been installed which reduces the regulated or life-cycle CO_2 emissions by 30%
Ene05: Energy-efficient cold storage	1	The installed refrigeration system is of a type described in the Future Technologies section of the Carbon Trust's Refrigeration Road Map and demonstrates a saving in indirect greenhouse emissions (CO_{2eq})
Wat01: Water consumption	1	Where the building's water consumption shows a 65% improvement on the notional baseline performance calculation
Mat01: Life-cycle impacts	1	Where four or five building elements are assessed and the building achieves at least 2 points more than the total points required to achieve the normal maximum number of credits **or** where fewer than four building elements are assessed, the building achieves at least 1 point more than the total points required to achieve the normal maximum number of credits
Mat03: Responsible sourcing of materials	1	Where 70% of available responsible sourcing points have been achieved
Wst01: Construction waste management	1	• Non-hazardous construction waste generated by the design is ≤ 1.6 m^3 or ≤ 1.9 tonnes per 100 m^2 (gross internal area) • 85% by volume or 90% by tonnage of non-demolition waste and 85% by volume or 95% by tonnage of demolition waste is diverted from landfill • All key waste groups have been identified for diversion from landfill in the pre-construction stage Site Waste Management Plan

- a description of the innovation and its aims
- its environmental and/or social benefits
- whether the proposed innovation has been made previously and whether it could be replicated on other projects
- the benefits expected from the proposed innovation and when these will be realised in the building's life cycle
- how the success of the innovation will be objectively measured, the criteria for measurement and the evidence that will be provided to demonstrate this success
- how the experience of implementing the innovation will be disseminated to the wider community.

It is important to realise that this method of achieving an Innovation credit does incur an additional fee, payable to BRE. Note also that BRE charges for each Innovation credit application and that the application might be unsuccessful. Although it is possible to appeal BRE's decision, this process will attract yet another fee, refundable if the appeal is successful. It is recommended that you consult your Assessor before following this route.

2.5 When do Issues have to be considered and who leads the process of providing evidence?

Design teams commonly try to understand what is needed for an Assessment by looking at the performance standards required for credits to be awarded Category by Category, starting with the Management Category. This approach tends to overwhelm the design team and leave the client with reams of indigestible information. It also fails to differentiate between the differing values of Issues and masks the importance of timing in the process.

A better approach is to consider the requirements of the Issues in relation to the building's design life-cycle stages prior to works commencing on site, as outlined in Table 2.4. This shows when Issues should be considered in relation to design stages. It highlights when decisions should be taken to avoid inadvertently losing credits. It groups Issues together to illustrate which design team member is expected to lead the process of gathering evidence for submission to the Assessor. It also shows when the architect should advise the client to appoint specialist consultants to provide the required evidence for a number of Issues.

A building's design life-cycle stages, illustrated in Table 2.4, are based on the *RIBA Outline Plan of Work*,[3] which comprises 11 key work stages grouped under five principal headings:

- **Preparation** – Stages A (Appraisal) and B (Design Brief)
- **Design** – Stages C (Concept), D (Design Development) and E (Technical Design)
- **Pre-Construction** – Stages F (Production Information), G (Tender Documentation) and H (Tender Action)
- **Construction** – Stages J (Mobilisation) and K (Construction to Practical Completion)
- **Use** – Stage L (Post-Practical Completion).

Timing is all-important. For example, as recommended in Figure 1.1, the appointment of the Assessor and the pre-assessment meeting should take place *before* the end of RIBA Stage B (Design Brief)

TABLE 2.4: When do Issues have to be considered and who leads the process of providing evidence

	Pre-Appraisal	Preparation (A, B)	Required?	Achieved?	Design (C, D, E)	Required?	Achieved?	Pre-Construction (F, G, H)	Required?	Achieved?
Architect		Man01: Sustainable procurement (Project brief and design criterion)			Man04: Stakeholder participation (Inclusive and accessible design criterion)			Man01: Sustainable procurement (part of Construction and handover criterion)		
		Tra01: Public transport accessibility			Hea01: Visual comfort (Daylighting criterion)			Man02: Responsible construction practices		
		Tra02: Proximity to amenities			Hea01: Visual comfort (Glare control and view out criterion)			Man03: Construction site impacts		
		Tra04: Maximum car parking capacity			Hea02: Indoor air quality (part of Minimising sources of air pollution criterion)			Hea02: Indoor air quality (two parts of Minimising sources of air pollution criterion)		
		LE01: Site selection (Previously developed land criterion)			Hea02: Indoor air quality (Potential for natural ventilation criterion)			Wat01: Water consumption		
					Hea06: Safety and security (Safe access criterion)			Mat03: Responsible sourcing of materials		
					Hea06: Safety and security (Security of site and building criterion)			Mat04: Insulation		
					Ene09: Drying space			Mat05: Designing for robustness		
					Tra03: Cyclist facilities					
					Wat01: Water consumption					
					Mat01: Life-cycle impacts					
					Mat02: Hard landscape and boundary protection					
					Wst03: Operational waste					
Services engineer					Man01: Sustainable procurement (part of Construction and handover criterion)			Man01: Sustainable procurement (part of Aftercare criterion)		
					Hea01: Visual comfort (Daylighting criterion)			Hea04: Water quality (Building services water systems: minimising risk of contamination criterion)		
					Hea01: Visual comfort (Internal/external lighting criterion)			Ene03: External lighting		
					Hea02: Indoor air quality (Laboratory fume cupboard and containment area criterion)			Ene05: Energy-efficient cold storage		
					Hea03: Thermal comfort			Ene06: Energy-efficient transport systems		
					Hea04: Water quality (Building occupants: Provision of fresh drinking water criterion)			Ene07: Energy-efficient laboratory systems		
					Ene01: Reduction of CO_2 emissions			Ene08: Energy-efficient equipment		
					Ene02: Energy monitoring			Wat01: Water consumption		
					Ene04: Low- and zero-carbon technologies			Wat02: Water monitoring		
					Wat01: Water consumption			Wat03: Water leak detection and prevention		
					Pol01: Impact of refrigerants			Wat04: Water-efficient equipment		
					Pol04: Reduction of night time light pollution			Mat04: Insulation (in relation to Building services)		
								Pol02: NO_x emissions		

Role			
Structural engineer	LE01: Site selection (Contaminated land criterion) Pol03: Surface water run-off (Flood risk criterion)	Wst01: Construction waste management Pol03: Surface water run-off (Surface water run-off criterion) Pol03: Surface water run-off (Minimising watercourse pollution criterion)	Mat03: Responsible sourcing of materials Wst02: Recycled aggregates
Quantity surveyor		Man05: Life-cycle cost and service life planning	
Client	Hea01: Visual comfort (Visual arts healthcare buildings criterion) Hea05: Acoustic performance Tra01: Public transport accessibility Tra05: Travel plan LE02: Ecological value of site and protection of ecology LE04: Enhancing site ecology	Man01: Sustainable procurement (part of Project brief and design criterion) Man01: Sustainable procurement (part of Construction and handover criterion) Man04: Stakeholder participation (Post-occupancy evaluation and information dissemination criterion) Hea03: Thermal comfort (Thermal model criterion) Hea05: Acoustic performance Wst03: Speculative floor and ceiling finishes LE03: Mitigating ecological impact LE05: Long-term impact on biodiversity Pol05: Noise attenuation	Man01: Sustainable procurement (part of Aftercare criterion) Ene08: Energy-efficient equipment
Specialist consultants — **Ecologist**	LE02: Ecological value of site and protection of ecology LE04: Enhancing site ecology	LE03: Mitigating ecological impact LE05: Long-term impact on biodiversity	
Acoustic engineer	Hea05: Acoustic performance	Pol05: Noise attenuation	
Highway engineer	Tra01: Public transport accessibility Tra05: Travel plan		

Note: the 'Required?' and 'Achieved?' columns are for use by readers of this Guide to use this table as a checklist through the BREEAM process.

to maximise the opportunities offered by an Assessment. This allows the client and design team to understand and adopt a large number of the required BREEAM Issues' performance standards from the outset. Evidence demonstrating compliance with performance standards being targeted for the Design Assessment will normally be developed during RIBA Design and Pre-Construction Stages C to H. Note, however, that some actions will have to be taken earlier, during RIBA Preparation Stages A–B, and some evidence might only be available during RIBA Stage J (Mobilisation) just after a main contractor has been appointed.

The performance standards of a number of Issues have to be considered and incorporated into a building's design as early as possible. Do not leave the preparation of evidence for these Issues until the completion of the tender design information as this will swamp the already busy design team with extra work.

Of the 48 BREEAM Issues, just over one-fifth have to be considered during RIBA Preparation Stages A and B. For example, whether some Issue credits can be awarded or not is dependent on site selection, which takes place during these stages. Other Issues will influence the development of the building's design brief. Over half of the Issues need to be considered during RIBA Design Stages C–E as the required performance standards will have an impact on a building's design, both in appearance and layout. Decisions on the requirements of the remaining third of Issues can be dealt with during RIBA Pre-Construction Stages F–H.

Equally important, evidence to demonstrate compliance with the performance standards of some Issues must be gathered over a comparatively long period of time. For example, the decision to target a particular Issue performance standard might be agreed during RIBA Design Stages C–E, but the full evidence required by the Assessor might not be ready for issue until during RIBA Pre-Construction Stages F–H. In some instances, confirmation of evidence might even be required from appointed contractors during RIBA Construction Stages J–K. The evidence required for the post-construction stage assessment will be developed towards the end of RIBA Stage K (Construction to Practical Completion) with the post-construction assessment being completed and submitted to BRE during RIBA Stage L1 (Post Practical Completion).

The following section describes which BREEAM Issues need to be addressed in relation to each of the key stages of the *RIBA Outline Plan of Work*.[3] The Issues have also been grouped to show which design team member is usually expected to lead the process of providing or gathering evidence. That design team member is also generally responsible for submitting this evidence to the Assessor for auditing prior to the design stage assessment. Although the following list is not exhaustive and more detailed information is provided in Chapters 3 and 4, it does provide a quick checklist of those persons who must consider the Issues and when the criteria have to be addressed, along with the number of credits that can be awarded if the performance standards are adopted.

2.6 Issues that should be first addressed during RIBA Preparation Stages A (Appraisal) and B (Design Brief)

Just over one-fifth of the Issues should be considered at the very start of a project, and include those which should be dealt with by the architect or structural engineer and certain decisions that must be taken by the client.

Architect responsibility

The architect will have to deal directly with half of the Issues arising during RIBA Preparation Stages A and B, including:

- *Man01: Sustainable procurement* (*Project brief and design* criterion): **one credit** can be awarded where the client, designers, building occupier, contractor, etc. contribute to the decision-making process from RIBA Stage B onwards.
- *Tra01: Public transport accessibility*: up to **three** or **five credits**, depending on the building type, can be awarded as a result of a site's proximity to local public transport networks, which determines its Accessibility Index. This might influence site selection as sites where few or no credits are available in relation to this Issue may require other Issues to be targeted to achieve a desired BREEAM rating, with resultant cost implications.
- *Tra02: Proximity to amenities*: **one credit** can generally be awarded as a result of a site's proximity to local amenities, except in the case of multi-residential buildings where **two credits** can be awarded and prisons where none are awarded. This aspect might also influence the choice of a site.
- *Tra04: Maximum car parking capacity*: up to **two credits** can be awarded by limiting the number of car parking spaces in relation to the following building types:
  - offices
  - industrial buildings
  - multi-residential buildings
  - further and higher educational buildings
  - other buildings.
  This fundamental design decision should be agreed with the client during RIBA Stage B (Design Brief) as it might affect a site's viability for future letting.
- *LE01: Site selection* (*Previously developed land* criterion): **one credit** can be awarded where 75 per cent of the development's footprint is on land previously used for industrial, commercial or domestic purposes, within the past 50 years. Again, this consideration might influence site selection.

The architect should also advise the client on approximately half of the Issues that should be considered during RIBA Preparation Stages A and B relating to specific issues and on whether specialist consultants should be appointed:

- *Hea01: Visual comfort* (*Visual arts for healthcare buildings* criterion): **one credit** can be awarded in relation to healthcare buildings only where an art policy and strategy is prepared and endorsed during RIBA Stage B (Design Brief).
- *Hea05: Acoustic performance*: up to **two** or **four credits**, depending on building type, can be awarded where the client appoints a suitably qualified acoustic engineer to provide early design advice on possible external sources of noise that will impact on the site layout and zoning of activities within the building during RIBA Stage B (Design Brief). The acoustic requirements vary between each building type.
- *Tra01: Public transport accessibility*: the client might consider appointing a Highway Engineer to assist in determining a site's Accessibility Index and how many credits can be awarded.
- *Tra05: Travel plan*: the client might consider appointing a Highway Engineer to commence the development of a site-specific travel plan during RIBA Stage B (Design Brief) to influence the concept design process.

- *LE02: Ecological value of site and protection of ecological features*: **one credit** can be awarded where a site is 'land of low ecological value'. The client might consider appointing a suitably qualified ecologist to undertake a survey of a site to determine its ecological value as this can influence the subsequent concept design development.
- *LE04: Enhancing site ecology*: up to **three credits** can generally be awarded, except for prisons where **two credits** can be awarded, where the client appoints a suitably qualified ecologist to carry out a survey of a site's existing ecology during RIBA Stage B (Design Brief) and make recommendations for protecting and enhancing its ecological value.

Structural engineer responsibility

The structural engineer will have to consider the impact of just two Issues during RIBA Preparation Stages A and B:

- *LE01: Site selection (Contaminated land criterion)*: **one credit** can be awarded if a site is significantly contaminated and remedial action is undertaken. This should be determined during the site selection process so the client is aware of the costs associated with the level of remediation needed.
- *Pol03: Surface water run-off (Flood risk criterion)*: up to **two credits** can be awarded in relation to a site's susceptibility to flooding, which should be a decisive factor in its selection for development.

2.7 Issues that should be addressed during RIBA Design Stages C (Concept), D (Design Development) and E (Technical Design)

Just over half of the Issues must be considered during RIBA Design Stages C–E as their requirements will have direct impact on a building's design, in terms of appearance, layout, specification and budget costs.

Architect responsibility

The architect will have to consider the implications of just over one-third of these Issues during the RIBA Design Stages C–E, including:

- *Man04: Stakeholder participation (Inclusive and accessible design criterion)*: **one credit** can be awarded for commencing the development of a building's Access Statement during RIBA Stage C (Concept) to allow its strategies to be fully integrated into the design.
- *Hea01: Visual comfort (Daylighting criterion)*: either **one** or **two credits** can be awarded, depending on the building type. It is important that the design features that influence whether or not a building will achieve the required daylight performance standards for credits to be awarded are understood and incorporated from RIBA Stage C (Concept) onwards.
- *Hea01: Visual comfort (Glare control and view out criterion)*: **one credit** is generally awarded, except in relation to healthcare buildings where two credits can be awarded. The design features that can adequately control glare and ensure that all work positions are provided with a compliant view out have to be understood and incorporated from RIBA Stage C (Concept) onwards.

- *Hea02: Indoor air quality* (part of *Minimising sources of air pollution* criterion): **one credit** can be gained by positioning a building so its openable windows or ventilation intakes/exhausts are located away from sources of external pollution. This must be resolved at the start of the design process in RIBA Stage C (Concept) so that a building's position on a site is fixed and its Indoor Air Quality Plan set in motion from the outset.
- *Hea02: Indoor air quality* (*Potential for natural ventilation* criterion): **one credit** can be awarded where a building is designed so that fresh air can be provided by a natural ventilation strategy. The design strategies required to achieve this are fundamental to a building's design solution and must be integrated from RIBA Stage C (Concept) onwards. This requires coordination with the services engineer. They need to separate a building's air intakes and exhausts.
- *Hea06: Safety and security* (*Safe access* criterion): **one credit** can be awarded where safe footpaths and cycle lanes across a site are provided. These must be considered from the earliest development of a site's layout to ensure that this credit is not lost.
- *Hea06: Safety and security* (*Security of site and building* criterion): **one credit** can be awarded where the layout of the site incorporates guidance from Secured by Design[4] or Safer Parking Scheme.[5] In addition, the architect should hold a meeting with the local police Crime Prevention Design Advisor or Architectural Liaison Office[6] during the RIBA Design Stages and incorporate their advice into the design.
- *Ene09: Drying space*: **one credit** can be awarded, in connection with multi-residential buildings only, where appropriately sized secure internal or external drying areas are provided. These should be considered from the start of RIBA Design Stages C–E to ensure that they are integrated into the design to avoid the credit being lost.
- *Tra03: Cyclist facilities*: **one** or up to **two credits**, depending on the building type, can be awarded where an adequate level of cycle storage and appropriate cyclist facilities are provided. These must be integrated into the site layout and building design during RIBA Design Stages C–E to ensure that adequate space is available for the required provision to be incorporated successfully.
- *Wat01: Water consumption*: up to **five credits** can be awarded for reducing a building's water consumption and, while detailed specification of water-efficient equipment to reduce water consumption will take place during RIBA Pre-Construction Stages F–H, the decision on whether or not to adopt rainwater harvesting and/or greywater recycling should be considered during RIBA Design Stages C–E to ensure that any design implications, such as the impact roof design, are fully integrated.
- *Mat01: Life-cycle impacts*: up to **two** or **six credits**, depending on the building type, can be awarded where the choice of materials for major building elements with low environmental impacts is maximised. This must be decided during RIBA Design Stages C–E as these choices are essential for the planning application. The impact of a material is based on a building element's rating, either derived from the *Green Guide to Specification*[7] or a bespoke rating agreed with the Assessor.
- *Mat02: Hard landscape and boundary protection*: **one credit** can be awarded where 80 per cent of a site's external hard landscaping and boundary protection materials achieve an A or A+ rating, defined in BRE's *Green Guide to Specification*.[7]
- *Wst03: Operational waste*: **one credit** can be awarded where a dedicated space is provided for the segregation and storage of operational recyclable waste. This should be integrated into a building's design or site layout during RIBA Design Stages C–E to ensure sufficient space is available.

Service engineer responsibility

During RIBA Design Stages C–E the project's service engineer has to consider more Issues than the architect, these being:

- *Man01: Sustainable procurement* (part of *Construction and handover* criterion): **one credit** can be awarded where a *specialist commissioning manager* is appointed during RIBA Design Stages C–E to provide commissioning advice on the commissioning of complex systems that could affect the design and construction programme. This service might be part of the service engineer's brief, if they have sufficient in-house expertise, or a specialist consultant/contractor might be appointed by the client at this stage.

- *Hea01: Visual comfort* (*Daylighting* criterion): while the fundamental design features required to ensure that the **one** or **two credits** available can be awarded are the responsibility of the architect, the service engineer may be required to provide calculations to check whether the building's design features provide the required daylight performance standards. This will have to be done during RIBA Design Stages C–E so that the required design features are fully integrated.

- *Hea01: Visual comfort* (*Internal and external lighting* criterion): **one credit** can be awarded where a building's internal lighting design strategies meet the requirements of:
  - CIBSE's *Code for Lighting* (2009), and other relevant standards
  - CIBSE's *Lighting Guide 7* for areas containing computers
  - zoning for occupant control in relation to internal lighting, except in prisons
  - *BS5489 – Part 1: Code of practice for the design of road lighting. Lighting of roads and public amenity areas* for external lighting
  - compliant lighting controls are provided.

- *Hea02: Indoor air quality* (*Laboratory fume cupboards and containment areas* criterion): up to **two credits** can be awarded where specific performance standards for laboratory fume cupboards and containment areas are achieved.

- *Hea03: Thermal comfort*: **one credit** can be awarded where a dynamic thermal modelling analysis is undertaken to confirm that thermal comfort levels required by CIBSE's *Guide to Environmental Design* for occupied spaces are achieved. Another credit can be awarded where zoning and control strategies based on occupancy patterns, user interactions and expectations of space heating and cooling systems are provided. It is important to agree these during RIBA Design Stages C–E so it is clear that the design submitted for planning meets the required standards.

- *Hea04: Water quality* (*Building occupants: Provision of fresh drinking water* criteria): **one credit** can be awarded where the requirements for the provision of fresh drinking water, for some building types, are integrated into a design and the minimising risk of contamination criteria (described later in this chapter) being satisfied. The space requirements to accommodate chilled, mains-fed water coolers must be addressed during RIBA Design Stages C–E.

- *Ene01: Reduction of CO_2 emissions*: up to **15 credits** can be awarded for this Issue. The calculations necessary to assess this Issue should be completed during the RIBA Design Stages to ensure that the building design, after the grant of planning permission, incorporates all the design features that will maximise the number of credits that can be awarded.

- *Ene02: Energy monitoring*: up to **two credits** can generally be awarded where sub-meters to monitor energy consumption of major energy-consuming systems and tenanted/functional areas are provided. This should be considered during RIBA Design Stages C–E to ensure their successful integration. Only **one credit** can be awarded in relation to:

- pre-schools and primary schools
- courts
- prison buildings
- multi-residential and other residential buildings.

- *Ene04: Low- and zero-carbon technologies*: up to **five credits** can be awarded in relation to this Issue. For the first credit to be awarded a feasibility study must be carried out by an energy specialist to establish the most appropriate local (on-site or near-site) low- and zero-carbon technologies for the building during RIBA Design Stage C (Concept). Understanding whether any low and zero carbon technologies will be incorporated into the design and how much they can reduce carbon emissions is important in order to demonstrate compliance with planning policies designed to reduce carbon emissions by set amounts.

- *Wat01: Water consumption*: up to **five credits** can be awarded where a building's water consumption is reduced. As discussed above, a decision has to be taken regarding whether or not to adopt rainwater harvesting and/or greywater recycling during RIBA Design Stage C (Concept) so that any special design features can be included in the design development of the building services.

- *Pol01: Impact of refrigerants*: up to **three credits** can be awarded, depending on whether a building requires the use of any refrigerants and, if so, whether they have reduced environmental impacts. The decision on whether a building requires refrigerants for comfort cooling, etc. is fundamental to a design decision and will have to be taken during RIBA Stage C (Concept). This is because maintaining comfort conditions without the use of refrigerant-based cooling systems requires the building form to work harder to reduce and control internal and external heat gains and provide passive cooling.

- *Pol04: Reduction of night time light pollution*: **one credit** can be awarded where external lighting does not create light pollution and does not come on during daylight hours. The reduction of night time light pollution is a common planning issue for many building types and so should be addressed during RIBA Design Stages C–D.

Structural engineer responsibility

The structural engineer must deal with just two Issues during RIBA Design Stages C–E, as follows:

- *Wst01: Construction waste management*: up to **four credits** can be awarded where certain benchmarks for non-hazardous construction waste are achieved. For any credits to be awarded, a compliant Site Waste Management Plan has to be commenced during RIBA Stage C (Concept) so that waste-saving strategies can be integrated into the design at the earliest opportunity. Where the development includes the demolition of an existing building, a pre-demolition audit should ideally be completed during RIBA Design Stages C–E.

- *Pol03: Surface water run-off* (*Surface water run-off* criterion): up to **two credits** can be awarded. One is awarded where a site's peak surface water run-off is no greater for the developed site than the undeveloped site. Another is awarded where a building will not be flooded if the local drainage network fails. These are issues which the Environment Agency would normally expect to have been addressed in submitted planning applications and so must be resolved during RIBA Design Stages C–D.

- *Pol03: Surface water run-off* (*Minimising watercourse pollution* criterion): **one credit** can be awarded where the structural engineer, if they are responsible for the below-ground drainage system, can confirm that the potential for any watercourse pollution is minimised by the adoption of sustainable drainage systems, oil/petrol interceptors, etc. These are issues that the Environment Agency would normally expect to have been addressed in submitted planning applications so must be considered during RIBA Design Stages C–D.

Quantity surveyor responsibility

The quantity surveyor is likely to have to deal with just one Issue during the RIBA Design Stages C–E:

- *Man05: Life-cycle costs and service life planning*: up to **three credits** can be awarded, with the first credit relating to this Issue awarded if a life-cycle cost analysis is undertaken on the design during RIBA Stages C(Concept) or D (Design Development). Further credits can be awarded depending on the scope of the analysis and whether it is updated during RIBA Stages D (Design Development) or E (Technical Design).

The architect will have to advise the client on what decisions to take or instructions to give in relation to around one-quarter of the Issues being considered during RIBA Design Stages C–E, as follows:

- *Man01: Sustainable procurement* (part of the *Project brief and design* criterion): up to **three credits** can be awarded, with the first credit awarded if a BREEAM Accredited Professional (AP) is appointed during RIBA Stage C (Concept) to assist in establishing a BREEAM rating target and provide advice on how this might be achieved. Further credits can be awarded where their appointment is extended for the duration of the procurement process.
- *Man01: Sustainable procurement* (part of *Construction and handover* criterion): as highlighted above under the list of Issues that the service engineer must address, the client may need to appoint a specialist commissioning manager to provide input into the design process if the service engineer is unable to provide this expertise.
- *Man04: Stakeholder participation* (*Post-occupancy evaluation and information dissemination* criterion): **one credit** can be awarded where the client instructs that a post-occupancy evaluation of the building is to be undertaken one year after its completion and the result of this study is disseminated.
- *Hea03: Thermal comfort* (*Thermal model* criterion): the client will have to ensure that the service engineer's terms of appointment include fees to undertake the necessary dynamic thermal analysis, as indicated above, required in relation to this Issue.
- *Wst04: Speculative floor and ceiling finishes*: **one credit** can be awarded where the client agrees to limit floor and ceiling finishes in speculative buildings to a show area which is less than 25 per cent of the net lettable floor area. If the building is for a specific occupant then they must confirm that they have chosen the specified floor and ceiling finishes.
- *LE03: Mitigating ecological impact*: up to **two credits** can be awarded, one credit where there is minimal change to the ecological value of a site or two credits where there is no negative change to the ecological value of a site, as explained in Chapter 3. This process can be made easier if the client appoints a suitably qualified ecologist to determine a site's initial 'plant species richness' and to provide design advice on limiting the development's impact.
- *LE05: Long-term impact on biodiversity*: up to **two credits** (or in the case of prison buildings up to **three credits**) can generally be awarded where the client appoints a suitably qualified ecologist, prior to works commencing on site, to:
  - confirm that all relevant legislation relating to the protection and enhancement of ecology will be complied with
  - produce a site-specific landscape and habitat management plan covering the first five years after a building's completion

     – advise on additional recommendations for the development.

- *Pol05: Noise attenuation*: **one credit** can be awarded where the client appoints an acoustic engineer to undertake a Noise Impact Assessment to determine the impact of noise generated by the building on noise-sensitive areas/buildings within 800 m of the site. This kind of study is often required for planning applications.

2.8 Issues that can be dealt with during RIBA Pre-Construction Stages F (Production Information), G (Tender Documentation) and H (Tender Action)

The remaining Issues need only be considered during the detailed design stages covered by RIBA Pre-Construction Stages F–H, so that any requirements can be included within the tender documentation for prospective principal contractors to price accurately.

Service engineer responsibility

Unlike the previous design stages, the service engineer needs to consider the majority of the Issues being considered during RIBA Pre-Construction Stages F–H, including:

- *Man01: Sustainable procurement* (part of the *Aftercare* criterion): **one credit** can be awarded where seasonal commissioning responsibilities, for the first 12 months of a building's occupation, are included in the contact specification.
- *Hea04: Water quality* (*Building services water systems: minimising risk of contamination* criterion): **one credit** can be awarded where all water systems comply with HSE's *Legionnaires' Disease – The Control of Legionella Bacteria in Water Systems: Approved Code of Practice and Guidance* (2000) and the provision of fresh drinking water (described earlier in this chapter) criteria being satisfied.
- *Ene03: External lighting*: **one credit** can be awarded where appropriate luminous efficacy for external light fittings for buildings, footpaths, car parks, access roads, etc. and controls to prevent operation during daylight hours are specified.
- *Ene05: Energy-efficient cold storage*: up to **two credits** can be awarded where energy-efficient commercial/industrial-sized refrigeration storage systems are specified to reduce operation greenhouse gas emissions. This will typically apply to supermarkets and cold storage warehouses, but it could also apply to laboratory and healthcare buildings.
- *Ene06: Energy-efficient transport systems*: up to **two credits** can be awarded where an analysis of transportation demand is undertaken to determine the optimum provision and energy-efficient lifts, escalators or movable walkways are specified.
- *Ene07: Energy-efficient laboratory systems*: **one credit** can be awarded where energy-efficient laboratory systems or areas are specified. Up to **two additional credits** can be awarded if the laboratories account for at least 10 per cent of a building's area and up to **four additional credits** where they account for 25 per cent of the area if improved performance standards are achieved.
- *Ene08: Energy-efficient equipment*: **two credits** can be awarded where the service engineer works with the client/building occupier to check whether certain building functions or equipment which are responsible for the *significant majority* of unregulated energy consumption meet the specified criteria.
- *Wat01: Water consumption*: up to **five credits** can be awarded for reducing a building's

water consumption and, while the architect may specify some products, such as those relating to sanitary ware, the bulk of evidence showing that the performance standards related to this Issue are achieved is likely to be provided by the service engineer. Water consumption figures will be required for specified WCs, urinals, taps, showers, baths, dishwashers and washing machines. If greywater and/or rainwater harvesting systems are specified, then any water generated by these systems can be offset against non-potable demand.

- *Wat02: Water monitoring*: **one credit** can be awarded where a water meter (with a pulsed output to enable its connection to a BEMS) is specified for each building or tenanted space in a development and for any areas or plant within a building which consume 10 per cent or more of a building's water demand.
- *Wat03: Water leak detection and prevention*: **two credits** can be awarded in relation to this Issue. One credit can be awarded where an appropriate leak detection system, capable of detecting major water leaks, is specified for the mains water supply. The other credit can be awarded where flow control devices are specified to the water supply of a building's toilet area to ensure that water is only supplied when required.
- *Wat04: Water-efficient equipment*: **one credit** can be awarded in relation to this Issue where appropriate irrigation systems for internal and external planting areas are specified. Additionally, where a vehicle-wash facility is provided, a full or partial water reclaim system should be specified.
- *Mat04: Insulation*: up to **two credits** can be awarded in relation to this Issue; one where a building's Insulation Index is equal to or greater than 2 and another where 80 per cent of the insulation types specified are responsibly sourced. Responsibility for action in relation to the requirements for this Issue is shared between the service engineer and the architect, as the Issue also relates to the insulation used for building services.
- *Pol02: NO_x emissions*: up to **two** or up to **three credits**, depending on building type, can be awarded where the nitrous-oxide (NO_x) emissions from the space heating and cooling plant are limited to certain values.

Architect responsibility

The architect will still have to deal directly with one-third of the Issues that have to be considered during RIBA Pre-Construction Stages F–H, including:

- *Man01: Sustainable procurement* (part of the *Construction and handover* criterion): **one credit** can be awarded where the contractor undertakes a thermographic survey of the completed building prior to practical completion to check for the continuity of insulation, excessive thermal bridging and air leakage through the building fabric. The principal contractor will also be required to rectify any defects identified.
- *Man02: Responsible construction practices*: up to **two credits** can be awarded where the principal contractor is required to use the Considerate Constructors Scheme (or a similar scheme) to assess site practices. One credit is awarded where a Considerate Constructors Scheme score of between 24 and 31.5 is achieved and two credits for a score of between 32 and 35.5.
- *Man03: Construction site impacts*: up to **five credits** can be awarded in relation to this Issue as follows:
  - one credit for monitoring, recording and reporting on the energy consumption of site operations
  - one credit for monitoring, recording and reporting on the site's net water consumption

- one credit for monitoring, recording and reporting on transportation energy consumption for delivering materials to site and removing construction waste
- one credit if all site timber used to facilitate construction is sourced in accordance with the UK Government's Timber Procurement Policy[8]
- one credit where the principal contractor operates a certified environmental management system and implements the best practice pollution prevention policies described in *Section 2.25 – Preventing Pollution* of the Environmental Checklist contained in the Environment Agency's *Building a Better Environment: A Guide for Developers.*[9]

- *Hea02: Indoor air quality* (two parts of *the Minimising sources of air pollution* criterion): up to **two credits** can be awarded in relation to this Issue. One credit is awarded if all decorative paints and varnishes are specified to meet emission levels for volatile organic compounds (VOC) and five of eight additional products (wood panels, timber structures, wood flooring, resilient or textile or laminate floor coverings, suspended ceiling tiles, flooring or rigid wall coverings adhesives) meet set VOC emission standards. The second credit is awarded if, post-construction and pre-occupancy, measurement of formaldehyde and VOC concentration levels is specified.

- *Wat01: Water consumption*: as discussed earlier in this chapter, up to **five credits** can be awarded in relation to this Issue. The architect will have to consider the water efficiency of the following products:
  - WC systems
  - urinals
  - taps (except taps to baths)
  - showers
  - baths
  - dishwashers
  - washing machines.

- *Mat03: Responsible sourcing of materials*: up to **three credits** can be awarded for maximising the extent of responsible sourcing of certain materials within some or all of the following main building elements:
  - foundations/substructure
  - ground floors
  - structural frame
  - upper floors
  - roof
  - external walls
  - internal walls
  - significant fittings, such as staircases, windows, doors, floor finishes, etc.
  - hard landscaping.

There are seven, so called, responsible sourcing *Tier Levels* against which the materials in the above elements are classified. These Tier Levels are graded to reflect the rigour of the responsible sourcing certification schemes used by material suppliers or product manufacturers. The BREEAM Assessor uses a web-based *Mat03: Responsible sourcing of materials* calculator to calculate how many points can be achieved and credits awarded. Within any given element, 80 per cent of the materials must be classified between Tier Levels 1 and 6 for any points to be allocated. In addition, all timber used in the building must be sourced in accordance with the UK Government's

Timber Procurement Policy.[8] This is a complex Issue which is described in more detail in Chapter 4.

- *Mat04: Insulation*: up to **two credits** can be awarded in relation to this Issue. The first credit is awarded where the insulation specified in the following achieves an overall Insulation Index equal to or greater than 2:
    - external walls
    - ground floors
    - roofs
    - building services.

  The Insulation Index is calculated by the BREEAM Assessor using a *Mat04: Insulation* calculator tool based on the insulations':
    - volumes
    - thermal resistances
    - *Green Guide to Specification* ratings.[7]

  The second credit is awarded where at least 80 per cent, by volume, of the insulation specified is responsibly sourced and certified in accordance with the requirements for either Tier Levels 1, 2, 3, 4 or 5 as described for *Issue Mat03: Responsible sourcing of materials.*
- *Mat05: Design for robustness*: **one credit** can be awarded where internal and external areas of the building are protected against vehicular, trolley and pedestrian movement in order to prevent damage.

There are only two Issues where the architect will be required to advise the client, during RIBA Pre-Construction Stages F–H, on decisions to be taken:

- *Man01: Sustainable procurement* (part of the *Aftercare* criterion): **a further credit**, in addition to that described above in the services engineer's responsibilities for RIBA Pre-Construction Stages F–H, can be awarded if seasonal commissioning is undertaken and the client instructs contractors and the design team to obtain feedback on the building occupants' comfort. This must be carried out during the first 12 months of occupation and is described in detail in Chapter 3.
- *Ene08: Energy-efficient equipment*: up to **two credits** can be awarded where the client includes the requirement for the service engineer to work collaboratively with the client or the building's occupant within their appointment to:
    - identify equipment which will be responsible for a significant proportion of unregulated energy use
    - ensure that the chosen equipment complies with the required performance standards.

Structural engineer responsibility

The structural engineer will have to deal with just two Issues during RIBA Pre-Construction Stages F–H, as follows:

- *Mat03: Responsible sourcing of materials*: in addition to the architect specifying materials, the structural engineer is responsible for specifying concrete, steel and timber structural products within the foundations, structural frame, upper floors and roof and should specify suppliers that use appropriate certified responsible sourcing schemes for their key production and supply chain process stages.

- *Wst02: Recycled aggregates*: **one credit** can be awarded where more than 25 per cent (by weight or volume) of the total high-grade aggregates proposed in a building or development are either recycled (sourced from the site or from within a distance of 30 km) or secondary aggregates. In addition, there are different minimum percentage levels of recycled aggregate for different applications and elements within the building areas, as described in Chapter 4.

2.9 RIBA Construction Stages J (Mobilisation) and K (Construction to Practical Completion)

While all Issues have to be considered prior to the tender process, and the performance standards required for credits to be awarded, a number require written confirmation from the principal contractor for certain credits to be awarded in the design stage assessment.

Principal contractor responsibilities

Examples of documents that a principal contractor may be required to provide in the immediate post-tender period include:

- *Man01: Sustainable procurement* (part of the *Construction and handover* criterion): the appointment letter of a specialist commissioning manager (if appointed by the principal contractor), a commission schedule and a copy of the principal contractor's programme showing that sufficient time has been allocated for the commissioning process.
- *Wat01: Water consumption*: a letter of instruction to subcontractors and suppliers requiring them to provide sufficient information to allow a water consumption calculation to be completed.
- *LE01: Site selection* (*Contaminated land* criteria): a letter may be required from the principal contractor or remediation contractor confirming the remediation strategy for the site and providing a summary of the implementation plan.
- *LE05: Long-term impact on biodiversity* (additional criteria): a letter from the principal contractor:
  - confirming appointment of a biodiversity champion, their job title, site role and responsibilities
  - providing a training schedule or letter confirming their commitment to provide relevant training to site operatives on protecting a site's ecology
  - detailing how they intend to monitor and report on actions taken to protect a site's biodiversity during the construction period
  - providing a copy of their programme confirming that any works needed to minimise disturbance to a site's existing wildlife have been taken into account.

2.10 Post-construction stage

It should not be forgotten that all the credits awarded in the design stage assessment will be reviewed at the post-completion stage and reassessed. This is accomplished in the following ways:

- the BREEAM Assessor visiting site to verify that the as-constructed status of the building is in accordance with the information provided for the design stage assessment
- the client, design team and contractors providing evidence which confirms that the project has been constructed in accordance with the assurances given at the design stage or
- where there has been a change in the design, providing new evidence for the Assessor to audit and award credits as appropriate in the post-construction assessment.

2.11 How a shell-only approach impacts on the BREEAM Assessment

Speculative shell-only development, where the tenant will be completing some of the building's elements, components, etc., is a special case. The evidence required for an Assessment is slightly different.

There are four options, each with a different level of robustness and consequential impact on the value of credits that can be awarded:

- **Option 1 – Use of a Green Lease Agreement between developer and tenant(s)**: the client can use a legally binding Green Lease Agreement between themselves and their tenants. If this commits the tenant to meeting the full extent of the BREEAM Issue Assessment criteria, the full value of the available credits can be awarded. In multi-tenanted developments compliant Green Lease Agreements need to cover at least 75 per cent of the net lettable floor area for the full value of credits to be awarded.
- **Option 2 – A Green Building Guide for tenant fit-outs**: alternatively the client can commission a Green Building Guide for future tenants, which provides building-specific guidance on how the fit-out works can be implemented to standards required to comply with assessment criteria of BREEAM Issues. If this approach is adopted, however, then only half of the value of the credits can be awarded.
- **Option 3 – Developer and tenant collaboration**: where future tenants are known, then a collaborative assessment can be carried out involving both the client and the tenant. In this case, compliance with assessment criteria can be demonstrated by using evidence either from the shell-only design team or from the tenant's fit-out design and specification. In this case the full value of the credits can be awarded.
- **Option 4 – No evidence provided for a tenant(s) fit-out specification**: if the client or shell-only design team cannot confirm compliance with the assessment criteria of any particular Issue, or are unable to provide a Green Lease Agreement or a Green Building Guide covering the issue in question, then no credit can be awarded.

The Assessment process of a shell-only building is the same as for a fully fitted-out building. It should be noted, however, that over 60 per cent of Issues can be influenced by the fit-out specification. Where this occurs is indicated in the detailed description of Issues in Chapters 3 and 4. For example, in relation to *Ene01: Reduction of CO$_2$ emissions*, use of the Green Building Guide option is not permitted and the energy modelling for the building must be based on either the actual fit-out specification or the most energy-intensive fit-out specification permissible for a Building Regulations compliant building's TER calculation to be achieved.

References

1   *BREEAM New Construction: Non-Domestic Buildings – Technical Manual*, see:
    www.breeam.org/BREEAM2011SchemeDocument/

2   For details of the Considerate Constructors Scheme, see: www.ccscheme.org.uk/

3   For an explanation of the *RIBA Outline Plan of Work* see Nigel Ostime and David Standford, *Architect's Handbook of Practice Management*, 8th edition, RIBA Publishing (2010)

4   Secured by Design website at: www.securedbydesign.com/index.aspx

5   For Safer Parking Scheme documents, see:
    www.britishparking.co.uk/Documents-Guidelines-for-the-Safer-Parking-Scheme

6   For contact details for Crime Prevention Design Advisors or Police Architectural Liaison Officers, see:
    www.securedbydesign.com/professionals/design_advisors.aspx

7   BRE, *Green Guide to Specification* at: www.bre.co.uk/greenguide/podpage.jsp?id=2126

8   UK Government's Timber Procurement Policy, see: www.cpet.org.uk/uk-government-timber-procurement-policy

9   Environment Agency, *Building a Better Environment: A Guide for Developers*, see:
    www.environment-agency.gov.uk/business/sectors/32695.aspx

chapter three

Maximising the benefits and some quick wins

Chapter 2 showed how important it is to understand how the BREEAM process works. You must know what the client and the design team have to do, when they should do it and who is responsible for giving evidence to the BREEAM Assessor who audits and awards credits. This chapter looks at how Issues linked by common themes contribute to a BREEAM score in order to achieve some quick wins. These themes are:

- the environmental impact of the chosen site
- the relationship between Issues' *performance standards* and a building's design and services. Once the design team understand this relationship, earning credits in this group of Issues will be easier
- including certain performance standards for the construction process in the tender
- the potential benefits of appointing specialist consultants and/or a BREEAM Accredited Professional (AP).

The guidance below does not offer an exhaustive list of compliance performance standards. Always discuss the details and requirements of any building with the appointed BREEAM Assessor. Discussions should start at the pre-assessment stage, in order to understand the sort of evidence required by the Assessor. This will allow sufficient time for the design team to compile the necessary evidence for the Issues being audited. Poor quality information can delay the preparation of a BREEAM Assessment Report. If the evidence provided to the Assessor does not comply with the relevant performances standards, then the Assessor cannot award a credit. Clients must understand exactly when to appoint specialist consultants or to instruct the design team to undertake specific tasks; these requirements must be met at the right time for the credits to be awarded.

You must understand what evidence is needed for the Issues targeted and when clients have to make decisions; this is of key importance in the BREEAM process.

3.1 Measuring a site's impact on an Assessment

There are six Issues which relate to choosing the right site and setting out buildings correctly that can yield some comparatively easy and inexpensive credits (see Table 3.1). Admittedly, there is frequently little room for manoeuvre in site selection or in how you orientate and design your building. But bear these credits in mind at the start of a project because they account for about 10 per cent of the value of a final BREEAM score. If you are targeting a Very Good rating, these credits amount to one-fifth of your target score; for Excellent, one-seventh.

If these credits are not awarded, then you will have to consider replacing them from other Issues. It is likely that these other credits will be harder and more costly to achieve.

The six Issues that deal with choosing the site and setting out are detailed below.

TABLE 3.1: The value of a site's impact on the overall score

	Commercial buildings		Non-housing buildings							
	Offices	Retail	Industrial	Educational (schools)	Educational (higher education)	Healthcare	Prisons	Courts	Multi-residential buildings	Other buildings
Management Category	No Issues in this Category relate to a site's impact									
Health and Wellbeing Category										
Hea02: Indoor air quality (*Minimising sources of air pollution* criterion)	1	1	1	1	1	1	1	1	1	1
Weighted % value of the above credit to the final BREEAM score	1.36	1.36	1.36	1.07	1.15	1.15	1.36	1.36	1.15	1.15
Energy Category	No Issues in this Category relate to a site's impact									
Transport Category										
Tra01: Public transport accessibility (*Accessibility Index* criterion)	3	5	3	3	5	5	2	5	3	5
Tra02: Proximity to amenities	1	1	1	1	1	1	0	1	2	1
Weighted % value of the above credits to the final BREEAM score	3.56	5.33	3.56	4.57	4.36	4.80	4.00	5.33	4.44	4.36
Water Category	No Issues in this Category relate to a site's impact									
Materials Category	No Issues in this Category relate to a site's impact									
Waste Category	No Issues in this Category relate to a site's impact									
Land Use and Ecology Category										
LE01: Site selection (*Previously developed land* criterion)	1	1	1	1	1	1	1	1	1	1
LE01: Site selection (*Contaminated land* criterion)	1	1	1	1	1	1	1	1	1	1
LE02: Ecological value of site and protection of ecological features	1	1	1	1	1	1	1	1	1	1
Weighted % value of the above credits to the final BREEAM score	3.00	3.00	3.00	3.33	3.00	3.00	3.33	3.00	3.00	3.00
Pollution Category										
Pol03: Surface water run-off (*Flood risk* criterion)	2	2	2	2	2	2	2	2	2	2
Weighted % value of the above credits to the final BREEAM score	1.54	1.54	1.67	1.54	1.54	1.54	1.54	1.54	1.54	1.54
Overall % value of the site towards the overall BREEAM score	9.46	11.24	9.59	10.51	10.06	10.49	10.24	11.24	10.14	10.06

Hea02: Indoor air quality (first part of Minimising sources of air pollution criterion)

CREDITS AVAILABLE

1

INNOVATION CREDITS

0

The aim of this Issue criterion is to create healthy internal environments by siting buildings away from sources of external pollution.

PREREQUISITES: An Indoor Air Quality Plan must be produced covering:
* removal of contaminant sources
* dilution and control of contaminated sources
* procedures for pre-occupancy flushing out of a building
* third-party testing and analysis requirements.

MINIMUM STANDARDS: None

PERFORMANCE STANDARD REQUIRED: One credit can be awarded where:
* in naturally ventilated buildings, openable windows are located 10 m from sources of external pollution
* in air-conditioned and mixed mode buildings, air intakes and exhausts are located over 10 m apart and intakes over 20 m away from sources of external pollution.

These distances are measured in three dimensions, combining horizontal and vertical distances. Sources of external pollution include:
* roads
* car parks
* delivery areas
* exhausts from other buildings.

It may be possible to discount service and access roads with restricted or infrequent access as sources of external pollution. One example is roads that only provide access for waste collections. Check with the BREEAM Assessor in this case.

INNOVATION CREDITS: None

BUILDING-TYPE VARIATIONS: None

CONSEQUENTIAL IMPACTS ON DESIGN/TIPS: A site's location can impact on the award of this credit. It is important to analyse potential sources of pollution on a site to determine whether the proposed building can be located far enough from sources of external pollution to allow this credit to be awarded. On some sites of pollution this can prove very difficult, either due to the proposed density of development or existing sources that are located close to the site beyond the control of the client or the design team.

→

Hea02: Indoor air quality (first part of *Minimising sources of air pollution* criterion) (continued)

EVIDENCE TO BE PROVIDED FOR DESIGN STAGE ASSESSMENT:
- A copy of the Indoor Air Quality Plan.
- Design drawings showing locations of air intakes and exhausts, sources of external pollution, etc.
- A copy of the contract specification clauses confirming the requirements.

EVIDENCE TO BE PROVIDED FOR POST-CONSTRUCTION STAGE ASSESSMENT: As at the design stage, updated to show the as-constructed status:
plus
- for naturally ventilated buildings, a letter from the design team or principal contractor confirming that the building's construction complies with the BREEAM criteria
- for mechanically ventilated buildings, a Commissioning Manager's performance testing report confirming that the required fresh air rates are achieved.

IMPLICATION FOR SHELL-ONLY DEVELOPMENTS: None

Tra01: *Public transport accessibility*

CREDITS AVAILABLE

2, 3, 4 or 5
(depending on building type)

INNOVATION CREDITS

0

The aim of this Issue criterion is to recognise developments near to good public transport networks which contribute to reducing transport-related pollution and congestion arising from development.

PREREQUISITES: None

MINIMUM STANDARDS: None

PERFORMANCE STANDARD REQUIRED: The number of credits awarded is determined by a site's *Accessibility Index* (AI) as follows:
- For offices and industrial buildings, multi-residential buildings and other buildings predominately occupied by staff with occasional business-related visitors, pre-schools, schools and sixth-form colleges:
  - AI ≥ 2 – **one credit**
  - AI ≥ 4 – **two credits**
  - AI ≥ 8 – **three credits**.

→

- For retail developments, law courts, further education colleges, higher education buildings on a campus with less than 25 per cent of students resident on or within one kilometre of the campus, other buildings occupied by core employees with a large number of frequent visitors, healthcare hospital buildings:
  - AI ≥ 2 – **one credit**
  - AI ≥ 4 – **two credits**
  - AI ≥ 8 – **three credits**
  - AI ≥ 12 – **four credits**
  - AI ≥ 18 – **five credits**.
- For higher education buildings on a campus with 25 per cent or more of students resident on or within 1 km of the campus, GP surgeries, health centres, community hospitals:
  - AI ≥ 2 – **one credit**
  - AI ≥ 4 – **two credits**
  - AI ≥ 8 – **three credits**
  - AI ≥ 10 – **four credits**
  - AI ≥ 12 – **five credits**.
- For rural location-sensitive buildings – this applies to sites that are in locations or villages with a population of less than 3,000:
  - AI ≥ 2 – **one credit**
  - AI ≥ 4 – **two credits**.
- For prisons and MOD sites:
  - AI ≥ 2 – **one credit**
  - AI ≥ 4 – **two credits**.
- For transport hubs:
  - AI ≥ 2 – **one credit**
  - AI ≥ 4 – **two credits**
  - AI ≥ 8 – **three credits**
  - AI ≥ 18 – **four credits**.

A site's AI is determined by the Assessor using the *Tra01: Public transport accessibility* calculator based on the following:

- The distance from a building's main entrance to safe pedestrian routes to each compliant transport node (for bus stops 650 m and for railway stations 1,000 m). Where a public transport service has more than one node close to a site, only the closest is considered.
- The type of public transport and whether it provides transport to or from an urban centre, major transport node or community focal points (for instance doctor's surgery, library, school or village centre).
- The average number of services per hour during the building type's standard operating hours. Table 7-1 in the online *Technical Manual*[1] provides default operating hours for different building types.

To gain the **additional credit** for providing a dedicated bus service to buildings with fixed shift patterns:

- no other credits must have been awarded as a result of a site's AI

→

- the bus service must be provided at the beginning and at the end of each shift or day
- the bus service must provide transport to a local population centre or public transport exchange.

INNOVATION CREDITS: None

BUILDING-TYPE VARIATIONS: Only those detailed above.

CONSEQUENTIAL IMPACTS ON DESIGN/TIPS: Sites close to good public transport networks will obviously be awarded more credits. While this element might be beyond the control of the design team, they may have to target other Issues to make up the shortfall of credits arising from a site's location.

Sites within the Greater London area can use the following to calculate their AI:
- London's public transport accessibility map[2]
- Transport for London's Planning Information Database website.[3]

EVIDENCE TO BE PROVIDED FOR DESIGN STAGE ASSESSMENT: For an Assessor to calculate a site's AI using the *Tra01: Public transport accessibility* calculator, you must provide the following:
- a scale map showing location and types of public transport nodes with distances to the site
- timetables for each service.

For the **additional credit for** the dedicated bus service you must provide:
- a letter from the future building occupier confirming the provision of the details of the dedicated bus service.

EVIDENCE TO BE PROVIDED FOR POST-CONSTRUCTION STAGE ASSESSMENT: As at the design stage, but if the period between the design and post-construction stages is more than 12 months, then a site's AI should be recalculated.

IMPLICATION FOR SHELL-ONLY DEVELOPMENTS: None

Tra02: Proximity to amenities

CREDITS AVAILABLE

1 or 2
(for multi-residential buildings)

INNOVATION CREDITS

0

The aim of this Issue criterion is to reduce the need for extended travel or multiple trips by locating buildings close to local amenities.

PREREQUISITES: None

MINIMUM STANDARDS: None

PERFORMANCE STANDARD REQUIRED: Where the local amenities listed below are located within 500 m of a building's main entrance (measured along a safe pedestrian route) the following credits can be awarded:

- For pre-school, schools, sixth-form colleges, further education buildings, offices, industrial and retail buildings, law courts – all of the following for **one credit**:
    - grocery shop or food outlet
    - post box
    - cash machine.
- For higher education buildings – five of the following for **one credit**:
    - grocery shop or food outlet
    - post box
    - cash machine
    - GP surgery or medical centre
    - leisure or sports centre
    - library
    - students' union.
- For healthcare buildings – all of the following for **one credit**:
    - grocery shop or food outlet
    - post box
    - cash machine
    - pharmacy.
- For multi-residential buildings – all of the following for **one credit**:
    - grocery shop or food outlet
    - post box
    - cash machine.
- For multi-residential buildings – eight of the following for **two credits**:
    - grocery shop or food outlet
    - post box
    - cash machine

→

- pharmacy
- GP surgery or medical centre
- leisure or sports centre
- outdoor open public access area
- public house
- community centre
- place of worship.
- For other building types – two of the following for **one credit**:
  - grocery shop or food outlet
  - post box
  - cash machine
  - pharmacy
  - GP surgery or medical centre.

More than one of the above amenities may exist within another or within the site (for example, a cash machine and a pharmacy may be located within a supermarket).

INNOVATION CREDITS: None

BUILDING-TYPE VARIATIONS: As indicated above. Note that no credit can be awarded for prison buildings.

CONSEQUENTIAL IMPACTS ON DESIGN/TIPS: If a number of sites are being investigated, check the location of local amenities in relation to each to see if this will influence the final choice of site. If this check is made early enough in the design process it may affect the award of this credit.

EVIDENCE TO BE PROVIDED FOR DESIGN STAGE ASSESSMENT: You must provide a plan of the site and surrounding area indicating:

- the location of the assessed building
- the location of amenities
- routes to amenities with distances.

If the amenities do not currently exist but will be developed, the client must confirm in writing:

- the location and types of amenities to be provided
- the timescale for their development.

EVIDENCE TO BE PROVIDED FOR POST-CONSTRUCTION STAGE ASSESSMENT: As at the design stage, updated to show the as-constructed status.

IMPLICATION FOR SHELL-ONLY DEVELOPMENTS: None

LE01: Site selection
(Previously developed land criterion)

CREDITS AVAILABLE

1

INNOVATION CREDITS

0

The aim of this Issue criterion is to encourage building on previously developed land, rather than on undisturbed sites which may have a greater ecological value.

PREREQUISITES: None

MINIMUM STANDARDS: None

PERFORMANCE STANDARD REQUIRED: One credit is awarded where at least 75 per cent of a new building's construction zone is on a site used previously for industrial, commercial or domestic purposes within the past 50 years. A building's construction zone includes:
* buildings
* hard-standing areas
* landscaping
* site access

plus
* the area within a site boundary around the above, set at a distance of 3 m from the construction zone up to the edge of the actual site boundary.

In assessing this criterion, 'previously developed land' is defined in *Planning Policy Guidance (2000)*[4] as land which

is or was occupied by a permanent structure, including the curtilage of the developed land and any associated fixed surface infrastructure.

This definition means that the following cannot be classed as previously developed land for a BREEAM assessment:
* agricultural or forestry buildings
* land developed for mineral extraction or waste disposal by landfill
* urban land, such as gardens
* parks
* recreation grounds
* allotments
* previously developed land where remains of permanent structures have blended into the landscape.

If a site has not been used over the past 50 years, this credit can only be awarded if the site is contaminated (see below).

INNOVATION CREDITS: None

→

BUILDING-TYPE VARIATIONS: In relation to the following building types, 'previously developed land' includes:

- for prisons, all land within a secure perimeter fence on an existing prison site
- for schools, an existing playing field if an equivalent area is to be reinstated as a playing field within one year of the works being completed.

CONSEQUENTIAL IMPACTS ON DESIGN/TIPS: If a number of sites are being investigated, check which are on previously developed land to see if this will influence the final choice of site. If this check is made early enough in the design process it may affect the award of this credit.

EVIDENCE TO BE PROVIDED FOR DESIGN STAGE ASSESSMENT: Design drawings, site plans, historic maps, reports and photographs confirming:

- type and duration of previous land use
- the area of previous land use
- the location and footprint of proposed development and temporary works, with areas.

EVIDENCE TO BE PROVIDED FOR POST-CONSTRUCTION STAGE ASSESSMENT: As at the design stage, updated to show the as-constructed status.

IMPLICATION FOR SHELL-ONLY DEVELOPMENTS: None

LE01: Site selection (*Contaminated land* criterion)

CREDITS AVAILABLE

1

INNOVATION CREDITS

0

The aim of this Issue criterion is to encourage the development of contaminated sites.

PREREQUISITES: None

MINIMUM STANDARDS: None

PERFORMANCE STANDARD REQUIRED: One credit is awarded where a contaminated land specialist's report is provided which confirms that the site is 'significantly contaminated' and identifies:

- the degree of contamination
- the sources or type of contamination
- options for remediation.

→

LE01: Site selection (Contaminated land criterion) (continued)

Plus you must confirm that a strategy and an Implementation Plan are in place showing how remediation will be, or has been, implemented to enable the proposed development to take place.

The credit can still be awarded for a small plot on a larger site which was previously contaminated, regardless of the smaller plot's location in relation to the contamination. If remediation of the contamination on the larger site had to take place to allow the development to occur, the credit can be awarded.

If asbestos is removed from within an existing building, then the whole site cannot be classed as contaminated, but the site will be classed as contaminated if the asbestos is removed from the ground.

The credit cannot be awarded for historic remediation which is not related to the current proposed development.

INNOVATION CREDITS: None

BUILDING-TYPE VARIATIONS: None

CONSEQUENTIAL IMPACTS ON DESIGN/TIPS: Highly contaminated sites will restrict the possibilities for development. As in previous BREEAM Schemes, there is still the anomaly of no credits being available for uncontaminated sites, whether previously developed or not.

EVIDENCE TO BE PROVIDED FOR DESIGN STAGE ASSESSMENT:
- A copy of the specialist's land contamination report for the site, with drawings showing areas of contamination/remediation in relation to the proposed development.

Plus
- a letter from the principal contractor or remediation contractor (or from the client if no contractors are appointed) confirming:
  - the remediation strategy for the site

  and
  - summary details of their Implementation Plan.

If the site is not contaminated or if historic remediation has taken place, this credit cannot be awarded.

EVIDENCE TO BE PROVIDED FOR POST-CONSTRUCTION STAGE ASSESSMENT: As for the design stage **plus** a copy of a specialist report confirming:
- the remediation works undertaken
- a description of any relevant pollution linkages addressed.

IMPLICATION FOR SHELL-ONLY DEVELOPMENTS: None

LE02: Ecological value of site and protection of ecological features

CREDITS AVAILABLE

1

INNOVATION CREDITS

0

The aim of this Issue criterion is to encourage the development of sites with limited ecological value and to protect existing ecological features from damage during construction.

PREREQUISITES: None

MINIMUM STANDARDS: None

PERFORMANCE STANDARD REQUIRED: One credit can be awarded where a site is defined as land of low ecological value. This can be determined:

either

by completing the BREEAM Checklist in the online *Technical Manual*,[1] answering '**No**' to all five of these questions:

1   Has the planning authority requested an ecological survey/statement?
2   Is the site within 2 km of a Special Area of Conservation (SAC), Special Protection Area (SPA) or a Ramsar Convention site?[5]
3   Is the site within 500 m of a Site of Special Scientific Interest (SSSI)?[5]
4   Are the following habitats present on or within 100 m of the construction zone:
    –   broad-leaved woodlands
    –   watercourses
    –   wetlands
    –   flower-rich meadows or grasslands
    –   heathland?
5   Are any of following within or on the boundary of the construction zone (for a definition, see below):
    –   trees more than ten years old
    –   mature field hedgerows – over 1 m tall and 500 mm wide
    –   an existing building with pitched tile, slate or shingle roof, lofts, hanging tiles, weather-boarding, dense climbing plants, soffits, cellars, basements, ice houses, etc?

Or if a *suitably qualified ecologist* is appointed to:

- undertake a survey of the site's ecology
- produce an Ecological Assessment Report, based on the requirements of Appendix F in the online *Technical Manual*,[1] which identifies the site as being land of low ecological value.

A building's construction zone includes:

- buildings
- hardstanding areas
- landscaping
- site access

→

plus
- a site boundary is established around the area containing the above, set at a distance of 3 m from the construction zone up to the edge of the actual site boundary.

Plus all existing features of ecological value surrounding the site's construction zone and site boundary must be adequately protected from damage prior to any preliminary site works and during site clearance, site preparation and construction activities.

Protection applies to:
- trees of over 100 mm trunk diameter and/or of significant ecological value – protect with barriers
- trees – prevent direct impact and severance or asphyxiation of roots
- hedges and natural areas – erect barriers or, if remote, protect by prohibiting construction activity in vicinity
- watercourses and wetlands – provide cut-off ditches and site drainage to prevent run-off to natural watercourses.

This credit can be awarded by default if the site is defined as being of low ecological value and containing no features of ecological value.

If a site has been cleared within five years of the proposed development, then the ecologists will have to estimate its ecological value immediately prior to the clearance. A definition of 'suitably qualified ecologist' is given later in this chapter.

INNOVATION CREDITS: None

BUILDING-TYPE VARIATIONS: None

CONSEQUENTIAL IMPACTS ON DESIGN/TIPS: If a number of sites are being investigated, their ecological value might influence which is developed if this credit is to be awarded.

EVIDENCE TO BE PROVIDED FOR DESIGN STAGE ASSESSMENT: A completed copy of the Checklist and Tables, signed by the client or design team:
plus either
- plans or site photographs confirming the presence or absence of ecological features
- drawings or contract specification clauses confirming the protection measures

or
- a copy of the ecologist's report.

EVIDENCE TO BE PROVIDED FOR POST-CONSTRUCTION STAGE ASSESSMENT: As at the design stage, updated to show any changes to the design.

IMPLICATION FOR SHELL-ONLY DEVELOPMENTS: None

Pol03: Surface water run-off (Flood risk criterion)

CREDITS AVAILABLE

2

INNOVATION CREDITS

0

The aim of this Issue criterion is to minimise the risk of localised flooding on and off a site by avoiding, reducing and delaying the discharge of rainfall into public sewers and watercourses.

PREREQUISITES: A site-specific Flood Risk Assessment must be prepared which shows that the development is:
- appropriately flood resilient

and
- resistant to all sources of flooding to the satisfaction of local or statutory bodies.

The Assessment must consider the flood risk from the following sources (as defined in *Planning Policy Statement 25: Development and Flood Risk*):[6]
- rivers
- tidal flow
- surface water run-off from adjacent land
- groundwater
- sewers
- other artificial sources of flooding (e.g. reservoirs).

MINIMUM STANDARDS: None

PERFORMANCE STANDARD REQUIRED: Two credits can be awarded for sites with a low annual probability of flooding. This is defined:
- for England and Scotland, as Zone 1 sites with less than 1 in 1,000 (<0.1) per cent chance of river and sea flooding
- for Wales, as Zone A and Zone B sites (if site levels are higher than the flood levels used to define adjacent extreme flooding).

Only **one credit** can be awarded for:
- sites with a medium or high probability of flooding (if not within a functional floodplain)
- building(s) whose ground level and access is 600 mm above the design flood level.

For smaller sites, 2,000 m² or less, the Flood Risk Assessment could be a brief report carried out by the contractor's engineer confirming the risk from all sources of flooding, including information from:
- the Environment Agency
- a water company or sewerage undertaker
- other relevant statutory bodies
- a site investigation
- local knowledge.

→

Pol03: Surface water run-off (Flood risk criterion) (continued)

INNOVATION CREDITS: None

BUILDING-TYPE VARIATIONS: The credit is awarded for multi-residential buildings where self-contained dwellings achieve the requirements of the Code for Sustainable Homes (CSH) Issues Sur 1 and Sur 2, provided that the whole site is compliant.

CONSEQUENTIAL IMPACTS ON DESIGN/TIPS: While initial guidance on flood risk potential can be obtained from the Environment Agency's Flood Maps,[7] showing areas that have a 1 in 1,000 chance of flooding each year, you also need a site-specific Flood Risk Assessment as Flood Maps do not show all sources of flooding. The Scottish Environment Protection Agency provides similar maps.[8]

EVIDENCE TO BE PROVIDED FOR DESIGN STAGE ASSESSMENT: The following are required:
- a Flood Risk Assessment
- design drawings
- correspondence from the statutory body confirming annual probability of flooding in light of existing flood defences.

EVIDENCE TO BE PROVIDED FOR POST-CONSTRUCTION STAGE ASSESSMENT: As for the design stage, updated as necessary,
plus
- confirmation that the basis for the Flood Risk Assessment has not changed if it was written more than five years ago.

IMPLICATION FOR SHELL-ONLY DEVELOPMENTS: None

3.2 Issues whose performance standards are more easily achieved through good design and specification

You should next consider those Issues where simple good design and specification make the performance standards easier to achieve. What is meant by the term 'good practice design and specification'? The former Commission for Architecture and the Built Environment (CABE) included in its six-point description of good building design:

> a building that responds to environmental imperatives and minimises its carbon footprint.
>
> *Creating Excellent Buildings: A Guide for Clients*[9]

Meeting the performance standards of any Issue will help to achieve the above aim, but some are difficult to achieve, depending on the required levels of performance and compliance. These Issues are considered in Chapter 4. The Issues whose requirements are easier to achieve are shown in Table 3.2 and if you can maximise these credits you can add over 25 per cent to a final BREEAM score. The relevant Issues are listed below, divided into sections for the architect, service engineer and structural engineer, depending on who is usually responsible for submitting evidence to the BREEAM Assessor.

TABLE 3.2: Issues that might be easier to achieve with good design and specification

	Commercial buildings		Non-housing buildings							
	Offices	Retail	Industrial	Educational (schools)	Educational (higher education)	Healthcare	Prisons	Courts	Multi-residential buildings	Other buildings
Management Category										
Man01: Sustainable procurement (*Project brief and design* criterion)	1	1	1	1	1	1	1	1	1	1
Man01: Sustainable procurement (part of *Construction and handover* criterion)	1	1	1	1	1	1	1	1	1	1
Man01: Sustainable procurement (part of *Aftercare* criterion)	1	1	1	1	1	1	1	1	1	1
Man04: Stakeholder participation (*Inclusive and accessible design* criterion)	1	1	1	1	1	1	1	1	1	1
Man04: Stakeholder participation (*Building user information* criterion)	1	1	1	1	1	1	1	1	1	1
Weighted % score of 1 credit in Management Category	2.73	2.73	2.73	2.73	2.73	2.73	2.73	2.73	2.73	2.73
Health and Wellbeing Category	15% weighting towards BREEAM score									
Hea01: Visual comfort (*Glare control and view out* criterion)	1	1	1	1	1	2	1	1	1	1
Hea01: Visual comfort (*Internal and external lighting* criterion)	1	1	1	1	1	1	1	1	1	1
Hea03: Thermal comfort	2	2	2	2	2	2	2	2	2	2
Hea04: Water quality	1	1	1	1	1	1	1	1	1	1
Hea06: Safety and security (*Safe access* criterion)	1	1	1	1	1	1	1	1	1	1
Hea06: Safety and security (*Security of site and building* criterion)	1	1	1	1	1	1	1	1	1	1
Weighted % score of 1 credit in Health and Wellbeing Category	7.50	7.00	7.50	6.18	6.18	6.67	7.50	7.50	6.56	6.56
Energy Category										
Ene02: Energy monitoring	2	2	2	2	2	2	1	1	1	2
Ene03: External lighting	1	1	1	1	1	1	1	1	1	1
Ene04: Low- or zero-carbon technologies (*Feasibility study/renewable supply contract*)	1	1	1	1	1	1	1	1	1	1
Ene06: Energy-efficient transportation systems	2	2	2	2	2	2	2	2	2	2
Ene07: Energy-efficient laboratory systems	0	0	0	1	1	0	0	0	0	1
Ene09: Drying space	0	0	0	0	0	0	0	0	1	0
Weighted % score of 1 credit in Energy Category	4.22	3.80	3.80	4.75	3.80	3.80	3.65	3.65	4.22	3.80
Transport Category										
Tra05: Travel plan	1	1	1	1	1	1	1	1	1	1
Total credits available in Transport Category	9	9	9	7	11	10	4	9	9	11
Weighted % score of 1 credit in Transport Category	0.89	0.89	0.89	1.14	0.73	0.80	2.00	0.89	0.89	0.73

	Commercial buildings		Non-housing buildings							
	Offices	Retail	Industrial	Educational (schools)	Educational (higher education)	Healthcare	Prisons	Courts	Multi-residential buildings	Other buildings
Water Category										
Wat02: Water monitoring	1	1	1	1	1	1	1	1	1	1
Wat03: Water leak detection and prevention (System to detect major leaks criterion)	1	1	1	1	1	1	1	1	1	1
Wat03: Water leak detection and prevention (Flow control devices criterion)	1	1	1	1	1	1	1	1	1	1
Weighted % score of 1 credit in Water Category	2.00	2.00	2.00	2.00	2.00	2.00	2.00	2.00	2.00	2.00
Materials Category										
Mat02: Hard landscaping and boundary protection	1	1	1	1	1	1	1	1	1	1
Mat04: Insulation	2	2	2	2	2	2	2	2	2	2
Mat05: Designing for robustness	1	1	1	1	1	1	1	1	1	1
Weighted % score of 1 credit in Materials Category	4.17	4.17	5.56	3.85	3.85	3.85	4.55	3.85	3.85	3.85
Waste Category										
Wst03: Operational waste	1	1	1	1	1	1	1	1	1	1
Wst04: Speculative floor and ceiling finishes	1	0	0	0	0	0	0	0	0	0
Weighted % score of 1 credit in Waste Category	2.14	1.25	1.25	1.25	1.25	1.25	1.25	1.25	1.25	1.25
Land Use and Ecology Category	Issues in this category are considered elsewhere									
Pollution Category	10% weighting towards BREEAM score									
Pol02: NO_x emissions from heating source	3	3	2	3	3	3	3	3	3	3
Pol03: Surface water run-off (Surface water run-off criterion)	1	1	1	1	1	1	1	1	1	1
Pol04: Reduction of night time light pollution	1	1	1	1	1	1	1	1	1	1
Weighted % score of 1 credit in Pollution Category	3.85	3.85	3.33	3.85	3.85	3.85	3.85	3.85	3.85	3.85
Overall % value of good design and specification towards the overall BREEAM score	27.49	25.68	27.06	25.74	24.37	24.94	27.52	25.71	25.34	24.76

3.3 Issues for which the architect is normally responsible

Man01: *Sustainable procurement* (first part of the *Project brief and design* criterion)

CREDITS AVAILABLE

1

INNOVATION CREDITS

0

The aim of this Issue criterion is to deliver functional and sustainable building design through correct briefing.

PREREQUISITES: The briefing process must start during RIBA Preparation Stage B (Design Brief).

MINIMUM STANDARDS:
- For BREEAM ratings Pass, Good, Very Good and Excellent – **one credit** from any of the criteria in this Issue, including this one.
- For BREEAM Outstanding rating – **two credits** from any of the criteria in this Issue, including this one.

PERFORMANCE STANDARD REQUIRED: One credit can be awarded where meetings are held during the design, construction, commissioning and handover stages, and when the building is occupied. These meetings must include those involved in making design-related decisions, namely:
- the client
- design team members
- the contractor
- the building occupier.

These meetings must establish roles and responsibilities relating to:
- end-user requirements
- the aims of the design strategy
- installation and construction requirements
- the occupier's budget and available technical expertise to maintain installed systems
- usability and manageability of design proposals
- the supporting documentation
- commissioning, training and aftercare.

A schedule of training for the building's operation should be established for relevant occupants and must cover:
- the Building User Guide
- design strategies behind how the building functions

Man01: Sustainable procurement (first part of the *Project brief and design* criterion) (continued)

- key features for the operation, maintenance, repair and replacement of installed systems
- all documentation provided
- training responsibilities.

INNOVATION CREDITS: None

BUILDING-TYPE VARIATIONS: None

CONSEQUENTIAL IMPACTS ON DESIGN/TIPS: The necessary activities for this credit resemble the good practice design process recommended by CABE,[9] which involves stakeholders (such as a building's future occupants) in the development of the outline brief. Note, however, that the standard approach described in the *Architects' Job Book*[10] does not necessarily include a building's future occupants.

EVIDENCE TO BE PROVIDED FOR DESIGN STAGE ASSESSMENT: Documentation showing when collaboration began and the roles and responsibilities of the project team, including:
- meeting minutes
- the construction programme
- a responsibilities schedule
- the contract specification clauses confirming requirements
- a copy of the proposed training schedule.

EVIDENCE TO BE PROVIDED FOR POST-CONSTRUCTION STAGE ASSESSMENT: As for the design stage, updated to show the as-constructed status.

IMPLICATION FOR SHELL-ONLY DEVELOPMENTS: For speculative buildings, you must consider the general end-user requirements, relevant to the expected type of tenant. Training documentation is still needed and, if any services are to be installed by tenants, a space should be left for these to be completed later.

Man04: *Stakeholder participation*
(Inclusive and accessible design criterion)

CREDITS AVAILABLE

1

INNOVATION CREDITS

0

The aim of this Issue criterion is to deliver buildings which are accessible, functional and inclusive by implementing an appropriate design.

PREREQUISITES: None

MINIMUM STANDARDS: None

PERFORMANCE STANDARD REQUIRED: One credit is awarded if an Access Statement is developed describing the strategies adopted for inclusive design. The statement must be prepared in accordance with CABE's guidance[11] and must cover:
- the removal or management of obstacles that define disability
- identification of the age groups, genders, ethnicity and fitness levels of the building users
- provision for parents and children.

The Access Statement has to confirm how the public and community will access the following facilities without gaining access to non-public areas:
- sports facilities
- meeting and conference rooms
- drama and theatre spaces
- amenity spaces for staff and visitors
- home office areas within multi-residential buildings.

INNOVATION CREDITS: None

BUILDING-TYPE VARIATIONS: None

CONSEQUENTIAL IMPACTS ON DESIGN/TIPS: Inclusive and accessible design solutions must be included from the earliest concept design development stages. This will allow them to be integrated at minimal cost.

EVIDENCE TO BE PROVIDED FOR DESIGN STAGE ASSESSMENT: A copy of the Access Statement is required **and/or:**
- copies of design drawings illustrating the inclusive design solutions
- contract specification clauses covering issues from the Access Statement, if necessary.

EVIDENCE TO BE PROVIDED FOR POST-CONSTRUCTION STAGE ASSESSMENT: Copies of as-constructed drawings confirming that the proposed inclusive design features have been completed.

IMPLICATION FOR SHELL-ONLY DEVELOPMENTS: None

Man04: Stakeholder participation
(Building user information criterion)

CREDITS AVAILABLE

1

INNOVATION CREDITS

0

The aim of this Issue criterion is to deliver accessible, functional and inclusive buildings by providing sufficient information to enable the building occupiers to operate the building efficiently.

PREREQUISITES: None

MINIMUM STANDARDS: This credit must be gained for either a BREEAM Excellent or Outstanding rating to be achieved.

PERFORMANCE STANDARD REQUIRED: One credit can be awarded where a Building User Guide is provided to enable building occupants to operate the building efficiently. It should be written to meet the needs of the general users and residents, non-technical facility management staff and visitors, and should include information on:

- the building's environmental strategies and provisions (relating to energy, water, waste, etc.) and suggestions on how users can best engage with them
- a building services overview detailing access to controls
- the provision for visitors relating to access, security procedures, etc.
- any facilities shared with the community, public and adjoining building users, and details of access to them
- safety and emergency procedures, with detailed instructions
- specific building operational procedures
- incident reporting and feedback procedures
- training in the use of the building services, etc.
- the site and local transport network, cyclist facilities, pedestrian routes, etc.
- access to local amenities
- refurbishment, re-fit and maintenance arrangements and considerations
- links to sources of assistance and contact details of facility management teams, etc.

INNOVATION CREDITS: None

BUILDING-TYPE VARIATIONS: None

CONSEQUENTIAL IMPACTS ON DESIGN/TIPS: Architects may be asked to prepare this Guide. It may fall outside their normal scope of service so it is important to include it within their terms of appointment and make provision for an appropriate fee.

→

Man04: Stakeholder participation (Building user information criterion) (continued)

EVIDENCE TO BE PROVIDED FOR DESIGN STAGE ASSESSMENT: You must provide:
either
- contract specification clauses requiring the principal contractor to develop the Building User Guide

or
- a letter from the client confirming that they will develop a Building User Guide.

EVIDENCE TO BE PROVIDED FOR POST-CONSTRUCTION STAGE ASSESSMENT:
- A copy of the completed Building User Guide.

Plus
- written confirmation from the client or design team that the Guide will be given to the building's tenant or owner
- details of how information relating to the building, site and local amenities will be made available to the building's tenant or owner.

IMPLICATION FOR SHELL-ONLY DEVELOPMENTS: In speculative developments it may not be possible to include all the information required for the Building User Guide. If some elements are to be installed by future tenants, compliance with the above performance standards can be established by:
either
- a Green Lease Agreement

or
- developer and tenant collaboration.

Hea01: Visual comfort
(Glare control and view out criterion)

CREDITS AVAILABLE

1 or 2
(for healthcare buildings)

INNOVATION CREDITS

0

The aim of this Issue criterion is to provide best practice visual comfort for building users by reducing glare and providing a view to the outside.

PREREQUISITES: All fluorescent and compact fluorescent lamps must be fitted with high-frequency ballasts.

→

Hea01: Visual comfort (Glare control and view out criterion) (continued)

MINIMUM STANDARDS: For any BREEAM rating, all fluorescent and compact fluorescent lamps must be fitted with high-frequency ballasts.

PERFORMANCE STANDARD REQUIRED: One credit can be awarded where all 'relevant building areas' have:

- a glare-control strategy in place that does not conflict with the lighting controls (avoiding higher energy use)
- a 'compliant view out' from workstation positions, places where close work is undertaken or where visual aids are used.

'Relevant areas' of buildings are those which have workstations/desks where building users will spend a significant amount of time and close work will be undertaken or where visual aids will be used. Some areas within certain buildings are excluded from this requirement. It is best to agree these with the BREEAM Assessor but they can include:

- nurse bases that are located centrally to enable patient observation
- courtrooms or interview rooms with security and privacy requirements
- prison staff areas for security or observational purposes, including workstations
- workstations in nurseries.

A 'compliant view' is a view out through a window or opening that must meet certain criteria. In rooms less than 7 m deep, the view must be through windows or openings that make up 20 per cent or more of the internal wall area in which they are located. In rooms that are deeper than 7 m:

- the window or opening areas must meet the requirements of Table 1 in BS8206 – Part 2[12]
- a building or landscape as well as sky must be visible
- the view must be visible at seated eye level (between 1.2 and 1.3 m from the floor level)
- if the view is into courtyards or atria these must be at least 10 m deep.

INNOVATION CREDITS: None

BUILDING-TYPE VARIATIONS:

- Prison buildings – cells: adequate view out is from a normal standing or sitting position with a minimum distance of 10 m between the window and external solid object (wall, fence, etc.).
- Prison buildings – cells: where existing features prevent compliance with the view out criteria in less than 20 per cent of cells, the credit can still be awarded.
- Multi-residential buildings – all positions in living rooms in self-contained flats, communal lounges, individual bedrooms and bed-sits in sheltered housing must be within 5 m of the wall with a window or permanent opening (of at least 20 per cent of the wall area) providing a view out.
- Healthcare buildings with in-patient areas – for patient-occupied spaces (such as wards and dayrooms): the distance between the wall with the window or opening and the nearest external object (walls, buildings, fence, etc.) is at least 10 m.

CONSEQUENTIAL IMPACTS ON DESIGN/TIPS: Glare can be reduced through:

- building layout (e.g. providing low eaves)
- building design (e.g. providing blinds, brise soleil, bioclimatic design solutions that shade in the summer and allow solar gain in winter).

→

Curtains do not meet the criteria for glare control. However, controllable internal blinds, which provide flexibility by allowing some sunlight into a room, are acceptable.

EVIDENCE TO BE PROVIDED FOR DESIGN STAGE ASSESSMENT: This must include:
- design drawings showing position of workstations and a window schedule
- the relevant contract specification clauses for any glare-control equipment.

EVIDENCE TO BE PROVIDED FOR POST-CONSTRUCTION STAGE ASSESSMENT: As for the design stage, updated to show the as-constructed status.

IMPLICATION FOR SHELL-ONLY DEVELOPMENTS: If it is not possible to determine which areas of a building will contain workstations then all areas must provide a compliant view out. If glare control is to be provided by the tenant, any of the Options 1, 2 or 3 (described in Chapter 2, section 2.11) can be used to establish compliance with the performance standards.

Hea06: Safety and security (*Safe access* criterion)

CREDITS AVAILABLE

1

INNOVATION CREDITS

0

The aim of this Issue criterion is to promote low-risk, safe and secure access to buildings.

PREREQUISITES: None, except where buildings are accessed directly from public highways or footpaths, then the *Security of site and building* criterion of this Issue must be achieved.

MINIMUM STANDARDS: None

PERFORMANCE STANDARD REQUIRED: One credit can be awarded if the site includes:
- direct footpath access from the building's entrance to off-site footpaths, allowing access to local public transport and amenities
- pedestrian crossing points raised to pavement level on access roads
- drop-off areas located so that pedestrians do not have to cross access roads to reach the building
- dedicated cycle lanes providing direct access from local cycle networks to the site's cycle storage (if provided), designed to meet the National Cycle Network *Guidelines and Practical Details: Issue 2*[13] and Appendix IV of National Cycle Network *Design and Construction Checklist*[14]

→

- lighting in accordance with BS5489 Part 1[15]
- signposted pedestrian access routes to off-site local amenities and public transport nodes for larger developments with high numbers of visitors (e.g. retail parks).

Buildings with dedicated delivery areas must have:

- access that avoids crossing general parking areas or shared pedestrian and cycle routes (which may require a separate delivery access road, although this stipulation can be relaxed for smaller sites if deliveries to the building will be made by small vans rather than heavy goods vehicles)
- turning areas designed for simple manoeuvring
- separate parking or waiting areas for goods vehicles, whether sited away from or adjacent to manoeuvring areas and staff or visitor parking
- dedicated storage space for refuse skips and pallets.

INNOVATION CREDITS: None

BUILDING-TYPE VARIATIONS: This credit can be awarded for self-contained dwellings in multi-residential buildings if the requirements of CSH Issue Man 4 are achieved, provided the whole building and car-parking areas are compliant.

CONSEQUENTIAL IMPACTS ON DESIGN/TIPS: Safe access across sites is part of normal good practice design, so this criterion should be easy to achieve, but it is vital to consider the detailed requirements of this Issue at an early stage.

EVIDENCE TO BE PROVIDED FOR DESIGN STAGE ASSESSMENT:
- Design drawings showing all the required features

and/or
- any contract specification clauses referring to the required design features.

EVIDENCE TO BE PROVIDED FOR POST-CONSTRUCTION STAGE ASSESSMENT: As for the design stage, updated to show the as-constructed status.

IMPLICATION FOR SHELL-ONLY DEVELOPMENTS: None

Hea06: Safety and security
(Security of site and building criterion)

CREDITS AVAILABLE

1

INNOVATION CREDITS

0

The aim of this Issue criterion is to promote low-risk, safe and secure access to, around and within buildings.

PREREQUISITES: Consultation with a security consultant, local Police Architectural Liaison Officer or Crime Prevention Design Advisor must occur prior to or during RIBA Design Stage C (Concept).

MINIMUM STANDARDS: None

PERFORMANCE STANDARD REQUIRED: One credit can be awarded if the architect:
either
- consults with the local Police Architectural Liaison Officer or Crime Prevention Design Advisor and incorporates any resulting recommendation into the building design and site layout

or
- designs the site layout to incorporate the principles and guidance of Secured by Design[16] and/ or the Safer Parking Scheme.[17]

If neither of the above schemes is relevant, a site-specific security risk and threat assessment will have to be carried out by a suitably qualified security consultant to establish appropriate security measures for the building and site.

A 'suitably qualified security consultant' must:
- have at least three years' relevant experience, gained within the past five years
- hold a recognised qualification in design and crime prevention, including Secured by Design training
- be a member of a relevant industry professional body or accreditation scheme (such as the Association of Security Consultants).

INNOVATION CREDITS: None

BUILDING-TYPE VARIATIONS: None

CONSEQUENTIAL IMPACTS ON DESIGN/TIPS: The architect should contact either their local Police Architectural Liaison Officer or Crime Prevention Design Advisor during the initial stages of site design so that their advice can be incorporated into the design before any decisions are made. Contact details for Crime Prevention Design Advisors can be obtained from the Secure by Design website.[16]

→

Hea06: Safety and security (Security of site and building criterion) (continued)

EVIDENCE TO BE PROVIDED FOR DESIGN STAGE ASSESSMENT:
- Design drawings showing security features

and/or
- any contract specification clauses stipulating security features

plus
- a copy of the report from the Police Architectural Liaison Officer, Crime Prevention Design Advisor or security consultant confirming:
  - the scope of their advice and involvement
  - the design stage during which their advice was sought
  - their recommendations in a summarised format.

EVIDENCE TO BE PROVIDED FOR POST-CONSTRUCTION STAGE ASSESSMENT: As for the design stage, updated to show the as-constructed status.
Plus (if relevant) **either**:
- copies of correspondence from the Police Architectural Liaison Officer, Crime Prevention Design Advisor or security consultant

or
- a copy of the development's Secured by Design and/or Park Mark® Award Certificate.

IMPLICATION FOR SHELL-ONLY DEVELOPMENTS: None

Ene09: Drying space

CREDITS AVAILABLE

1

INNOVATION CREDITS

0

The aim of this Issue criterion is to reduce the energy needed to dry clothes.

PREREQUISITES: None

MINIMUM STANDARDS: None

PERFORMANCE STANDARD REQUIRED: One credit can be awarded in multi-residential buildings where secure internal or external space is incorporated into the design. The drying space must incorporate posts and footings or fixings to accommodate:
- for self-contained dwellings with one or two bedrooms, at least 4 m of drying line
- for self-contained dwellings with three or more bedrooms, at least 6 m of drying line

and/or

→

- for developments of up to 30 individual bedrooms, at least 2 m of drying line per bedroom
- for developments of over 30 individual bedrooms, 1 m of additional drying line for each bedroom over the 30-bedroom threshold.

Internal drying spaces should be:

- heated and adequately ventilated in accordance with Part F of the Building Regulations and the service engineer must provide a copy of the calculations confirming compliance.

INNOVATION CREDITS: None

BUILDING-TYPE VARIATIONS: This Issue only applies to multi-residential buildings. The credit is awarded where self-contained dwellings comply with the requirements of CSH Issue Ene 4.

CONSEQUENTIAL IMPACTS ON DESIGN/TIPS: In self-contained dwellings, a 'secure space' is one that is enclosed and only accessible by the residents. Where communal drying space is provided, it also should be enclosed and accessible only by residents via a secure entrance. Drying spaces in living rooms, kitchens, dining rooms, halls and bedrooms do not comply with the requirements of this Issue.

EVIDENCE TO BE PROVIDED FOR DESIGN STAGE ASSESSMENT:

- Copies of design drawings

and/or

- contract specification clauses confirming that the required performance standards are being achieved

and/or

- a letter of instruction from the client to the contractor or supplier stipulating the standards that must be met.

EVIDENCE TO BE PROVIDED FOR POST-CONSTRUCTION STAGE ASSESSMENT:

- As-constructed design drawings showing installed provision

plus

- a purchase order or receipt for equipment to be installed.

IMPLICATION FOR SHELL-ONLY DEVELOPMENTS: None

Tra05: Travel plan

CREDITS AVAILABLE

1

INNOVATION CREDITS

0

One credit is awarded for the provision of a compliant Travel Plan (see later in this chapter under *Tra05: Travel plan*).

If no highway engineer is appointed, then the architect will be responsible for developing the Travel Plan. If this duty is not included within their terms of appointment an appropriate fee must be negotiated.

Mat02: Hard landscaping and boundary protection

CREDITS AVAILABLE

1

INNOVATION CREDITS

0

The aim of this Issue criterion is to encourage specification of materials and products with low environmental impact, taking into account the full life cycle of the materials.

PREREQUISITES: None

MINIMUM STANDARDS: None

PERFORMANCE STANDARD REQUIRED: One credit can be awarded where:
- materials for at least 80 per cent of the external hard landscaping and site boundary protection achieve either A+ or A *Green Guide to Specification* ratings.

'Hard landscaping' includes parking areas, but excludes main access roads and designated vehicle manoeuvring areas. Ratings for hard landscaping and boundary protection can be found on BRE's *Green Guide to Specification* website.[18]

If the element is not indicated in the *Green Guide to Specification*, one of the following steps can be taken:

Either
- The Assessor can obtain a bespoke Green Guide rating by completing the online Green Guide calculator or submitting a bespoke Green Guide query pro-forma to BRE, with detailed drawings and specification of the element.

→

Or

- Use an independently verified third-party Environmental Product Declaration (EPD), produced in accordance with the requirements of the ISO 14020 series. Where a product within an element has an EPD, its impact can be assessed by requesting a bespoke Green Guide rating, as described above. Consider the extent of the EPD: a Tier 1 EPD covers the whole life cycle of a product (i.e. cradle to grave); a Tier 2 EPD only covers part of a product's life cycle (i.e. cradle to gate).

In addition to the elements described in the *Green Guide to Specification*, the following examples will also be given an A+ rating:

- retained hard landscaping or boundary treatment, if no more than 20 per cent of its area is subject to minor alterations, repair or maintenance
- any existing hedges and living barriers
- external facades of buildings forming a site boundary.

If there are no site boundary elements, the credit is awarded solely on the hard landscaping assessment.

INNOVATION CREDITS: None

BUILDING-TYPE VARIATIONS: For prison buildings, the criterion for hard surfaces is only applicable to areas outside the secure perimeter zone but within the overall site curtilage.

CONSEQUENTIAL IMPACTS ON DESIGN/TIPS: You must carefully consider the specification of proposed materials: for example, areas of external concrete paving in heavily trafficked areas will only be A rated if laid on a recycled sub-base.

EVIDENCE TO BE PROVIDED FOR DESIGN STAGE ASSESSMENT: Copies of design drawings and contract specification clauses giving:

- detailed descriptions of each applicable element and its materials
- the location and area of each element

plus

- copies of the Green Guide ratings, element reference numbers and assessed specifications.

EVIDENCE TO BE PROVIDED FOR POST-CONSTRUCTION STAGE ASSESSMENT: Copies of design drawings and contract specification clauses showing the as-constructed status,

plus

- written confirmation of any changes to the specification from the principal contractor or design team
- copies of updated specifications, area calculations, Green Guide rating information and assessed specifications.

IMPLICATION FOR SHELL-ONLY DEVELOPMENTS: None

Mat04: Insulation

CREDITS AVAILABLE

2

INNOVATION CREDITS

0

This Issue criterion encourages the use of responsibly sourced insulation materials with low embodied environmental impact relative to their thermal properties.

PREREQUISITES: All insulation used in the following building elements must be assessed:
- external walls
- ground floor
- roof
- building services.

MINIMUM STANDARDS: None

PERFORMANCE STANDARD REQUIRED: The **first credit** can be awarded if the Insulation Index for the assessed insulation is equal to or greater than two.

The Insulation Index is calculated by the BREEAM Assessor using the *Mat04: Insulation* calculator. The calculation uses the volume-weighted thermal resistance (VWTR) of each insulation type, where:

VWTR = area of insulation (m2) x thickness (m)/thermal conductivity (W/mK)

The VWTR of each insulation type is then multiplied by the points allocated in its *Green Guide to Specification* rating, as follows:
- A+ rating = 3.0 points
- A rating = 2.0 points
- B rating = 1.0 point
- C rating = 0.5 points
- D rating = 0.25 points
- E rating = 0.0 points

The Insulation Index is the sum of the VWTR values corrected by the *Green Guide to Specification* rating divided by the sum of the VWTR values.

A+ ratings can also be given to insulation materials which:
- are incorporated as a component of another element manufactured off-site where this element has been assessed under *Mat01: Life-cycle impacts*
- fulfil a significant additional function, such as providing structural support in structural insulated panels.

→

An independently verified third-party Environmental Product Declaration (EPD) can increase a material's contribution to the Insulation Index if:

- it is produced in accordance with the requirements of the ISO 14020 series
- the calculation procedures described for *Mat01: Life-cycle impacts* are used to assess its impact.

The **second credit** can be awarded where:

- 80 per cent of the insulation types specified are responsibly sourced and certified in accordance with the requirements of Tier Levels 1, 2, 3, 4 or 5.

Table 12.2 in the online *Technical Manual*[1] indicates the key processes and supply chain processes required for common insulation products. The allocation of Tier Levels is considered in more detail in Chapter 4 in relation to *Mat03: Responsible sourcing of materials*.

INNOVATION CREDITS: None

BUILDING-TYPE VARIATIONS: None

CONSEQUENTIAL IMPACTS ON DESIGN/TIPS: Ensure that the service engineer is aware of the requirements of this Issue so that insulation used in the building services is correctly specified.

EVIDENCE TO BE PROVIDED FOR DESIGN STAGE ASSESSMENT: For the **first credit**, copies of design drawings and contract specification clauses confirming:

- the location of insulation materials
- the area and thickness of insulation specified

plus

- manufacturers' literature confirming the thermal conductivity of the insulation
- a copy of the *Mat04: Insulation* calculator output
- a copy of the Green Guide ratings, element number, etc.

For the **second credit**, in addition to the above:

- copies of relevant responsible source certificates for the insulation products confirming (or contract specification clauses requiring) that the insulation will be responsibly sourced from suppliers capable of providing certification to Tier Levels 1, 2, 3, 4 or 5.

EVIDENCE TO BE PROVIDED FOR POST-CONSTRUCTION STAGE ASSESSMENT: As for the design stage, updated to show the as-constructed status.

IMPLICATION FOR SHELL-ONLY DEVELOPMENTS: Where the shell works does not involve installing the majority of the insulation, any of the Options 1, 2 or 3 (described in Chapter 2, section 2.11) can be used to assess compliance with the required performance standards.

Mat05: Designing for robustness

CREDITS AVAILABLE

1

INNOVATION CREDITS

0

The aim of this Issue criterion is to ensure that adequate protection is provided to exposed building elements to minimise the need to replace materials.

PREREQUISITES: None

MINIMUM STANDARDS: None

PERFORMANCE STANDARD REQUIRED: One credit is awarded where adequate protection is provided in internal and external areas where vehicular, trolley and high levels of pedestrian movement occurs. Protection must be provided against the effects of:

- high levels of pedestrian traffic in main entrances, public areas, corridors, lifts, stairs, through doors, etc.
- internal vehicular or trolley movements in storage, delivery, corridor and kitchen areas
- vehicular collision in car-parking areas within 1 m of the building fabric
- vehicular collision in delivery areas within 2 m of the building fabric.

Vehicle impact protection must be positioned to protect the building fabric.

Suitable durability measures that can be employed include:

- specifying that corridor walls and linings must meet the Severe Duty (SD) category in BS5234 Part 2: *Partitions (including matching linings): Specification for performance requirements for strength and robustness including methods of test*
- providing protection rails to walls and kick plates to doors
- specifying hard-wearing, easily washable floor finishes in heavily used circulation areas
- providing bollards, barriers, raised kerbs or robust external wall construction up to a height of 2 m
- designing out risk, avoiding the need to specify additional protection measures
- providing protection in sales areas where customer goods trolleys are in use to vulnerable parts of the buildings (such as glass curtain walling) within 1 m of the trolley movement.

You should also consider which materials will provide maximum protection against malicious damage or physical abuse in public and common areas.

INNOVATION CREDITS: None

BUILDING-TYPE VARIATIONS: None

CONSEQUENTIAL IMPACTS ON DESIGN/TIPS: You must ensure that the specification of internal protection measures is not overlooked and that sufficient external space is set aside to provide protection that complies with the performances standards of this Issue.

→

EVIDENCE TO BE PROVIDED FOR DESIGN STAGE ASSESSMENT: Copies of design drawings showing vulnerable areas of the building with drawings and contract specification clauses detailing the protection and durability measures adopted.

EVIDENCE TO BE PROVIDED FOR POST-CONSTRUCTION STAGE ASSESSMENT: As for the design stage, updated to show the as-constructed status.

IMPLICATION FOR SHELL-ONLY DEVELOPMENTS: None

Wst03: Operational waste

CREDITS AVAILABLE

1

INNOVATION CREDITS

0

The aim of this Issue criterion is to divert operational waste from landfill by providing space for operational recycling of waste streams.

PREREQUISITES: None

MINIMUM STANDARDS: This credit is essential to achieve a BREEAM Excellent or Outstanding rating.

PERFORMANCE STANDARD REQUIRED: One credit is awarded where a dedicated segregated recyclable waste storage area for operational recyclable waste is included in a design, in addition to space allocated for general waste storage. This must be:
- clearly labelled as a store for recyclable waste
- accessible to the building occupants (no more than 20 m from the building's entrance)
- provided with vehicular access for collections (even if located within a building)
- designed to accommodate the predicted volume of waste likely to be generated by the building's use.

The area has to be suitable for the quantity of recyclable waste generated, the minimum space required in most buildings is:
- 2 m² per 1,000 m² (or part thereof) if the net floor area of the building is less than 5,000 m²
- 10 m² if building is over 5,000 m²
- an additional 2 m² per 1,000 m² of net floor area (or part thereof) if catering facilities are provided in the building – with an additional minimum of 10 m² for buildings over 5,000 m².

→

Consistent generation of operational recyclable waste, such as large amounts of packaging in retail units or compostable waste in restaurants, will require:

- a static waste compactor or baler, located in a service or delivery area
- vessels suitable for composting organic waste
- a water outlet where organic waste is stored or composted on a site.

Where the assessment covers a number of buildings (such as a number of industrial units), the dedicated storage space for operational recyclable waste can be sited in a centralised location to serve all the buildings on the site.

INNOVATION CREDITS: None

BUILDING-TYPE VARIATIONS: Additional performance standards apply to the following building types:

- Healthcare buildings: facilities must comply with Health Technical Memorandum 07-1: *Safe Management of Healthcare Waste.*[19]
- Schools: a school recycling policy must be in place on completion, comprising procedures for recycling paper, magazines, cardboard, plastic, metals, printer and toner cartridges and (if undertaken) the collection of composting materials.
- All multi-residential buildings: each dwelling should be provided with three internal dedicated recycling storage containers, none smaller than 7 litres, providing a total of 30 litres of storage.
- Multi-residential buildings with individual bedrooms and communal facilities: 30 litres of storage, comprising three containers, none smaller than 7 litres, should be provided for every six bedrooms, located within a communal kitchen or space. Home-composting facilities should also be provided and a home-composting leaflet issued to the occupants, usually by the architect, giving guidance on:
  - how composting works and why it is important
  - what materials can be composted
  - details of how the communal composting scheme or local authority green kitchen waste collection scheme works.
- Shopping centre and retail parks: flagship and anchor tenants should be provided with their own dedicated storage, while smaller units can share storage space. Adequate space must be provided to suit tenants' predicted recycling waste volumes.
- Small industrial units: where a development consists of a number of industrial units (each equal to or less than 200 m^2), a shared facility must be provided, based on the area of the whole development.
- Self-contained dwellings in multi-residential buildings: see the online *Technical Manual*[1] for the impact on BREEAM 2011 of credits awarded under CSH Issues Was 1 and Was 3.

CONSEQUENTIAL IMPACTS ON DESIGN/TIPS: Simply providing individual recycling bins throughout a building is not sufficient to gain the credit. You can obtain additional guidance on waste storage area design and waste management from:

→

- the *Metric Handbook*[20]
- BS5908: *Waste Management in Buildings – Code of Practice*
- the online *Technical Manual*[1] (for typical sizes of skips, bins, compactors and balers, etc.).

EVIDENCE TO BE PROVIDED FOR DESIGN STAGE ASSESSMENT:
- Design drawings and/or contract specification clauses confirming the size and location of the dedicated storage area for operational recyclable waste and general waste storage (including any home-composting provision).
- Meeting minutes or a letter from the design team confirming the building's likely waste streams and predicted volumes.
- For healthcare buildings, a letter confirming compliance with the relevant Healthcare Technical Memorandum.
- For schools, a copy of the school's recycling policy and a description of its waste management procedures or a written commitment from the school to develop and implement these.
- For multi-residential buildings, design drawings and/or contract specification clauses detailing the home-composting provision and a copy of the guidance leaflet.

EVIDENCE TO BE PROVIDED FOR POST-CONSTRUCTION STAGE ASSESSMENT: As for the design stage, updated to show the as-constructed status,
plus
- for schools, a copy of the school's recycling policy and a description of its waste management procedures.

IMPLICATION FOR SHELL-ONLY DEVELOPMENTS: The requirements are the same as those detailed above, except for the provision of a compactor or baler and composting requirements. Where the occupier is known, then:
either
- the compactor or baler and/or composting facilities must be provided
or
- the occupier must commit to providing a dedicated space for a compactor or baler and/or composting facilities, which includes
  - suitable concrete hardstanding
  - a three-phase electricity supply
  - access for collection.
If the occupier is not known then:
either
- a compactor or baler and/or composting facilities are not required if the building type is unlikely to generate a need for them
or
- the future occupier must commit to providing a compactor or baler and/or composting facilities.

Wst04: Speculative floor and ceiling finishes

CREDITS AVAILABLE

1

INNOVATION CREDITS

0

The aim of this Issue criterion is to avoid unnecessary waste of materials by encouraging the building's future occupant to select the floor and ceiling finishes.

PREREQUISITES: None

MINIMUM STANDARDS: None

PERFORMANCE STANDARD REQUIRED: If the future occupant is unknown, **one credit** is awarded where:
- carpets, other floor finishes and ceiling finishes are only installed in a limited show area
- the show area is less than 25 per cent of the net lettable floor area of the building.

If an office building is being developed for a specific occupant, you must provide evidence that they have specified or agreed to the floor and ceiling finishes to gain **one credit**.

INNOVATION CREDITS: None

BUILDING-TYPE VARIATIONS: This Issue only applies to office buildings.

CONSEQUENTIAL IMPACTS ON DESIGN/TIPS: In speculative buildings, agents often want a show area in excess of the 25 per cent limitation. You must resolve this conflict with the client to avoid losing this credit.

EVIDENCE TO BE PROVIDED FOR DESIGN STAGE ASSESSMENT:
- Design drawings and/or contract specification clauses confirming the size and location of the show area for the floor and ceiling finishes

and/or
- a letter from the client, design team or future building occupant confirming that they have chosen the floor and ceiling finishes.

EVIDENCE TO BE PROVIDED FOR POST-CONSTRUCTION STAGE ASSESSMENT: As for the design stage.

IMPLICATION FOR SHELL-ONLY DEVELOPMENTS: The provision of a limited show area, as described above.

3.4 Issues for which the service engineer is normally responsible

The service engineer plays a similar role to the architect in achieving the credits for the Issues indicated in Table 3.2. The service engineer will specify a range of good practice design solutions for building services for the Issues detailed below.

Man01: Sustainable procurement (second part of Construction and handover criterion)

CREDITS AVAILABLE

1

INNOVATION CREDITS

0

The aim of this part of this Issue criterion is to deliver a functional and sustainable building by ensuring that the performance of each of the building services is properly tested prior to practical completion.

PREREQUISITES: The client must appoint a specialist commissioning manager during RIBA Design Stages C–D for a building with complex service systems.

MINIMUM STANDARDS:
- For BREEAM ratings Pass, Good, Very Good and Excellent – **one credit** from any of the criteria in this Issue, including this one
- For BREEAM Outstanding rating – **two credits** from any of the criteria in this Issue, including this one.

PERFORMANCE STANDARD REQUIRED: For **one credit**:
- An appropriate project team member must be appointed to monitor and programme the pre-commissioning, commissioning and re-commissioning (if necessary) of the building services, on the client's behalf.
- All building services must meet the requirements of the current Building Regulations, BSRIA and CIBSE commissioning guidelines.
- The Building Management System (BMS) must include the following commissioning procedures:
  - air and water system commissioning must be carried out when all controls are installed and functional
  - measurements of key parameters (such as room temperatures) must be included
  - satisfactory internal conditions must be achieved when the BMS or control installation is running in automatic mode
  - the BMS schematics or graphics and user interface must be fully installed and functional
  - the building occupier must be trained to operate the BMS.

→

Man01: Sustainable procurement (second part of Construction and handover criterion) (continued)

- The principal contractor must prepare a construction programme incorporating appropriate commissioning periods.
- Where a building design includes complex service systems, a specialist commissioning manager must be appointed during RIBA Design Stages C–D to advise on:
  - design impacts arising from commissioning requirements
  - the proposed construction programme, to ensure that sufficient time is allocated
  - commissioning management input during installation stages
  - commissioning and performance testing at handover and post-handover stages.

Complex building service systems include:

- air conditioning
- mechanical and displacement ventilation
- complex passive ventilation
- building management systems (BMS)
- renewable energy sources
- microbiological safety cabinets and fume cupboards
- cold storage systems.

INNOVATION CREDITS: None

BUILDING-TYPE VARIATIONS: None

CONSEQUENTIAL IMPACTS ON DESIGN/TIPS: The service engineer should advise the client on the appointment of the specialist commissioning manager during the design stages if the necessary expertise is not available within their own company. The specialist commissioning manager can work for the subcontractor who is installing the services, etc. but must not be personally involved in the installation of the works.

EVIDENCE TO BE PROVIDED FOR DESIGN STAGE ASSESSMENT:

- A letter of appointment confirming the commissioning manager's responsibilities, if appointed by the client.
- Contract specification clauses requiring the appointment of the commissioning manager and setting out responsibilities.
- A copy of the principal contractor's programme showing the commissioning period.
- A copy of the commissioning schedule.

EVIDENCE TO BE PROVIDED FOR POST-CONSTRUCTION STAGE ASSESSMENT:

- A copy of commissioning records and reports.
- A copy of the principal contractor's programme showing the commissioning period.
- A copy of the commissioning schedule.

IMPLICATION FOR SHELL-ONLY DEVELOPMENTS: If some building services are installed as part of the tenant's fit-out works, one of the Options 1, 2 or 3 (described in Chapter 2, section 2.11) can be used to assess compliance with the required performance standards.

Man01: Sustainable procurement (Aftercare criterion)

CREDITS AVAILABLE

2

INNOVATION CREDITS

1

The aim of this Issue criterion is to deliver a functional and sustainable building by setting up commissioning and aftercare systems that offer an extended period of support to building occupants.

PREREQUISITES: None

MINIMUM STANDARDS:

- For BREEAM ratings Pass, Good, Very Good and Excellent – **one credit** from any of the criteria in this Issue including this one.
- For BREEAM Outstanding rating – **two credits** from any of the criteria in this Issue including this one.

PERFORMANCE STANDARD REQUIRED: One credit can be awarded where a specialist commissioning manager is appointed to undertake seasonal commissioning. In air-conditioned or ventilated buildings, this will include procedures to:

- test all building services under full load conditions (e.g. heating systems in mid-winter and cooling or ventilation systems in mid-summer)
- test all building services under part-load conditions in spring and autumn
- test in periods of high or low occupancy (if appropriate)
- interview building occupants to identify any problems or concerns to do with the effectiveness of the systems
- re-commission systems, if necessary, and incorporate any revisions to operating procedures into the Operations and Maintenance Manuals
- test specialist systems (e.g. fume cupboards, cold storage system) if installed.

In naturally ventilated buildings, seasonal commissioning requires:

- review of thermal comfort, ventilation and lighting at periods of three, six and nine months after occupation by measurement or occupant feedback
- re-commissioning of systems, if necessary, following the review
- updating of the Operations and Maintenance Manuals to incorporate any revisions.

Two credits can be awarded, although this may not be a 'quick win', where the seasonal commissioning detailed above is undertaken **and**, in addition to occupant comfort feedback, the contractor establishes a mechanism or installs equipment to:

- collect energy- and water-consumption data for 12 months after occupation
- compare collected data with projected usage
- analyse discrepancies and adjust systems if they fail to operate as expected.

Plus, the contractor must demonstrate a commitment to providing aftercare support for the building occupier by:

- arranging a meeting with the building occupier shortly after completion to introduce the contractor's aftercare team, hand over the Building User Guide (if one is in place) and present key information about how the building operates

→

Man01: Sustainable procurement (Aftercare criterion) (continued)

- providing initial aftercare by weekly site visits in the first month following completion
- providing on-site training for the occupier's facility management team
- providing longer term aftercare through a helpline or nominated individual.

INNOVATION CREDITS: One Innovation credit can be awarded where, during the first three years of occupation, the facility manager or team is contracted to undertake the following at quarterly intervals:
- collect data on occupant satisfaction, energy and water consumption
- use data to check that the building is performing as expected and, if not, make the necessary adjustments
- set targets for reducing energy and water consumption and monitor progress towards achieving them
- feed back any lessons learned to the client and design team for future use
- provide annual data on occupant satisfaction, energy and water consumption to BRE Global for publication.

BUILDING-TYPE VARIATIONS: None

CONSEQUENTIAL IMPACTS ON DESIGN/TIPS: The BSRIA Soft Landings Framework[21] requirements provide a framework for achieving the performance standards of this Issue criterion. These requirements must be included from an early stage in order to assess the additional costs associated with this extended service and commit to meeting them.

EVIDENCE TO BE PROVIDED FOR DESIGN STAGE ASSESSMENT: For the **first credit**:
- a copy of the commissioning manager's appointment letter

and/or
- the commissioning responsibilities schedule.

For the **second credit**, in addition to the above, a copy of a written commitment or contract to establish procedures to:
- collect, compare and analyse relevant data
- undertake necessary adjustments to services
- provide aftercare support and training.

EVIDENCE TO BE PROVIDED FOR POST-CONSTRUCTION STAGE ASSESSMENT: For the **first credit**:
- a copy of the seasonal commissioning records and reports

and/or
- the specialist commissioning manager's letter of appointment and the commissioning responsibilities schedule.

For the **second credit**, as for the design stage **plus**, in addition to the above:
- written evidence that the relevant procedures are in place or that there is a commitment to provide them.

→

IMPLICATION FOR SHELL-ONLY DEVELOPMENTS: It may not be possible to achieve all of the performance standards of this Issue criterion. If some elements that require seasonal commissioning, as described above, are part of the fit-out, the following (see Chapter 2 for details) can be used to assess compliance with the performance standards:

either

- a Green Lease Agreement

or

- developer and tenant collaboration.

Hea01: Visual comfort
(Internal and external lighting criterion)

CREDITS AVAILABLE

1

INNOVATION CREDITS

0

The aim of this Issue criterion is to achieve best practice performance and comfort for building occupants through the correct specification of artificial lighting systems.

PREREQUISITES: All fluorescent and compact fluorescent lamps must be fitted with high-frequency ballasts.

MINIMUM STANDARDS: For any BREEAM rating to be achieved, all fluorescent and compact fluorescent lamps have to be fitted with high-frequency ballasts.

PERFORMANCE STANDARD REQUIRED: One credit can be awarded where:

- internal illuminance levels (measured in lux) are specified in accordance with the CIBSE *Code for Lighting* (2009)
- in areas where computers are to be used, lighting is specified to comply with sections 3.3, 4.6, 4.7, 4.8 and 4.9 of CIBSE *Lighting Guide 7: Office Lighting*
- in areas used for teaching, lighting is specified to comply with CIBSE *Lighting Guide 5: Lighting for Education*
- external illuminance (lux) levels are specified to meet BS5489: *Part 1 – Lighting of roads and public amenity areas* (2008).

Other standards that might apply are:

- for pre-schools, schools and sixth-from colleges – *Building Bulletin 90: Lighting Design for Schools*
- for care homes housing people with dementia – *Design Lighting for People with Dementia*, University of Stirling.[22]

→

Hea01: Visual comfort (Internal and external lighting criterion) (continued)

Plus, lighting controls need to be zoned to accommodate varying uses and levels of occupancy and to allow for occupant control of zones, such as:

- office and circulation areas
- groups of no more than four workplaces, usually spaced at 40 m² intervals
- workstations adjacent to windows and atria with independent controls
- presentation and audience areas in seminar and lecture rooms
- teaching, seminar and lecture areas, where controls should comply with CIBSE Lighting Guide 5
- stacks, reading and counter areas in libraries
- teaching and demonstration areas
- whiteboards or display screens
- audience seating, circulation and lectern areas in auditoria. Controls must allow: full lighting; demonstrating area lighting to be off and audience seating lighting low; all lighting off and separate localised lectern lighting
- seating and servery areas in dining rooms, restaurants and cafes
- display and counter areas in retail units
- bar and seating areas in bars
- individual bed spaces and staff control areas in wards
- seating and activity areas and circulation spaces with controls for staff in treatment areas, day rooms, waiting areas, etc.

INNOVATION CREDITS: None

BUILDING-TYPE VARIATIONS:
- For educational buildings, manual lighting controls should be accessible to teachers as they enter or leave teaching areas.
- For court buildings, separate zoning is needed for the judge's or magistrate's bench, the dock, jury area and public seating. Lighting control in these spaces must allow for full lighting for cleaning, normal lighting for court sessions and dimmed lighting for showing audio-visual evidence which is still sufficient for note taking.
- For prison buildings:
  - a cell illuminance level of 200 lux at table-top height, with the facility for the cell occupant to select a lower level
  - an exercise yard illuminance level of 10 lux or 100 lux if used for sports.

CONSEQUENTIAL IMPACTS ON DESIGN/TIPS: Where no external light fittings are specified, the credit is awarded solely on the performance of the internal lighting systems. The following internal areas can be excluded from the lighting zone requirements:
- media and arts production spaces
- sports facilities (exercise spaces only, including hydrotherapy and physiotherapy areas).

→

Hea01: Visual comfort (Internal and external lighting criterion) (continued)

EVIDENCE TO BE PROVIDED FOR DESIGN STAGE ASSESSMENT:
- Design drawings showing lighting and controls systems
- Contract specification clauses stipulating the required performance standards or a letter from the service engineer confirming compliance with the required standards.

EVIDENCE TO BE PROVIDED FOR POST-CONSTRUCTION STAGE ASSESSMENT: As for the design stage, updated to show the as-constructed status **plus** a letter of confirmation from the contractor confirming that the installed lighting systems meet the design requirements.

IMPLICATION FOR SHELL-ONLY DEVELOPMENTS: Where part of the lighting system is to be provided by tenants, any of the Options 1, 2 or 3 (described in Chapter 2, section 2.11) can be used to assess compliance with the performance standards.

Hea03: Thermal comfort

CREDITS AVAILABLE

2

INNOVATION CREDITS

0

The aim of this Issue criterion is to achieve appropriate thermal comfort levels and provide controls that maintain a comfortable environment for the building's occupants.

PREREQUISITES: None

MINIMUM STANDARDS: None

PERFORMANCE STANDARD REQUIRED: The **first credit** can be awarded if a dynamic thermal simulation model is developed using software complying with CIBSE AM11 *Building Energy and Environmental Modelling*, to demonstrate that:
- the building design and services deliver the thermal comfort levels set out in CIBSE *Guide A: Environmental Design* (or another recognised industry standard) for occupied spaces
- the building services specification includes criteria on an acceptable 'time out of range' metric for maximum and minimum temperatures for both summer and winter
- the building complies with recognised industry standards for 'time out of range' results.

A **second credit** can be awarded where it is shown that, in addition to achieving the above standards, a temperature-control strategy for the building will be installed, based on the thermal modelling analysis. The heating and cooling strategies also need:

→

- separate zones for central spaces and perimeter spaces within 7 m of windows
- occupant-control systems based on discussions with end users (or, alternatively, specific design guidance or case studies for the building type) that consider user knowledge, occupancy, room function, user interaction with and expectations of the systems
- to consider how each system interacts with the others (an example of this is the interaction of external shading to reduce solar gain interacting with cooling systems)
- manual override of automatic controls to enable users to adapt their immediate environment.

INNOVATION CREDITS: None

BUILDING-TYPE VARIATIONS: Specific building types with additional requirements include:
- Schools – it is acceptable to use the ClassCool software for schools with a straightforward servicing strategy rather than a full CIBSE AM11 dynamic model.
- Education and prison buildings – occupant controls are for use by staff only.
- Industrial units – if they contain no office space, this Issue does not apply.

CONSEQUENTIAL IMPACTS ON DESIGN/TIPS: Any recognised industry or sector best-practice guidance that sets out a thermal performance level in terms of a design temperature and a 'time out of range' metric is considered an appropriate standard for this Issue criterion. For example:
- for pre-schools, schools and sixth-form colleges: internal summer temperatures must not exceed 28°C for more than 60 hours a year
- for patient and clinical areas in healthcare buildings: internal summer temperatures must not exceed 28°C for more than 50 hours a year, as stated in Health Technical Memorandum (HTM) 03-01.

CIBSE *Guide A*, Table 1.7 lists acceptable internal operative temperatures for a number of different building types.

For smaller and more basic buildings with less complex heating and cooling systems and controls:
- an alternative and less complex means of analysis is acceptable, such as the use of ClassCool in certain schools
- controls such as thermostatic radiator values to control heating around a building's perimeter or local occupant controls, such as fan coil units, are acceptable.

Examples of potentially compliant heating controls can be found in the Carbon Trust's *Guide CTG002: Heating Control.*[23]

EVIDENCE TO BE PROVIDED FOR DESIGN STAGE ASSESSMENT: For the **first credit**:
- contract specification clauses or a letter from the service engineer confirming that performance standards are being met
- thermal modelling results
- confirmation from the design team of the 'time out of range' metric adopted.

For the **second credit**, in addition to the above:
- a copy of the building's thermal comfort strategy confirming the proposed performance standards

→

- a contract specification clause confirming the required performance standards
- design drawings confirming the location and types of controls, etc.

EVIDENCE TO BE PROVIDED FOR POST-CONSTRUCTION STAGE ASSESSMENT: As for the design stage, updated to show the as-constructed status, with the thermal modelling updated to reflect any design changes.

IMPLICATION FOR SHELL-ONLY DEVELOPMENTS: The thermal modelling will have to be completed for a notional layout. If the tenant is to install any of the systems or controls, any of the Options 1, 2 or 3 (described in Chapter 2, section 2.11) can be used to assess compliance with the required performance standards.

Hea04: Water quality

CREDITS AVAILABLE

1

INNOVATION CREDITS

0

The aim of this Issue criterion is to minimise the risk of water contamination in building services and to provide fresh sources of water for building users.

PREREQUISITES: None

MINIMUM STANDARDS: For any BREEAM rating to be awarded, the requirements relating to minimising the risk of contamination to water systems must be achieved.

PERFORMANCE STANDARD REQUIRED: One credit can be awarded if all building services water systems are specified and installed to minimise the risk of contamination by compliance with the following:
- the Health and Safety Executive's *Legionnaires' Disease – The Control of Legionella Bacteria in Water Systems: Approved Code of Practice and Guidance* (2000)
- CIBSE TM13: *Minimising the Risk of Legionnaires Disease* (2002)
- other recognised industry standards – such as Health Technical Memorandum 04-1: *The Control of Legionella, Hygiene, Safe Hot Water, Cold Water and Drinking Water Systems*
- where humidification is required, a failsafe system is specified that will shut down the entire system if the unit that sterilises the water vapour fails.

INNOVATION CREDITS: None

→

BUILDING-TYPE VARIATIONS: Additionally, clean, fresh drinking water needs to be provided for the following building types:
- In education buildings and community centres:
  - chilled, mains-fed point-of-use water coolers must be provided for pupils, students, users and staff throughout the day – one per 200 building users
  - the water coolers must be sited in dining rooms, assembly halls, classrooms, common rooms, wide corridors, indoor social areas, changing rooms, concourses, etc., attached to both wall and floor to prevent vandalism and incorporate safety covers to protect the water and electricity connections.
- In permanently staffed buildings and office areas:
  - chilled, mains-fed point-of-use water coolers or point-of-use water coolers must be provided
  - the water coolers must be sited in each staff kitchenette or other suitable position on each floor and in the staff canteen (if provided).
- In sports, fitness and recreational areas or buildings:
  - chilled, mains-fed point-of-use water coolers must be provided
  - the water coolers must be sited in each changing room or on a public concourse, attached to both wall and floor to prevent vandalism and incorporate safety covers to protect the water and electricity connections.

The following do not comply:
- water fountains
- un-chilled mains-fed taps in toilets and kitchens
- bottled water.

CONSEQUENTIAL IMPACTS ON DESIGN/TIPS: The architect must ensure that sufficient space is allowed in areas where water coolers are required.

EVIDENCE TO BE PROVIDED FOR DESIGN STAGE ASSESSMENT: Copies of design drawings and contract specification clauses confirming that the required performance standards are met.

EVIDENCE TO BE PROVIDED FOR POST-CONSTRUCTION STAGE ASSESSMENT: As for the design stage, updated to show the as-constructed status
plus
- a letter from the principal contractor confirming compliance with the requirements of this Issue criterion.

IMPLICATION FOR SHELL-ONLY DEVELOPMENTS: If the tenant is to install any water-fed building services or fresh drinking water facilities, any of the Options 1, 2 or 3 (described in Chapter 2, section 2.11) can be used to assess compliance with the required performance standards.

Ene02: Energy monitoring

CREDITS AVAILABLE

2

(however, the second credit is
not awarded in certain building types)

INNOVATION CREDITS

0

The aim of this Issue criterion is to facilitate the monitoring of operational energy use through the installation of energy sub-meters.

PREREQUISITES: None

MINIMUM STANDARDS: For a BREEAM Very Good, Excellent or Outstanding rating the first credit for sub-meters must be awarded.

PERFORMANCE STANDARD REQUIRED: The **first credit** can be awarded where a building energy management system (BEMS) or separate sub-meters (with pulsed outputs) are specified to monitor the energy from, and the end energy use identified for, the following systems:
- space heating
- domestic hot water
- humidification
- cooling
- major ventilation fans
- lighting
- small power
- other major energy-consuming items (e.g. plant used for swimming pools, kitchens, cold storage, laboratories, lifts and escalators).

Combined sub-meters for lighting and small power meters can be provided if installed at each floor level or for each department.

A **second credit** can be awarded (for most building types) for providing an accessible BEMS or sub-meters for each tenanted building or area or for each function area or department. An extensive list of appropriate function areas for each building type is given in the online *Technical Manual*.[1] The second credit is **not** awarded for the following building types:
- pre-schools and primary schools
- courts
- prison buildings
- multi-residential buildings.

INNOVATION CREDITS: None

→

BUILDING-TYPE VARIATIONS:
- For healthcare buildings, in line with Department of Health requirements, all systems must be monitored using the BEMS or another type of automated control system (such as a remote computer). Large-scale medical equipment systems do not need to be sub-metered.
- Small office, industrial or retail units (less than 200 m²) can have a single sub-meter per unit.
- Large office, industrial or retail units (more than 200 m²) must have sub-meters for each relevant function area within each unit.

CONSEQUENTIAL IMPACTS ON DESIGN/TIPS: If separate energy sub-meters are installed to monitor the operational energy use they should be located to allow easy access for regular monitoring. Typically, this will be in the main plant room.

EVIDENCE TO BE PROVIDED FOR DESIGN STAGE ASSESSMENT: Design drawings showing the locations of sub-meters and contract specification clauses detailing the requirements of this criterion.

EVIDENCE TO BE PROVIDED FOR POST-CONSTRUCTION STAGE ASSESSMENT: As for the design stage, updated to show the as-constructed status.

IMPLICATION FOR SHELL-ONLY DEVELOPMENTS: Where the tenant is to install building services and associated sub-meters, any of the Options 1, 2 or 3 (described in Chapter 2, section 2.11) can be used to assess compliance with the required performance standards.

Ene03: External lighting

CREDITS AVAILABLE

1

INNOVATION CREDITS

0

The aim of this Issue criterion is to encourage the specification of energy-efficient light fittings to external areas.

PREREQUISITES: None

MINIMUM STANDARDS: None

PERFORMANCE STANDARD REQUIRED: One credit can be awarded for specifying external lighting (including decorative and floodlighting) that:

→

- achieves the required levels of efficiency
- does not operate during daylight hours (using time switches or daylight sensors).

The efficiency levels that different types of external lighting fittings must achieve are as follows:

Location of fittings	Where colour rendering index (Ra) greater than or equal to 60 then luminous efficacy is ...	Where colour rendering index (Ra) is less than 60 then luminous efficacy is ...
Fittings on buildings and footpaths	At least 50 lamp lumens/circuit watt	At least 60 lamp lumens/circuit watt
Fittings in car parking areas, associated roads and floodlighting	At least 70 lamp lumens/circuit watt	At least 80 lamp lumens/circuit watt
	Where lamp wattage is greater than or equal to 25W	Where lamp wattage is less than 25W
Signs and fittings up-lighting buildings	At least 60 lamp lumens/circuit watt	At least 50 lamp lumens/circuit watt

© BRE Global Ltd 2011

Plus, the external lighting must be prevented from working during daylight hours by using:
either
- time switches

or
- daylight sensors.

The credit can be awarded where a building is designed to operate with no external light fittings.

INNOVATION CREDITS: None

BUILDING-TYPE VARIATIONS:
- For prison buildings, lights used for security are excluded from the requirements of this Issue.
- Self-contained dwellings in multi-residential buildings that meet the requirements of the Code for Sustainable Homes (CSH) Issue Ene 6 qualify for this BREEAM credit.

CONSEQUENTIAL IMPACTS ON DESIGN/TIPS: Use of low-energy lighting (using LEDs) where each fitting consumes less than 5W should automatically comply with the requirements of this Issue, but the details should be confirmed with the BREEAM Assessor. The use of daylight sensors which override manual switches is also acceptable.

EVIDENCE TO BE PROVIDED FOR DESIGN STAGE ASSESSMENT:
- Design drawings showing the types and locations of external light fittings.
- Contract specification clauses confirming the required performance standards.

EVIDENCE TO BE PROVIDED FOR POST-CONSTRUCTION STAGE ASSESSMENT: As for the design stage, updated to show the as-constructed status, **plus**:
- manufacturers' literature confirming the efficiencies of installed systems.

IMPLICATION FOR SHELL-ONLY DEVELOPMENTS: None

Ene04: Low- and zero-carbon technologies

CREDITS AVAILABLE

5

INNOVATION CREDITS

1

The aim of this Issue criterion is to reduce CO_2 emissions and atmospheric pollution by using local energy generation from low- or zero-carbon technologies to supply a significant proportion of a building's energy demand.

PREREQUISITES: The feasibility study described below has to be undertaken during RIBA Design Stage C (Concept).

MINIMUM STANDARDS: If either a BREEAM Excellent or Outstanding rating is to be achieved, **one credit** must be awarded for this Issue.

PERFORMANCE STANDARD REQUIRED: The **first credit** can be awarded in two ways.
Either an energy specialist produces a feasibility study during RIBA Design Stage C (Concept) to establish the most appropriate low- or zero-carbon energy-generating technology for the building and at least one of the recommended technologies is specified to be installed. The feasibility study should include:

- all on-site or near-site low- or zero-carbon energy-generating technologies appropriate for the site
- the chosen low- or zero-carbon energy-generating technology(ies), with the reasons for rejecting others
- annual energy-generation potential from low- or zero-carbon energy-generating technologies
- life-cycle costs of specified low- or zero-carbon energy-generating technology, including payback periods
- local planning criteria, including land use and noise issues
- the feasibility of exporting heat or electricity from the system
- the availability of grants and tariffs (e.g. Feed-In Tariffs or the Renewable Heat Incentive)
- where appropriate, the potential for connecting to an existing local community combined heat and power (CHP) network or for specifying an on-site CHP system from which heat or electricity could be exported.

Or the credit can be awarded where the building occupant places a contract with an energy supplier to provide electricity for the building from a fully accredited, off-site renewable energy source. The contract has to run for at least three years from the date of the building occupation. Any proposed contract must be checked with the BREEAM Assessor for compliance.

Up to **three credits** can be awarded, although these may not be 'quick wins', where the feasibility study has been completed **and** a local low- or zero-carbon energy technology has been selected which reduces CO_2 emissions from energy regulated by the Building Regulations. **Two (out of a possible three) credits** can be awarded for a 10 per cent reduction. All **three credits** can be awarded for a 20 per cent reduction.   →

Ene04: Low- and zero-carbon technologies (continued)

Up to **four credits** can be awarded where the feasibility study has been completed **and** a local low- or zero-carbon energy technology has been selected for installation and a Life-Cycle Assessment (in accordance with ISO 14044[24] for a 60-year period covering any necessary replacements or maintenance requirements within this period) of the carbon impact of this technology has been carried out. The assessment must account for the chosen technology's embodied carbon emissions and operational carbon savings and emissions. Where the technology reduces the life-cycle CO_2 emissions:

- **two (out of a possible four) credits** can be awarded for undertaking the study only
- **three (out of a possible four) credits** can be awarded for a 10 per cent reduction
- **all four credits** can be awarded for a 20 per cent reduction.

Calculations showing percentage reductions in CO_2 emissions must be provided from approved energy modelling software.

An additional credit can be awarded in relation to this Issue's *Free cooling* criterion, regardless of the percentage reduction in the building's CO_2 emissions from low- or zero-carbon energy technologies and the number of credits already awarded, where:

- the first credit has been awarded in relation to Issue *Hea03: Thermal comfort*

and

- the design incorporates any of the following free-cooling strategies:
  - night-time cooling used with high thermal mass
  - ground coupled air cooling
  - displacement ventilation
  - groundwater cooling
  - surface water cooling
  - evaporative cooling
  - desiccant dehumidification
  - absorption cooling using waste heat.

The service engineer can be the energy specialist if they have suitable experience in low- and zero-carbon energy technologies, although Low Carbon Consultants and BREEAM APs may also have the necessary experience.

INNOVATION CREDITS: One Innovation credit can be awarded where the feasibility study has been completed **and**:

either

- a local low- or zero-carbon energy technology has been chosen which reduces CO_2 emissions from energy regulated by the Buildings Regulations by 30 per cent, qualifying for the award of four credits

or

- a local low- or zero-carbon energy technology has been chosen and a Life Cycle Assessment (as described above) has been carried out which shows that the chosen technology reduces the life-cycle CO_2 emissions by 30 per cent, qualifying for the award of five credits.

BUILDING-TYPE VARIATIONS: None

→

CONSEQUENTIAL IMPACTS ON DESIGN/TIPS: With planning policies increasingly demanding that CO_2 emissions are reduced by 10 or 20 per cent, achieving some of these additional credits is becoming easier, so long as the feasibility study is undertaken during RIBA Design Stage C.

Note that systems fuelled by first-generation biofuels (manufactured from sugars, starch, vegetable oil, animal fats, etc.) are not recognised as renewable by BREEAM 2011. However, second-generation biofuels (derived from lignocellulosic biomass feed stock using advance technical processes) or biofuels manufactured from biodegradable waste material (biogas or locally and sustainably sourced solid biofuels, such as woodchip and wood pellets) are recognised as renewable.

Where self-contained dwellings in multi-residential buildings have been assessed using the Code for Sustainable Homes (CSH), credits awarded for CSH Issue Ene 7 **cannot** be applied directly to a BREEAM 2011 Assessment.

EVIDENCE TO BE PROVIDED FOR DESIGN STAGE ASSESSMENT:
Either
- A copy of the feasibility study
- Design drawings and/or contract specification clauses confirming details of the chosen low- or zero-energy technology.

Or
- The name of the energy supplier providing electricity from an off-site renewable energy source
  plus
- a copy of the contract or other documentation confirming that the supplier is fully accredited.

For the **additional credits** relating to the reduction of CO_2 emissions, in addition to the above, the following evidence must be provided:
- a report, calculations from manufacturers or modelling software confirming the carbon savings, etc.
- a copy of the life-cycle assessment study demonstrating percentage carbon savings over the lifetime of the low- or zero-carbon energy technology system.

For the **free-cooling credit**:
- a report from the service engineer describing the free-cooling strategy
- results from a dynamic simulation model demonstrating the feasibility of the free-cooling strategy
- the evidence required for the first credit in relation to *Hea03: Thermal comfort.*

EVIDENCE TO BE PROVIDED FOR POST-CONSTRUCTION STAGE ASSESSMENT: For the **first credit**:
- as for the design stage, updated to show the as-constructed status.

For the **additional credits** relating to the reduction of CO_2 emissions:
- as for the design stage, updated to show the as-constructed status.

For the **free-cooling credit**:
- as for the design stage, updated to show the as-constructed status.

→

IMPLICATION FOR SHELL-ONLY DEVELOPMENTS: For speculative buildings, the feasibility study must be completed but, if the tenant is responsible for installing the chosen low- or zero-carbon energy technology, any of the Options 1, 2 or 3 (described in Chapter 2, section 2.11) can be used to assess compliance with the required performance standards.

Ene06: Energy-efficient transportation systems

CREDITS AVAILABLE	INNOVATION CREDITS
2	0

The aim of this Issue criterion is to encourage the specification of energy-efficient transport systems.

PREREQUISITES: None

MINIMUM STANDARDS: None

PERFORMANCE STANDARD REQUIRED: The **first credit** can be awarded if:
- an analysis is undertaken of the transportation demand and usage patterns to determine the optimum number and size of lifts, escalators and moving walkway systems
- the energy consumption for each transportation type is estimated for one of the following:
    - at least two types of systems
    - an arrangement of systems
    - a system strategy which is 'fit for purpose'.
    and the one using the least energy in each transportation type is specified.

The **second credit** can be awarded if, in addition to achieving the above, and if lifts are being installed, three of the following energy-efficiency options which offer the greatest energy savings are specified:
- the ability to operate in stand-by mode during off-peak periods (i.e. the power side of the lift controller and auxiliary equipment – lift car lighting, ventilation fans – is switched off) but this should not prevent the emergency lighting in a lift from working when required
- the installation of variable-speed lift motors, variable-voltage and variable-frequency controls
- the provision of a regenerative unit to return energy generated by the lift (due to running up empty and down full) back to the grid or to use elsewhere on site
- the use of energy-efficient lighting and display lighting consuming, on average, less than 55 lamp lumens/circuit watt and lighting which switches off when the lift is idle.

→

If escalators or moving walkway systems are being installed, they need to be fitted with:

either

- a load-sensing device to synchronise motor output to passenger demand

or

- a passenger-sensing device to operate in stand-by mode when there is no demand.

INNOVATION CREDITS: None

BUILDING-TYPE VARIATIONS: None

CONSEQUENTIAL IMPACTS ON DESIGN/TIPS: The parts of this Issue relating to lifts do not apply to lifting platforms, wheelchair stairlifts or platforms or other facilities to aid people with impaired mobility, installed with rated speeds of less than 0.15 m per second. This Issue is also not assessed if the building contains no lifts, escalators or moving walkway systems.

EVIDENCE TO BE PROVIDED FOR DESIGN STAGE ASSESSMENT: For the **first credit**:

- a copy of the transport analysis report with calculations.

For the **second credit**, in addition to the above:

- the contract specification clauses confirming the required performance standard

and either

- the manufacturer's literature confirming performance standards

or

- a letter from the system manufacturer containing a commitment to achieve the required performance standards.

EVIDENCE TO BE PROVIDED FOR POST-CONSTRUCTION STAGE ASSESSMENT: For **both credits**, the same as for the design stage, updated to show the as-constructed status, **plus**

- manufacturers' literature confirming that the required performance standards for the second credit have been implemented in the installed system.

IMPLICATION FOR SHELL-ONLY DEVELOPMENTS: None

Wat02: Water monitoring

CREDITS AVAILABLE

1

INNOVATION CREDITS

0

The aim of this Issue criterion is to provide the facility to monitor, manage and reduce a building's water consumption.

PREREQUISITES: A water meter for the mains water supply must be provided for each building in a development.

MINIMUM STANDARDS: To achieve a BREEAM Good, Very Good, Excellent or Outstanding rating a water meter for the mains water supply for each building on a site must be specified.

PERFORMANCE STANDARD REQUIRED: One credit can be awarded where the mains water supply to each building, and any supply to water-consuming plant or areas (such as swimming pools and kitchens) consuming 10 per cent or more of a building's water usage, is provided with a water meter which:

- has a pulsed output capable of being connected to a BMS
- is connected to any BMS that may already exist on a site where a new building or extension is being constructed.

On sites with multiple buildings or units (such as shopping centres, retail parks, industrial or warehouse units and educational campuses) compliant water meters must be specified for:

- each lettable unit
- common areas, such as toilets
- service and delivery areas
- ancillary and separate buildings.

INNOVATION CREDITS: None

BUILDING-TYPE VARIATIONS: For buildings containing laboratories, separate compliant water meters must be specified for:

- any process
- cooling loops for 'plumbed-in' laboratory process equipment.

For healthcare buildings or sites with multiple departments, compliant meters are typically provided for:

- staff and public areas
- clinical areas and wards
- any areas sub-let to tenants
- laundries
- main kitchens
- hydrotherapy pools

→

- laboratories
- the central sterile supply department and hospital sterilisation and disinfection unit, pathology, pharmacy, mortuary and any other major water usage
- supply from a cold water tank.

CONSEQUENTIAL IMPACTS ON DESIGN/TIPS: If a building contains no water-using equipment, a compliant water meter should be provided to the mains water supply of any existing building or water-consuming facilities that the occupants might use.

EVIDENCE TO BE PROVIDED FOR DESIGN STAGE ASSESSMENT: Copies of the design drawings and contract specification clauses confirming the required performance standards.

EVIDENCE TO BE PROVIDED FOR POST-CONSTRUCTION STAGE ASSESSMENT: As for the design stage, updated to show the as-constructed status.

IMPLICATION FOR SHELL-ONLY DEVELOPMENTS: Where the tenant is responsible for metering arrangements, any of the Options 1, 2 or 3 (described in Chapter 2, section 2.11) can be used to assess compliance with the required performance standards.

Wat03: Leak detection and prevention (Detecting a major leak criterion)

CREDITS AVAILABLE

1

INNOVATION CREDITS

0

The aim of this Issue criterion is to reduce the impact of water leaks that might otherwise go undetected.

PREREQUISITES: None

MINIMUM STANDARDS: None

PERFORMANCE STANDARD REQUIRED: One credit can be awarded where a leak detection system is provided for major water leaks in the mains water supply, both within the building and between the building and the site boundary. The system must be:
- audible
- activated by flow rates exceeding pre-set maximum levels for set periods of time

→

- capable of identifying different flow and potential leakage rates
- programmable to suit occupants' water consumption criteria
- designed to avoid false alarms caused by normal operation of large water-consuming plant (such as chillers).

There is no requirement for the system to shut off the water supply when the alarm is activated.

INNOVATION CREDITS: None

BUILDING-TYPE VARIATIONS: The criterion for this Issue does not apply to clinical areas in healthcare buildings.

CONSEQUENTIAL IMPACTS ON DESIGN/TIPS: Where a water utilities meter is installed at the site or building boundary it may be necessary to install an additional flow-rate meter immediately after the utility meter, towards the building, to detect leaks. If the water utility company agrees to some form of leak detection being installed on their meter, this option would be acceptable.

EVIDENCE TO BE PROVIDED FOR DESIGN STAGE ASSESSMENT:
- Copies of design drawings confirming the provision of a leak detection system.
- Contract specification clauses confirming the required performance standards.
- The manufacturer's product details.

EVIDENCE TO BE PROVIDED FOR POST-CONSTRUCTION STAGE ASSESSMENT: As at the design stage, updated to show the as-constructed status.

IMPLICATION FOR SHELL-ONLY DEVELOPMENTS: None

Wat03: Leak detection and prevention (*Flow control devices* criterion)

CREDITS AVAILABLE	INNOVATION CREDITS
1	0

The aim of this Issue criterion is to reduce the impact of water leaks that might otherwise go undetected.

PREREQUISITES: None

MINIMUM STANDARDS: None

→

Wat03: Leak detection and prevention (Flow control devices criterion) (continued)

PERFORMANCE STANDARD REQUIRED: One credit can be awarded where flow control devices are provided to the water supply in WC areas to ensure that water is only supplied when required. These devices can be:

- a time controller to switch the water supply off after use at a predetermined interval
- a programmed time controller to switch the water supply off or on at pre-determined times
- a volume controller to turn the water supply off once a pre-set maximum volume is reached
- presence detectors and controls to turn the water supply off when no people are present
- a central, computer-based unit providing a managed water control system utilising any of the above devices.

The above requirements still apply to buildings with a single WC, although the water supply shut-off can be activated by the same switch that controls the lighting.

INNOVATION CREDITS: None

BUILDING-TYPE VARIATIONS: The requirement of this criterion does not apply to residential en-suite facilities within multi-residential buildings, but it does apply to buildings with guest bed-rooms, such as hotels.

Note that the criterion for this BREEAM Issue does not apply to clinical areas in healthcare buildings.

CONSEQUENTIAL IMPACTS ON DESIGN/TIPS: A single control system may be fitted covering both male and female toilets within a single core.

If there is no water supply to a building then the criterion will be used to assess the facilities which the building occupants will use.

EVIDENCE TO BE PROVIDED FOR DESIGN STAGE ASSESSMENT:
- Copies of design drawings confirming the provision of a leak-detection system.
- Contract specification clauses confirming the required performance standards.
- The manufacturer's product details.

EVIDENCE TO BE PROVIDED FOR POST-CONSTRUCTION STAGE ASSESSMENT: As at the design stage, updated to show the as-constructed status.

IMPLICATION FOR SHELL-ONLY DEVELOPMENTS: Where the tenant is responsible for the installation of sanitary ware, any of the Options 1, 2 or 3 (described in Chapter 2, section 2.11) can be used to assess compliance with the required performance standards.

Mat04: Insulation

CREDITS AVAILABLE

2

INNOVATION CREDITS

0

The requirements of this Issue are described earlier in this chapter. However, since the performance standards also apply to any insulation used within the building services it is important for the service engineer to be aware of the specification requirements to gain the credit.

Pol02: NO_x emissions

CREDITS AVAILABLE

3 or 2

(for industrial buildings)

INNOVATION CREDITS

0

The aim of this Issue criterion is to reduce pollution of the local environment by specifying heating and cooling systems that minimise nitrous oxide (NO_x) emissions.

PREREQUISITES: None

MINIMUM STANDARDS: None

PERFORMANCE STANDARD REQUIRED: In offices, retail buildings, courts and other buildings where the dry NO_x emissions from plant specified for space heating and cooling systems are as described below, the following credits can be awarded:
- equal to or less than 100 mg/kWh (at 0 per cent excess O_2): **one credit**
- equal to or less than 70 mg/kWh (at 0 per cent excess O_2): **two credits**
- equal to or less than 40 mg/kWh (at 0 per cent excess O_2): **three credits**.

In education, healthcare, multi-residential and prison buildings, where the dry NO_x emissions from space heating and cooling system are as described below, the following credits can be awarded:
- equal to or less than 100 mg/kWh (at 0 per cent excess O_2): **one credit**
- equal to or less than 70 mg/kWh (at 0 per cent excess O_2): **two credits**
- equal to or less than 40 mg/kWh (at 0 per cent excess O_2) **plus** the NO_x emissions from the water heating equal to or less than 100 mg/kWh (at 0 per cent excess O_2): **three credits**.

→

For industrial buildings where dry NO$_x$ emissions from space heating and cooling system are as described below, the credits are awarded separately as follows:

- equal to or less than 70 mg/kWh (at 0 per cent excess O$_2$) in office and associated areas: **one credit**
- equal to or less than 70 mg/kWh (at 0 per cent excess O$_2$) in operational areas: **one credit**.

Typical concerns that are encountered in assessing this Issue, which might affect the award of credits, include the following:

- Manufacturers' NO$_x$ emission data may be supplied at levels of excess oxygen greater than zero or in different units (e.g. mg/m^3, mg/MJ or ppm). Ask the manufacturer to convert their data into the correct format, otherwise the BREEAM Assessor will convert it using factors included in the online *Technical Manual*,[1] which assume worst-case efficiencies.
- Heat pumps powered by grid electricity indirectly produce higher levels of NO$_x$ emissions than stated in the criteria. The BREEAM Assessor will have to carry out a separate calculation for these heat pumps.
- Any electricity from zero-emission renewable sources used by heating and cooling systems will be rated as having zero NO$_x$ emissions.
- Heat recovery is assumed to have zero NO$_x$ emissions.
- Biomass heating, although reducing the use of fossil fuel, can produce significant NO$_x$ emissions which may not meet the criteria.
- District heating systems using waste incineration usually have NO$_x$ emissions that do not meet the criteria.
- Point-of-use grid electric water heaters may be exempt from the calculation if the service engineer can show that their energy demand is less than 10 per cent of the total demand for space and water heating.
- Where more than one source is used for heating or cooling, an average NO$_x$ emission value will be calculated by the BREEAM Assessor.

INNOVATION CREDITS: None

BUILDING-TYPE VARIATIONS: In addition to the variations outlined above, if there are no offices within an industrial unit or there is no heating or cooling within the operational areas, the criterion is not assessed.

CONSEQUENTIAL IMPACTS ON DESIGN/TIPS: While the calculations for the evidence can be complex, if the service engineer specifies the correct type of heating or cooling plant, credits can be achieved relatively easily.

In highly insulated buildings, where the heating load is less than or equal to 7 per cent of the heating load of a Building Regulations compliant building of the same size and shape, **one credit** can be awarded regardless of the NO$_x$ emissions. Calculations of the percentage heat demand must be based on approved energy software.

The use of Green Electricity Tariffs does not provide adequate evidence of low NO$_x$ emissions.

→

EVIDENCE TO BE PROVIDED FOR DESIGN STAGE ASSESSMENT:
- Contract specification clauses confirming the required performance standards.
- The manufacturer's product details.
- Calculations confirming the NO$_x$ emissions.

EVIDENCE TO BE PROVIDED FOR POST-CONSTRUCTION STAGE ASSESSMENT: As for the design stage, updated to show the as-constructed status.

IMPLICATION FOR SHELL-ONLY DEVELOPMENTS: Where the tenant is responsible for specifying the heating or cooling system, any of the Options 1, 2 or 3 (described in Chapter 2, section 2.11) can be used to assess compliance with the required performance standards.

Pol04: Reduction of night time light pollution

CREDITS AVAILABLE

1

INNOVATION CREDITS

0

The aim of this Issue criterion is to reduce unnecessary light pollution, energy consumption and nuisance to neighbours by concentrating external lighting in appropriate areas and minimising upward lighting.

PREREQUISITES: None

MINIMUM STANDARDS: None

PERFORMANCE STANDARD REQUIRED: One credit can be awarded where:
- external lighting is designed to comply with Table 1 (and its accompanying notes) in the Institution of Lighting Engineers' GN01: *Guidance Notes for the Reduction of Obtrusive Light* (2005)
- all external lighting (including floodlighting, but with the exception of safety and security lighting) is specified to switch off automatically between 11.00pm and 07.00am using timed switches
- safety and security lighting is specified to comply with the lower illuminance levels in Table 1 of the ILE's GN01 by using automatic switches, allowing it to be used between 11.00pm and 07.00am
- illuminated signs comply with ILE Technical Report 5: *Brightness of Illuminated Advertisements* (1991).

→

If external lighting is essential for 24-hour operation, it should switch automatically to the lower illuminance levels recommended in the ILE Guidance for lighting between 11.00pm and 07.00am.

INNOVATION CREDITS: None

BUILDING-TYPE VARIATIONS: Buildings in Scotland must also comply with the light pollution criteria detailed in the checklists in Annexes B and C of the Scottish Executive Guidance Note: *Controlling Light Pollution and Reducing Lighting Energy Consumption.*

CONSEQUENTIAL IMPACTS ON DESIGN/TIPS: If there is no external lighting on or around the building, this credit can be awarded by default.
Flush stud lights used for safety reasons in vehicle manoeuvring areas may be excluded from the assessment of this Issue.

EVIDENCE TO BE PROVIDED FOR DESIGN STAGE ASSESSMENT:
- Design drawings indicating the design of the external lighting.
- Contract specification clauses confirming required performance standards.
- Examples provided by the service engineer or lighting designer indicating where and how the proposed lighting strategy complies with the required standards.

EVIDENCE TO BE PROVIDED FOR POST-CONSTRUCTION STAGE ASSESSMENT: As for the design stages, updated to show the as-constructed status.

IMPLICATION FOR SHELL-ONLY DEVELOPMENTS: None

3.5 Issues for which the structural engineer is normally responsible

Pol03: Surface water run-off (Minimising watercourse pollution criterion)

CREDITS AVAILABLE

1

INNOVATION CREDITS

0

The aim of this Issue criterion is to minimise the risk of watercourse pollution by avoiding, reducing and delaying the discharge of rainfall to watercourses.

PREREQUISITES: The appointment of an appropriate consultant (usually the structural engineer) to confirm that there will be no discharge from the developed site for rainfall depths up to 5 mm.

MINIMUM STANDARDS: None

PERFORMANCE STANDARD REQUIRED: One credit can be awarded where:
- sustainable drainage systems (SuDS) or permeable surfaces or infiltration trenches are specified for areas of low pollution risk
- oil and petrol separators, etc. are specified for areas of high contamination or spillage risk
- all water pollution prevention systems are in accordance with the Environment Agency's *Pollution Prevention Guideline 3*[25] and CIRIA's *SUDS Manual: C697* (2007)
- on sites that have chemical or liquid gas storage, shut-off values are fitted to the drainage system to prevent chemicals escaping off site
- all external storage and delivery areas are designed to comply with the Environment Agency's *Pollution Prevention Pays* guidance[26]
- a comprehensive Drainage Plan is issued to the building's occupant.

Areas that present a risk of pollution to watercourses include:
- vehicle manoeuvring areas
- car parks
- waste disposal facilities
- delivery and storage facilities
- plant areas – including those on roofs where there is a risk of oil or petrol leakage.

INNOVATION CREDITS: None

BUILDING-TYPE VARIATIONS: None

→

Pol03: Surface water run-off (Minimising watercourse pollution criterion) (continued)

CONSEQUENTIAL IMPACTS ON DESIGN/TIPS: The use of green roofs is deemed to comply with the requirement for no surface water discharge off-site for rainfall depths up to 5 mm.

If it can be demonstrated that an area of permeable paving is able to retain silts and degrade oils, this will meet the performance standard for minimising watercourse pollution for car parks and access roads.

EVIDENCE TO BE PROVIDED FOR DESIGN STAGE ASSESSMENT:
- The consultant's report detailing the design specification, calculations and drawings confirming the 5 mm rainfall discharge criterion.
- Design drawings showing high- and low-risk areas on the site and contract specification clauses confirming the required performance standards for SuDS, source control systems, oil and petrol separators and shut-off valves, etc.

Plus a letter from the structural engineer:
- confirming that water pollution prevention systems are designed meet the criteria in the Environment Agency's *Pollution Prevention Guide: PPG3* and CIRIA's *SUDS Manual*
- indicating examples of compliance with PPG3 and CIRIA's *SUDS Manual*
- confirming that a Drainage Plan will be produced and handed over to the building's occupant
- confirming that the design of all external storage and delivery areas complies with the requirements of the relevant PPG
- indicating examples of compliance with the PPG.

EVIDENCE TO BE PROVIDED FOR POST-CONSTRUCTION STAGE ASSESSMENT: As for design stage, updated to show the as-constructed status.

IMPLICATION FOR SHELL-ONLY DEVELOPMENTS: None

3.6 Tender specifications to ensure that the principal contractor operates in an environmentally friendly way

Table 3.3 shows that around 11 per cent of a total possible BREEAM score can be achieved by maximising the credits available in relation to environmentally friendly construction activities. The design team must ensure that the following Issues' performance standards are included in the contract requirements at the tender stage so that contractors are fully aware of their requirements and can make appropriate cost provisions.

TABLE 3.3: Issues relating to contractors constructing in an environmentally friendly manner

	Commercial buildings		Non-housing buildings							
	Offices	Retail	Industrial	Educational (schools)	Educational (higher education)	Healthcare	Prisons	Courts	Multi-residential buildings	Other buildings
Management Category										
Man01: Sustainable procurement (Construction and handover criterion)	2	2	2	2	2	2	2	2	2	2
Man01: Sustainable procurement (Aftercare criterion)	2	2	2	2	2	2	2	2	2	2
Man02: Responsible construction practices	2	2	2	2	2	2	2	2	2	2
Man03: Construction site impacts	5	5	5	5	5	5	5	5	5	5
Total credits available in Management Category	22	22	22	22	22	22	22	22	22	22
Weighted % score of 1 credit in Management Category	6.00	6.00	6.00	6.00	6.00	6.00	6.00	6.00	6.00	6.00
Health and Wellbeing Category	No Issues relate to environmental construction activities									
Energy Category	No Issues relate to environmental construction activities									
Transport Category	No Issues relate to environmental construction activities									
Water Category	No Issues relate to environmental construction activities									
Materials Category	No Issues relate to environmental construction activities									
Waste Category	7.5% weighting towards BREEAM score									
Wst01: Construction waste management (Construction resource efficiency criterion)	3	3	3	3	3	3	3	3	3	3
Wst01: Construction waste management (Diversion of resources from landfill criterion)	1	1	1	1	1	1	1	1	1	1
Total credits available in Waste Category	7	6	6	6	6	6	6	6	6	6
Weighted % score of 1 credit in Waste Category	4.29	5.00	5.00	5.00	5.00	5.00	5.00	5.00	5.00	5.00
Land Use and Ecology Category	No Issues relate to environmental construction activities									
Pollution Category	No Issues relate to environmental construction activities									
Overall % value of environmental construction activities towards overall BREEAM score	10.29	11.00	11.00	11.00	11.00	11.00	11.00	11.00	11.00	11.00

Man01: Sustainable procurement (Construction and handover criterion)

CREDITS AVAILABLE

2

INNOVATION CREDITS

0

The aim of this Issue criterion is to deliver a functional and sustainable building by ensuring that its performance is tested prior to practical completion.

The first part of this criterion is described above in section 3.3 dealing with the service engineer's responsibilities: it is repeated here to cover the principal contractor's responsibilities.

PREREQUISITES: None

MINIMUM STANDARDS:
- For BREEAM ratings Pass, Good, Very Good and Excellent – **one credit** from any of the criteria in this Issue, including this one.
- For BREEAM Outstanding rating – **two credits** from any of the criteria in this Issue, including the two for this criterion.

PERFORMANCE STANDARD REQUIRED: One credit can be awarded where the principal contractor is required to commission and programme a thermographic survey of the completed building fabric enclosing all heated and/or air conditioned areas of the building. The survey must:
- be undertaken by the holder of a Level 2 Certificate in thermography[27]
- identify the continuity of the insulation
- highlight any excessive thermal bridges within and air leakage paths through the fabric

and must
- meet the requirements of BS EN 13187 and CIBSE TM23

and
- carry the requirement for the contractor to rectify any faults found.

Another credit can be awarded where the principal contractor undertakes the following:
- Appoints a specialist commissioning manager to monitor and programme the pre-commissioning and commissioning of the building services on behalf of the client.
- Ensures that building services are commissioned to the current Building Regulations, BSRIA and CIBSE commissioning guidelines.
- Ensures that the commissioning of any Building Management System (BMS) includes the following checks:
    - commissioning of air and water systems are carried out when all controls are installed and functional
    - measurements of key parameters (e.g. room temperatures) are included
    - satisfactory internal conditions are achieved when the BMS and controls are running in automatic mode

→

Man01: Sustainable procurement (Construction and handover criterion) (continued)

- BMS schematics, graphics and user interfaces are fully installed and functional
- the building occupier is trained to operate the BMS.
- Prepares a programme to account for appropriate commissioning periods.

The specialist commissioning manager can work for the subcontractor who is installing the services, etc. but they must not be personally involved in installing the works.

INNOVATION CREDITS: None

BUILDING-TYPE VARIATIONS: None

CONSEQUENTIAL IMPACTS ON DESIGN/TIPS: If the building is naturally ventilated using cross-ventilation from windows and/or trickle vents, a specialist commissioning manager may not need to be appointed.

EVIDENCE TO BE PROVIDED FOR DESIGN STAGE ASSESSMENT: For the **credit relating to the thermographic survey**:

- contract specification clauses or a letter of appointment requiring the thermographic survey to be carried out
- the construction programme showing the thermographic survey.

For the **credit relating to commissioning**:

- a letter of appointment confirming commissioning responsibilities, if the specialist commissioning manager is appointed by the client
- contract specification clauses confirming the appointment and responsibilities of the commissioning manager
- a copy of the principal contractor's programme showing the commissioning period
- a copy of the commissioning schedule.

EVIDENCE TO BE PROVIDED FOR POST-CONSTRUCTION STAGE ASSESSMENT: For the **credit relating to the thermographic survey**:

- a copy of the thermographic survey
- a copy of the Level 2 thermography certificate from the surveyor
- written confirmation from the principal contractor that defects have been rectified.

For the **credit relating to commissioning**:

- a copy of the commissioning records and reports
- a copy of the principal contractor's programme showing the commissioning period
- a copy of the commissioning schedule.

IMPLICATION FOR SHELL-ONLY DEVELOPMENTS: None for the thermographic survey. If the shell spaces contain heating, ventilations, air-conditioning, domestic hot water and/or lighting, the commissioning part of this criterion can be assessed. If none of these systems is installed as part of the shell works, any of the Options 1, 2 or 3 (described in Chapter 2, section 2.11) can be used to assess compliance with the required performance standards.

Man01: Sustainable procurement (Aftercare criterion)

CREDITS AVAILABLE

2

INNOVATION CREDITS

1

The aim of this Issue criterion is to deliver a functional and sustainable building by setting up commissioning and aftercare systems that offer greater support.

PREREQUISITES: None

MINIMUM STANDARDS:

- For BREEAM ratings Pass, Good, Very Good and Excellent – **one credit** from any of the criteria in this Issue, including this one.
- For BREEAM Outstanding rating – **two credits** from any of the criteria in this Issue including this one.

PERFORMANCE STANDARD REQUIRED: The **first credit** can be awarded for air-conditioned and ventilated buildings where a specialist commissioning manager is appointed to undertake seasonal commissioning, including the following:

- Testing all building services under full load conditions (e.g. heating systems in mid-winter and cooling and ventilation systems in mid-summer).
- Testing all building services under part-load conditions in spring and autumn.
- Testing in periods of high or low occupancy, if appropriate.
- Interviewing building occupants to identify problems with and concerns about the effectiveness of systems.
- Re-commissioning systems, if necessary, and incorporating any revisions in operating procedures in the Operations and Maintenance Manuals.
- Checking specialist systems installed (e.g. fume cupboards, cold storage systems).

Or, in naturally ventilated buildings, the specialist commissioning manager undertakes the following:

- Reviews of thermal comfort, ventilation and lighting at three, six and nine months after occupation by measurement or occupant feedback.
- Re-commissioning of systems following review and incorporating revisions into the Operations and Maintenance Manuals.

Two credits can be awarded where either of the above seasonal commissioning procedures is undertaken, depending on the building being assessed **and**, in addition to the above occupant comfort feedback requirement, the contractor establishes a mechanism or installs equipment to:

- collect energy- and water-consumption data for 12 months after occupation
- compare collected data with projected usage
- analyse discrepancies and adjust systems if they fail to operate as expected.

Plus, in relation to both air-conditioned and ventilated buildings and naturally ventilated buildings, the contractor demonstrates commitment to providing aftercare support for the building occupier by:

→

- arranging a meeting with the building occupier shortly after completion to introduce the contractor's aftercare team, hand over the Building User Guide (if one is in place) and present key information about how the building operates
- providing initial aftercare by weekly site visits in the first month following completion
- providing on-site training for the occupier's facility management team
- providing longer term aftercare, through a helpline or nominated individual.

INNOVATION CREDITS: One Innovation credit can be awarded where, during the first three years of occupation, the facility manager or equivalent is contracted to undertake the following at quarterly intervals:

- collect data on occupant satisfaction, energy and water consumption
- use data to check that the building is performing as expected and, if not, make the necessary adjustments
- set targets for reducing energy and water consumption and monitor progress towards achieving them
- feed back any lessons learned to the client and design team for future use
- provide annual data on occupant satisfaction, energy and water consumption to BRE Global for publication.

BUILDING-TYPE VARIATIONS: None

CONSEQUENTIAL IMPACTS ON DESIGN/TIPS: The BSRIA Soft Landings Framework[21] requirements provide a framework for achieving the performance standards of this Issue criterion.

EVIDENCE TO BE PROVIDED FOR DESIGN STAGE ASSESSMENT: For the **first credit**:

- a copy of the commissioning manager's appointment letter confirming they have been appointed to undertake seasonal commissioning

and/or

- the commissioning responsibilities schedule.

For the **second credit**, in addition to the above, a copy of a written commitment or contract to put in place:

- a mechanism to collect, compare and analyse relevant data
- provisions to undertake the necessary adjustments to services
- any aftercare support and training necessary.

EVIDENCE TO BE PROVIDED FOR POST-CONSTRUCTION STAGE ASSESSMENT: For the **first credit**:

- a copy of the seasonal commissioning records and reports

and/or

- the specialist commissioning manager's letter of appointment and the commissioning responsibility schedule.

For the **second credit**, as for the design stage and, in addition to the above:

- written evidence that the relevant mechanisms and procedures are in place or that there is a commitment to provide them.

→

Man01: Sustainable procurement (Aftercare criterion) (continued)

IMPLICATION FOR SHELL-ONLY DEVELOPMENTS: The performance standards of this Issue criterion can be achieved if the above requirements are included in the fit-out works and credits awarded as described in Chapter 2, using:

either
- a Green Lease Agreement

or
- developer and tenant collaboration.

Man02: Responsible construction practices

CREDITS AVAILABLE

2

INNOVATION CREDITS

1

The aim of this Issue criterion is to promote the environmentally and socially considerate, responsible and accountable management of construction sites.

PREREQUISITES: The principal contractor must use a compliant considerate construction scheme to formally assess the construction site. One such scheme is the Considerate Constructors Scheme operated by the Construction Confederation.[28]

MINIMUM STANDARDS: To achieve a BREEAM Excellent rating, **one credit** must be awarded. For a BREEAM Outstanding rating, **two credits** must be awarded.

PERFORMANCE STANDARD REQUIRED: One credit can be awarded where the principal contractor meets the criteria of a compliant scheme. For the Considerate Constructors Scheme, this means achieving a score of between 24 and 31.5.

The **second credit** can be awarded where the principal contractor significantly exceeds compliance with the criteria of a relevant scheme. For the Considerate Constructors Scheme, this means achieving a score of between 32 and 35.5.

INNOVATION CREDITS: One Innovation credit can be awarded where the principal contractor achieves an exemplary level of practice in terms of the criteria of a compliant scheme. For the Considerate Constructors Scheme, this means achieving a score of 36 or more.

BUILDING-TYPE VARIATIONS: None

→

CONSEQUENTIAL IMPACTS ON DESIGN/TIPS: Nearly all principal contractors are now assessed under the Considerate Constructors Scheme, so compliance with the Scheme should be entered into the requirements in the tender documents. Achieving **two credits** should be the normal default position for any contractor.

EVIDENCE TO BE PROVIDED FOR DESIGN STAGE ASSESSMENT: For **both credits**: **either**
- contract specification clauses confirming the requirement to use a compliant Scheme and the score required

or
- written confirmation from the client that the principal contractor is obliged to comply with the requirements of this BREEAM Issue.

EVIDENCE TO BE PROVIDED FOR POST-CONSTRUCTION STAGE ASSESSMENT: For **both credits**, a copy of the Scheme certificate and/or compliance report confirming the score for the site.

IMPLICATION FOR SHELL-ONLY DEVELOPMENTS: None

Man03: Construction site impacts

CREDITS AVAILABLE

5

INNOVATION CREDITS

0

The aim of this Issue criterion is to ensure that construction sites are managed in an environmentally sound way.

PREREQUISITES: The principal contractor must name the individual within their organisation responsible for achieving the performance standards in relation to data on energy, water and transport energy consumption.

MINIMUM STANDARDS: None

PERFORMANCE STANDARD REQUIRED: Up to five credits can be awarded as follows:
- **One credit** for monitoring, recording and reporting energy consumption data from construction plant, equipment and site accommodation as energy used (kW) by fuel type or CO_2 emissions (total kg/tonnesCO_{2equiv} and tonnesCO_{2equiv} per £100 of project value).

→

- **One credit** for monitoring, recording and reporting water consumption data (m^3) from construction plant, equipment and site accommodation and reporting on net water consumption if any recycled water is used on site.
- **One credit** for monitoring, recording and reporting separately energy consumption data from transport used in delivering the majority of construction materials in the major building elements, groundworks and landscaping (from production gate to site gate) and the removal of construction waste (from site gate to waste disposal or recovery centre gate) as fuel consumption by type (litres) or CO_2 emissions (total kg/tonnesCO_{2equiv}) plus distances travelled in kilometres.
- **One credit** for ensuring that all site timber is sourced in accordance with the UK Government's Timber Procurement Policy.[29] Site timber is timber used to facilitate the construction process (e.g. formwork and site hoardings).
- **One credit** if the principal contractor operates a certified environmental management system, to BS EN ISO 14001[30] or BS8555[31] (and reaches stage four of the implementation stage – Implementation and Operation of Environmental Management system). The principal contractor must also implement a best practice pollution prevention policy as described in 'Section 2.25 – Preventing Pollution' of the Environment Agency's *Building a Better Environment: A Guide for Developers* Environmental Checklist.[32]

While BREEAM does not require specific benchmarks or targets to be achieved in relation to this Issue, it is recommended that site-specific targets are established and used as the basis for reports.

INNOVATION CREDITS: None

BUILDING-TYPE VARIATIONS: Where self-contained dwellings in multi-residential buildings have been assessed using the Code for Sustainable Homes (CSH), credits awarded for CSH Issue Man 3 **cannot** be applied directly to a BREEAM 2011 Assessment.

CONSEQUENTIAL IMPACTS ON DESIGN/TIPS: As there are no accepted protocols for the collection of data and reporting on energy and water consumption on construction sites, BREEAM requires confirmation of the method used. The Strategic Forum has produced a number of reports[33] offering guidance.

EVIDENCE TO BE PROVIDED FOR DESIGN STAGE ASSESSMENT:
Either
- contract specification clauses requiring the above performance standards to be achieved

or
- a written commitment from the principal contractor to achieving the required performance standards.

EVIDENCE TO BE PROVIDED FOR POST-CONSTRUCTION STAGE ASSESSMENT:
- The name of the individual responsible for monitoring, recording and reporting on data.
- A summary of the monitoring and data-gathering mechanism used to collect data.

→

- Collected data for:
  - the total site energy consumption by fuel type or CO_2 emissions
  - total site net water consumption
  - fuel consumption for both the delivery of materials and removal of waste by fuel type or CO_2 emission, plus distances travelled.
- A list of the certified and non-certified timber used on site, as required by *Mat03: Responsible sourcing of materials*.
- A copy of the principal contractor's ISO 14001 Certificate or evidence of status under BS8555.
- A completed copy of Section 2.2.5 of the Environment Agency's Environmental Checklist, signed by the principal contractor to confirm the site's compliance.

IMPLICATION FOR SHELL-ONLY DEVELOPMENTS: None

Wst01: *Construction waste management*

CREDITS AVAILABLE

4

INNOVATION CREDITS

1

The aim of this Issue criterion is to improve resource efficiency by effectively managing and reducing construction-related waste.

PREREQUISITES: A compliant Site Waste Management Plan (SWMP) must be in place. Since April 2008, all construction projects in England over a value of £300,000 require an SWMP by law.

MINIMUM STANDARDS: For a BREEAM Outstanding rating, **one credit** must be awarded.

PERFORMANCE STANDARD REQUIRED: Three credits can be awarded in relation to the *Construction resource efficiency* criterion where the principal contractor meets the following benchmarks in relation to non-hazardous construction waste (excluding demolition and excavation waste) generated by the development:
- **One credit** if the waste is equal to or less than 13.3 m³ (11.1 tonnes) per 100 m² gross internal floor area.
- **Two credits** if it is equal to or less than 7.5 m³ (6.5 tonnes) per 100 m² gross internal floor area.
- **Three credits** if it is equal to or less than 3.4 m³ (3.2 tonnes) per 100 m² gross internal floor area.

→

If an existing building is to be demolished, a pre-demolition audit, which is referenced in the SWMP, must be carried out to:

- identify key refurbishment or demolition materials
- identify potential materials for reuse and recycling.

A further credit can be awarded in relation to the *Diversion of resources from landfill* criterion where the following percentages of non-hazardous construction and demolition waste (if applicable) are diverted from landfill:

- 80 per cent by weight, or 70 per cent by volume, of non-demolition waste
- 90 per cent by weight, or 80 per cent by volume, of demolition waste.

This waste must be sorted into *key waste groups*, either on or off site, by a licensed recovery contractor. 'Diverted from landfill' includes:

- reusing on site in situ or for new applications
- reusing on other sites
- salvaging or reclaiming for reuse
- returning to the supplier via a 'take-back' scheme
- recovering by an approved waste management contractor and recycling
- being sent for energy recovery.

A list of what BREEAM considers 'key waste groups' is given in Table 10-1 in the online *Technical Manual*.[1]

A compliant SWMP includes:

- a target benchmark in relation to non-hazardous construction waste
- procedures for minimising non-hazardous construction waste in relation to this benchmark
- procedures for minimising hazardous waste
- procedures for monitoring, measuring and reporting hazardous and non-hazardous site waste
- procedures for sorting, reusing and recycling defined construction waste groups
- the name and job title of the individual on site responsible for implementing the SWMP.

INNOVATION CREDITS: One Innovation credit can be awarded if the following exemplary levels are achieved:

- Non-hazardous construction waste is equal to or less than 1.6 m^3 (1.9 tonnes) per 100 m^2 gross internal floor area.
- 90 per cent by weight, or 85 per cent by volume of non-hazardous non-demolition waste is diverted from landfill.
- 95 per cent by weight, or 85 per cent by volume of non-hazardous demolition waste is diverted from landfill.
- All key waste groups are identified for diversion from landfill in the pre-construction stage SWMP.

BUILDING-TYPE VARIATIONS: None

→

CONSEQUENTIAL IMPACTS ON DESIGN/TIPS: The SWMP should be started initially as part of the design process, then passed on to the principal contractor for development and implementation. This process will help to identify how waste can be reduced by making changes in the design and specification of products and materials. This is often the responsibility of the structural engineer, but sometimes the architect is responsible for the process up to the start of works on site. For further guidance on how to reduce construction waste, visit the Waste and Resources Action Programme (WRAP) Construction and the Construction Resources and Waste Platform websites.[34] The benchmarks listed above are derived from data collected through BRE's SMARTWaste scheme. BRE has indicated that the level of waste generated by projects using this scheme in terms of potential credits equates to:

- **one credit** = top 50 per cent
- **two credits** = top 25 per cent
- **three credits** = top 10 per cent
- **an Innovation credit** = top 5 per cent.

Registering the site with BRE's SMARTWaste[35] scheme will provide the principal contractor with the relevant tools to monitor and target resource efficiency on site in a structured way.

EVIDENCE TO BE PROVIDED FOR DESIGN STAGE ASSESSMENT: At least **one** of the following is required:

- a copy of the SWMP
- the contract specification clauses confirming requirements
- a letter from the principal contractor confirming how the requirements of this Issue will be achieved.

EVIDENCE TO BE PROVIDED FOR POST-CONSTRUCTION STAGE ASSESSMENT: A copy of the SWMP summary datasheets or equivalent monitoring reports and records confirming that the required performance standards were achieved during the construction period.

IMPLICATION FOR SHELL-ONLY DEVELOPMENTS: None

3.7 Benefits of appointing specialist consultants

As described in Chapter 2, it can be advantageous to appoint a number of specialist consultants, who can provide evidence of compliance with the performance standards of a range of Issues. The design team must know when the appointment of a specialist consultant is a prerequisite for the award of a credit so that they can advise the client.

Table 2.4 shows which specialist consultants the client might need to appoint and when they should be appointed. If all of these specialist consultants are appointed, approximately 17 per cent of a BREEAM Assessment's final score (Table 3.4) can be contributed from the Issues described below.

TABLE 3.4: Impact of appointing specialist consultants

	Commercial buildings		Non-housing buildings							
	Offices	Retail	Industrial	Educational (schools)	Educational (higher education)	Healthcare	Prisons	Courts	Multi-residential buildings	Other buildings
Management Category	Possible credits from appointing a BREEAM Accredited Professional and a specialist commissioning manager									
Man01: Sustainable procurement (part of Project brief and design criterion)	3	3	3	3	3	3	3	3	3	3
Man01: Sustainable procurement (part of Construction and handover criterion)	1	1	1	1	1	1	1	1	1	1
Weighted % score of 1 credit in Management Category	2.18	2.18	2.18	2.18	2.18	2.18	2.18	2.18	2.18	2.18
Health and Wellbeing Category	Possible credits from appointing an acoustic consultant									
Hea05: Acoustic performance	2	2	2	3	2	2	2	2	4	2
Weighted % score of 1 credit in Health and Wellbeing Category	2.14	2.00	2.14	2.65	1.76	1.67	2.14	2.14	3.75	1.88
Energy Category	No Issues in this category relate to specialists									
Transport Category	Possible credits from appointing a highway engineer									
Tra01: Public transport accessibility	3	5	3	3	5	5	2	5	3	5
Tra05: Travel plan	1	1	1	1	1	1	1	1	1	1
Weighted % score of 1 credit in Transport Category	3.56	5.33	3.56	4.57	4.36	4.80	6.00	5.33	3.56	4.36
Water Category	No Issues in this category relate to specialists									
Materials Category	No Issues in this category relate to specialists									
Waste Category	No Issues in this category relate to specialists									
Land Use and Ecology Category	Possible credits from appointing an ecologist									
LE02: Ecological value of site and protection of ecological features	1	1	1	1	1	1	1	1	1	1
LE03: Mitigating ecological impact	2	2	2	2	2	2	2	2	2	2
LE04: Enhancing site ecology	3	3	3	3	3	3	2	3	3	3
LE05: Long-term impact on biodiversity	2	2	2	2	2	2	3	2	2	2
Weighted % value of the above credits to the final BREEAM score	8.00	8.00	8.00	8.00	8.00	8.00	8.00	8.00	8.00	8.00
Pollution Category	Possible credits from appointing an acoustic consultant									
Pol05: Noise attenuation	1	1	1	1	1	1	1	1	1	1
Weighted % score of 1 credit in Pollution Category	0.77	0.77	0.83	0.77	0.77	0.77	0.77	0.77	0.77	0.77
Overall % value of client appointing specialist consultants towards overall BREEAM score	16.65	18.28	16.71	18.17	17.08	17.42	19.09	18.43	18.26	17.19

3.8 Appointing an ecologist

Of the five Issues in the *Land use and ecology* category, four can involve the appointment of a *suitably qualified ecologist*. These four Issues alone are responsible for around 8 per cent of a BREEAM score. A 'suitably qualified ecologist' is someone with:

- a degree or equivalent qualification in ecology or a related subject (e.g. biological sciences, zoology, botany, countryside management, environmental sciences, marine and freshwater management, earth sciences, agriculture, forestry, geography or landscape management)
- a minimum of three years' relevant and practical experience, gained within the past five years, of the factors affecting a site's ecology
- membership of a professional association, such as:
  - the Chartered Institution of Water and Environmental Management
  - the Institute of Ecology and Environmental Management
  - the Institute of Environmental Management and Assessment
  - the Landscape Institute.

Details of an ecologist's qualifications and experience must be provided to the BREEAM Assessor in order to verify their suitability. The Issues for which ecologists can provide suitable evidence for the award of credits are listed below.

LE02: Ecological value of site and protection of ecological features

CREDITS AVAILABLE	INNOVATION CREDITS
1	0

The requirements for awarding the credit for this Issue are described earlier in this chapter, in section 3.1 Measuring a site's impact on an Assessment. While appointing an ecologist is **not** a prerequisite for the award of the credit, it could greatly ease the task of providing the evidence required to show that a site is of low ecological value. An ecologist is far better placed to apply professional judgement to determine a site's ecological value, and whether certain features have an ecological value, than a layman using the simple BREEAM checklist.

BUILDING-TYPE VARIATIONS: Where self-contained dwellings in multi-residential buildings have been assessed using the Code for Sustainable Homes (CSH) and the requirements of CSH Issues Eco 1 and Eco 3 are met, this credit can be awarded.

LE03: Mitigating ecological impact

CREDITS AVAILABLE

2

INNOVATION CREDITS

0

The aim of this Issue criterion is to minimise the impact of a development on a site's existing ecology.

PREREQUISITES: None

MINIMUM STANDARDS: For a BREEAM Very Good, Excellent or Outstanding rating, **one credit** must be awarded.

PERFORMANCE STANDARD REQUIRED: One credit can be awarded where the change in a site's ecological value, as measured in plant species richness, is less than zero but equal to or greater than minus nine. This is determined in one of two ways.

Either provide the following information for the BREEAM Assessor to insert into the *LE03/LE04* calculator:

- the broad habitat types existing on the site and those proposed – this can be done using Tables 11-2 and 11-3 in the online *Technical Manual*[1]
- details of the areas of existing and proposed broad habitat types.

Or, if appointed by the client, a suitably qualified ecologist provides the information for the *LE03/LE04* calculator by:

- undertaking an ecological survey of the site to determine the existing broad habitat types, average plant species richness and areas
- confirming the broad habitat types proposed in the development, average plant species richness and areas.

Two credits can be awarded where the change in a site's ecological value, as measured in plant species richness, is equal to or greater than zero, as determined above.

The ecological value of a site is the sum of the average plant species richness for each habitat type, multiplied by its area, divided by the total area of the site.

INNOVATION CREDITS: None

BUILDING-TYPE VARIATIONS: Where self-contained dwellings in multi-residential buildings are assessed using the Code for Sustainable Homes (CSH), credits awarded for CSH Issue Eco 4 **cannot** be applied directly to a BREEAM 2011 Assessment.

CONSEQUENTIAL IMPACTS ON DESIGN/TIPS: It is important to note that derelict sites are **not** devoid of ecological habitats. Once a site has been derelict for more than five years, BREEAM presumes that flora and fauna will start to colonise it. So do not assume that a derelict site is devoid of ecological habitats: you must check.

If the client appoints an ecologist, assessing this BREEAM Issue can be much easier. →

A living roof can mitigate the ecological impact of a development, **but** an ecologist will have to be appointed to confirm its impact.

EVIDENCE TO BE PROVIDED FOR DESIGN STAGE ASSESSMENT: Design drawings (site plan, survey, etc.) must be provided showing existing and proposed habitat types and:
either
- a completed *LE03/LE04* calculation from the BREEAM Assessor

or
- an ecologist's report covering the issues in Appendix F in the online *Technical Manual*.[1]

EVIDENCE TO BE PROVIDED FOR POST-CONSTRUCTION STAGE ASSESSMENT: As at the design stage, updated to show the as-constructed status of the site and in large mixed-use developments, where the planting of the site being assessed has not yet been completed, confirmation that any planting will be completed within 18 months by:
either
- contract specification clauses

or
- a letter from the client or principal contractor.

IMPLICATION FOR SHELL-ONLY DEVELOPMENTS: None

LE04: Enhancing site ecology

CREDITS AVAILABLE

3 or 2
(for prison buildings)

INNOVATION CREDITS

0

The aim of this Issue criterion is to maintain and enhance the ecological value of sites.

PREREQUISITES: A suitably qualified ecologist must be appointed during RIBA Preparation Stage B (Brief).

MINIMUM STANDARDS: None

PERFORMANCE STANDARD REQUIRED: Except for prison buildings, **one credit** can be awarded where an ecologist is appointed and they:

→

- undertake a site ecological survey prior to initial site works during RIBA Preparation Stage B (Brief)
- produce an Ecology Report, based on the survey, making recommendations for the protection and enhancement of the site's ecology.

Plus

- confirmation is supplied that the ecologist's recommendations will be implemented.

Two credits can be awarded where, in addition to the above:

- the ecologist confirms that the Ecology Report recommendations increase the site's ecological value by up to (but not including) six plant species
- the increase in plant species is determined using the *LE03/LE04* calculator using actual plant species reported by the ecologist.

Three credits can be awarded where:

- the ecologist confirms that the Ecology Report recommendations increase the site's ecological value by six plant species or more
- the increase in plant species is determined using the *LE03/LE04* calculator using actual plant species reported by the ecologist.

A site's ecology can be protected and enhanced by the incorporation of design solutions such as:

- planting native species to attract and benefit local wildlife – see the Natural History Museum's online postcode plant database[36]
- adopting horticultural good practice (e.g. reduced use of pesticides)
- installing bird, bat and/or insect boxes
- developing a full Biodiversity Management Plan with recommendations on when clearance works should occur, to avoid breeding seasons, etc.
- the integration of sustainable drainage schemes, green roofs, community orchards, etc.

INNOVATION CREDITS: None

BUILDING-TYPE VARIATIONS: For prison buildings, **two credits** can be awarded where a suitably qualified ecologist:

- undertakes a site ecological survey prior to initial site works
- produces an Ecology Report, based on the survey, making recommendations for the protection and enhancement of the site's ecology.

Plus

- confirmation is supplied that the ecologist's recommendations will be implemented.

Where self-contained dwellings in multi-residential buildings are assessed using the Code for Sustainable Homes (CSH), credits awarded for CSH Issue Eco 4 **cannot** be applied directly to a BREEAM 2011 Assessment.

CONSEQUENTIAL IMPACTS ON DESIGN/TIPS: It is important to advise the client that a suitably qualified ecologist must be appointed during RIBA Preparation Stage B (Brief) for any credits to be awarded in relation to this Issue.

→

Guidance on the range of possible design solutions to improve a site's ecology is given in Dr Carol Williams' *Biodiversity for Low and Zero Carbon Buildings: A Technical Guide for New Build*.[37] This includes advice on living roofs, providing habitats for birds and bats and planting for wildlife.

EVIDENCE TO BE PROVIDED FOR DESIGN STAGE ASSESSMENT:
- The Ecology Report covering the issues in Appendix F of the online *Technical Manual*.[1]
- Design drawings, including site plans, surveys, etc.
- Written confirmation from the client or design team confirming how the ecologist's recommendations will be implemented.

EVIDENCE TO BE PROVIDED FOR POST-CONSTRUCTION STAGE ASSESSMENT: As for the design stage, updated to show the as-constructed status of the site **and**, in large mixed-use developments, where the planting of the site has not yet been completed, confirmation that any planting will be completed within 18 months by:
either
- contract specification clauses
or
- a letter from the client or principal contractor.

IMPLICATION FOR SHELL-ONLY DEVELOPMENTS: None

LE05: Long-term impact on biodiversity

CREDITS AVAILABLE

2 or 3
(for prison buildings)

INNOVATION CREDITS

0

The aim of this Issue criterion is to minimise the long-term impact of the development on the site and its surrounding area.

PREREQUISITES: A suitably qualified ecologist must be appointed.

MINIMUM STANDARDS: None

PERFORMANCE STANDARD REQUIRED: One credit can be awarded to all building types, except prison buildings, if a suitably qualified ecologist is appointed and they:
- confirm that all relevant UK and EU legislation relating to the protection and enhancement of a site's ecology will be a contract requirement

→

- produce a Landscape and Habitat Management Plan for the first five years after completion, to be handed over to the building occupants, which includes:
  - management of protected ecological features on site
  - details of any new, existing or enhanced habitats
  - references to local Biodiversity Action Plans.

Plus two of the following additional recommendations must be part of the contract requirements. Four of these recommendations require the principal contractor to:

- appoint a Biodiversity Champion to ensure that site activities do not impact detrimentally on site biodiversity
- train the site workforce on protecting the site's ecology during construction
- record actions taken to protect site biodiversity and monitor the effectiveness of these actions
- programme site preparation, ground and landscaping works to minimise disturbance to wildlife and phase clearance of vegetation to mitigate impact on site biodiversity.

The fifth additional recommendation requires:

- the creation of new ecologically valuable habitats to support nationally, regionally or locally important biodiversity issues. This will be difficult to achieve unless it is included in the design from the concept stage.

Two credits can be awarded for all building types, except prisons, where at least four of the above additional recommendations are contract requirements.

If the ecologist confirms that some of the additional recommendations cannot be undertaken due to site constraints or context, the number of additional recommendations that have to be implemented can vary, as described in the online *Technical Manual*.[1]

INNOVATION CREDITS: None

BUILDING-TYPE VARIATIONS: In the case of prison buildings, **up to three credits** can be awarded if a suitably qualified ecologist is appointed, as detailed above, and the following additional recommendations are implemented:

- two recommendations – **one credit**
- three recommendations – **two credits**
- four recommendations – **three credits**.

Additionally, in educational buildings the design team must establish a partnership with a local wildlife trust to provide:

- early advice on protecting species important to the locality by taking into account the local Biodiversity Action Plan
- advice on developing the design in harmony with the local environment
- ongoing help for the educational establishment in managing, maintaining and developing their outdoor spaces.

CONSEQUENTIAL IMPACTS ON DESIGN/TIPS: The client must be advised that unless a suitably qualified ecologist is appointed, **no credits** can be awarded in relation to this Issue.

EVIDENCE TO BE PROVIDED FOR DESIGN STAGE ASSESSMENT: For **one credit**, a copy of the Ecology Report covering the issues in Appendix F of the online *Technical Manual*[1] and:

either

- a copy of the site's Landscape and Habitat Management Plan

or

- contract specification clauses confirming the requirement to produce a Landscape and Habitat Management Plan

or

- written confirmation from the client confirming their commitment to producing a Landscape and Habitat Management Plan and its scope.

For the **second** and **third credits**, in addition to the above, any of the following, as appropriate for the additional recommendations being adopted:

- Contract specification clauses or a letter from the principal contractor confirming the appointment of a Biodiversity Champion.
- Contract specification clauses requiring the training of the site's workforce or a letter from principal contractor committing to training.
- Contract specification clauses requiring ongoing monitoring and reporting or a letter from the principal contractor confirming ongoing monitoring and reporting.
- A copy of plans showing new ecologically valuable habitat and an ecologist's report or letter confirming that the habitat will support the relevant Biodiversity Action Plan.
- Contract specification clauses requiring the programming of site works to minimise disturbance to wildlife or an ecologist's report or letter confirming the actions required to minimise disturbance and the principal contractor's programme of works demonstrating compliance.

In relation to educational buildings, written confirmation of the following must be provided:

- the scope of the partnership with the local wildlife group
- details and remit of the wildlife group
- the process established to provide ongoing support
- details of meetings and actions to date.

EVIDENCE TO BE PROVIDED FOR POST-CONSTRUCTION STAGE ASSESSMENT: For **one credit**:

- a letter from the ecologist confirming that all UK and EU legislation relating to the protection and enhancement of a site's ecology has been complied with
- a copy of the Landscape and Habitat Management Plan.

For the **second** and **third credits**, in addition to the above, **any** of the following, as appropriate for the additional recommendations being adopted:

either

- a copy of sections from the site log book confirming any actions taken by the Biodiversity Champion
- records and details of training undertaken by the site's workforce
- records of monitoring and actions taken to protect the site's biodiversity with records and outcomes of any requests to view this information
- photographs of completed new ecologically valuable habitat

→

or
- a letter or report from the ecologist confirming that site works were undertaken as recommended with minimum disturbance to wildlife.

For educational buildings, written confirmation from the design team and wildlife group of:
- meeting minutes, detailing advice given and actions taken
- the framework for future support by the wildlife group, including a timetable for future meetings and events.

IMPLICATION FOR SHELL-ONLY DEVELOPMENTS: None

3.9 Appointing an acoustic consultant

Appointing a suitably qualified acoustic consultant to advise the design team on achieving the performance standards of the next two Issues will have less impact than appointing an ecologist, since these Issues only account for between 2 and 3 per cent of the final BREEAM score. However, an acoustic consultant's appointment is a prerequisite for the award of any credits in both of these Issues. A 'suitably qualified acoustic consultant' is one who:

- holds a recognised acoustic qualification
- is a member of a professional body, such as the Institute of Acoustics.

Hea05: Acoustic performance

CREDITS AVAILABLE

2, 3 or 4
(depending on building type)

INNOVATION CREDITS

0

The aim of this Issue criterion is to ensure that a building's acoustic performance meets the standards appropriate to its purpose.

PREREQUISITES: The appointment of a suitably qualified acoustic consultant during RIBA Preparation Stage B (Brief) to provide design advice on:
- external sources of noise which impact on the building or site
- how to achieve good acoustics for a building through the site layout and zoning
- acoustic requirements of users with special hearing or communication needs
- acoustic treatment of different building zones and facades.

→

MINIMUM STANDARDS: None

PERFORMANCE STANDARD REQUIRED: The required performance standards vary between building types and may be quite complex, so check the online *Technical Manual*.[1] A summary of the requirements follows.

Up to two credits can be awarded for offices, retail and industrial buildings, prisons, courts and other building types where the following requirements are met:

For **the first credit**:

* indoor ambient noise levels must comply with good practice criteria in Tables 5 and 6 of BS8233

plus

* the acoustic consultant must carry out pre-completion testing to check that relevant spaces achieve the required performance standards

plus

* for teaching and lecturing spaces, airborne and impact sound levels must comply with Health Technical Memorandum 08-01 (HTM08-01)
* for medical treatment rooms, airborne and impact sound levels must comply with HTM08-01 **plus** the acoustic consultant must carry out pre-completion testing to check that relevant spaces achieve the required performance standards
* for acoustically sensitive rooms (e.g. cellular offices, meeting and interview rooms, witness and consultation rooms and jury rooms), sound insulation must comply with section 7.6.3.1 of BS8233 **plus** the acoustic consultant must carry out pre-completion testing to check that relevant spaces achieve the required performance standards.

For the **second credit**:

* reverberation times must meet the specification in Table 8 of BS8233 for rooms or areas for speech and performance or, if relevant, the specification for classrooms and seminar rooms or lecture theatres in Table 1.5 of Building Bulletin 93 (BB93).

Up to two credits can be awarded for healthcare buildings as follows:

* **One credit** is awarded if values for noise intrusion from external sources are achieved as specified in Table 1 of HTM08-01; for internal noise from mechanical and electrical services as specified in Table 2 of HTM08-01; and measured differences between rooms as Tables 4 and 3, **plus** the acoustic consultant carries out pre-completion testing to check that relevant spaces achieve the required performance standards.
* **One credit** is awarded if reverberation in rooms and circulation spaces is controlled with sound-absorbent materials as specified in paragraph 2.110 of HTM08-01.

Up to three credits can be awarded for pre-schools, schools and sixth-form colleges as follows:

* **One credit** is awarded if the performance standards set out by BB93 to suit each room function are achieved, based on the required sample measurement described in Section 1.3 of BB93 and The Association of Noise Consultants' *Good Practice Guide*,[38] **plus** the acoustic consultant carries out pre-completion testing to check that relevant spaces achieve the required performance standards.
* **One credit** is awarded if the noise of rain on lightweight (150 kg/m²) glazed roofs or roof lights in teaching and learning areas does not exceed acceptable limits **plus** the acoustic consultant carries out pre-completion testing to check that relevant spaces achieve the required performance standards.

→

- **One credit** is awarded if performance levels set in BB93 for all music rooms and spaces are achieved and suitable sound insulation is installed where noise levels will exceed 95 dB **plus** the acoustic consultant carries out pre-completion testing to check that relevant spaces achieve the required performance standards.

Up to two credits can be awarded for further or higher education buildings as follows:

- **One credit** is awarded if indoor ambient noise-level criteria are met for rooms as stipulated for secondary schools in section 1 of BB93 or if the criteria in BS8233 are met if the room use is not covered by BB93 **plus** the acoustic consultant carries out pre-completion testing to check that relevant spaces achieve the required performance standards.
- **One credit** is awarded if all teaching, training and education areas achieve reverberation times as specified in Table 1.5 of BB93 **plus** the acoustic consultant carries out pre-completion testing to check that relevant spaces achieve the required performance standards.

Up to four credits can be awarded for multi-residential buildings that meet the following criteria:

- **One credit** is awarded if airborne sound insulation values are at least 3 dB higher and impact sound insulation values at least 3 dB lower than required by the Building Regulations **plus** a compliant testing body carries out pre-completion testing to check that relevant spaces achieve the required performance standards or robust details approved by Robust Details Limited[39] are used.
- **Three credits** are awarded if airborne sound insulation values are at least 5 dB higher and impact sound insulation values at least 5 dB lower than required by the Building Regulations **plus** a compliant testing body carries out pre-completion testing to check that relevant spaces achieve the required performance standards or robust details approved by Robust Details Limited[39] are used.
- **Four credits** are awarded if airborne sound insulation values are at least 8 dB higher and impact sound insulation values at least 8 dB lower than required by the Building Regulations **plus** a compliant testing body carries out pre-completion testing to check that relevant spaces achieve the required performance standards or robust details approved by Robust Details Limited[39] are used.

Compliant test bodies for multi-residential buildings include those which:

either

- have appropriate United Kingdom Accreditation Service (UKAS) accreditation or are members of the International Accreditation Forum

or

- provide evidence that they meet the requirements of BS EN ISO/IEC 17024.[40]

Table 5-4 in the online *Technical Manual*[1] provides a selection of good practice indoor ambient noise-level targets from BS8233.

INNOVATION CREDITS: None

BUILDING-TYPE VARIATIONS: In addition to the above, buildings without areas used for speech (other than education, healthcare and multi-residential buildings) need not comply with reverberation time performance standards.

→

CONSEQUENTIAL IMPACTS ON DESIGN/TIPS: The performance standards associated with this Issue are complex and need careful consideration at the detailed design stage.

EVIDENCE TO BE PROVIDED FOR DESIGN STAGE ASSESSMENT:
- A letter of appointment confirming the date of appointment of a suitably qualified acoustic consultant.
- A report from the consultant confirming performance standards, including calculations.
- Contract specification clauses or a letter from the design team confirming commitment to achieving the required performance standards.

Plus for multi-residential buildings, if pre-completion testing is to be carried out:

either
- a letter from the client confirming commitment to meeting the required sound insulation performance levels

and
- using a compliant test body to complete the testing.

Or, if robust details are being used:
- confirmation that the chosen robust details meet the required performance standard
- confirmation that the development is registered with Robust Details Limited.

EVIDENCE TO BE PROVIDED FOR POST-CONSTRUCTION STAGE ASSESSMENT: A post-completion report and calculations from a suitably qualified acoustic consultant will be required for all building types

plus
- a letter or field-test report from the acoustic consultant confirming that required standards have been met
- a letter from the design team or principal contractor confirming that any remedial works required in the acoustic consultant's report have been carried out.

Plus, for multi-residential buildings:

either
- copies of sound insulation field-test results and/or a letter confirming that sound insulation as detailed has been achieved

and
- evidence that the tests were carried out by a compliant test body

or
- a completed Robust Details Limited Compliance Certificate signed by the client for all relevant details.

IMPLICATION FOR SHELL-ONLY DEVELOPMENTS: If it is not possible to define a type of office space, it will be assumed to be open plan with an occupancy rate of one person per 10 m^2. Performance standards for noise-sensitive rooms will not apply to buildings that are not fully fitted out.

Pol05: Noise attenuation

CREDITS AVAILABLE

1

INNOVATION CREDITS

0

The aim of this Issue criterion is to ensure that buildings or areas that might be sensitive to noise from the proposed development are not affected.

PREREQUISITES: None

MINIMUM STANDARDS: None

PERFORMANCE STANDARD REQUIRED: One credit can be awarded where no buildings or areas that might be sensitive to noise generated by the proposed development lie within an 800 m radius. Noise-sensitive buildings or areas include:

- houses and residential areas
- hospitals, health centres, care homes, surgeries, etc.
- schools, colleges, etc.
- libraries
- places of worship
- wildlife areas, parks, gardens or historic landscape
- areas of outstanding natural beauty or sites of special scientific interest.

If any of the above are located within 800 m of the development, for **one credit** to be awarded, the client must undertake the following:

- Appoint an acoustic consultant to carry out a Noise Impact Assessment, which complies with BS7445, of the proposed building's service plant to establish:
    - existing background noise levels at the nearest or most exposed noise-sensitive location
    - the rating noise level for proposed noise sources, confirming that it will be no greater than plus 5 dB compared to background noise levels during the day (07.00am to 10.00pm) and plus 3 dB at night (10.00pm to 07.00am).
- Instruct the acoustic consultant to produce a Noise Impact Assessment, calculations and specification clauses demonstrating:
    - attenuation measures needed to reduce noise levels at source where noise levels from the proposed development will be greater than identified in the survey.
- Ensure that any attenuation measures are incorporated into the contract requirements.

INNOVATION CREDITS: None

BUILDING-TYPE VARIATIONS: None

CONSEQUENTIAL IMPACTS ON DESIGN/TIPS: The presence of noise-sensitive buildings or areas close to the proposed development should be established early in the design process so that any necessary sound attenuation measures can be incorporated in the building design prior to submission for planning approval.

→

EVIDENCE TO BE PROVIDED FOR DESIGN STAGE ASSESSMENT: Design drawings are required showing:

- all existing and proposed noise-sensitive buildings or areas within 800 m of the development
- sources of noise from the development
- distances from noise sources to noise-sensitive buildings or areas.

Plus either

- an acoustic consultant's report, details of qualifications and experience

  or

- contract specification clauses requiring a Noise Impact Assessment to be carried out by a suitably qualified acoustic consultant to comply with BS4142

  or

- a letter from the client or design team confirming that they will appoint a suitably qualified acoustic consultant to carry out a Noise Impact Assessment to comply with BS4142.

Plus

- an acoustic consultant's report recommending suitable noise-attenuation measures.

  Plus either

- a marked-up plan showing the acoustic consultant's proposed attenuation measures

  or

- a letter from the client or design team confirming that the proposed attenuation measures will be installed.

EVIDENCE TO BE PROVIDED FOR POST-CONSTRUCTION STAGE ASSESSMENT: Photographic evidence must be provided identifying:

- all noise-sensitive buildings or areas within 800 m of the development
- sources of noise from the development
- distances from noise sources to noise-sensitive buildings or areas

plus

- the acoustic consultant's report with measurements based on installed and operating plant

plus either

- photographic evidence confirming the existence of specified noise-attenuation measures

  or

- a letter from the acoustic consultant confirming that all specified noise-attenuation measures have been installed to the required performance standards.

IMPLICATION FOR SHELL-ONLY DEVELOPMENTS: Where the tenant is responsible for the specification and installation of plant that can generate noise, the acoustic consultant must assume the worst-case noise rating levels for their proposals, based on existing examples. Alternatively, one of Options 1, 2 or 3 (described in Chapter 2, section 2.11) can be used to assess compliance with the required performance standards .

3.10 Appointing a highway engineer

Although not a prerequisite for either of the two Issues described below, the client may appoint a highway engineer to assist in providing the evidence of compliance with their performance standards. The highway engineer can:

- provide the necessary data for calculating a site's Accessibility Index (AI)
- investigate options for dedicated bus services, where required
- undertake site transport surveys for the Travel Plan.

Together, these two Issues could contribute around 4 per cent of a final BREEAM score.

Tra01: Public transport accessibility

CREDITS AVAILABLE

3, 4 or 5

(depending on building type)

INNOVATION CREDITS

0

The detailed requirements for awarding the credits relating to this Issue are described earlier in section 3.1 Measuring a site's impact on an Assessment. Appointing a highway engineer can make it easier to establish the location and frequency of compliant public transport nodes when calculating the AI.

The highway engineer can also help to establish the feasibility of providing a dedicated bus service to the site for a credit where the AI for a site is zero. This can apply to buildings with fixed shift patterns where the building occupants arrive and depart at certain times (such as offices, factories, schools and prisons) as discussed earlier.

Tra05: Travel plan

CREDITS AVAILABLE

1

INNOVATION CREDITS

0

The aim of this Issue criterion is to encourage the reduction in use of those forms of transport with the highest environmental impact (e.g. car-based travel).

PREREQUISITES: The Travel Plan has to be developed as part of a building's feasibility and design stages at RIBA Design Stages C (Concept) and D (Design Development).

MINIMUM STANDARDS: None

PERFORMANCE STANDARD REQUIRED: One credit can be awarded where a site-specific Travel Plan is developed. It must be:
- site specific
- based on the findings of a site-specific transport survey or assessment
- related to the proposed use and occupation.

The site-specific transport survey or assessment must cover:
- existing travel patterns and opinions of existing building or site users (where relevant) in terms of cycling and walking to identify constraints and opportunities
- travel patterns and transport impact of future occupants or users and operational transport (if appropriate)
- the existing local environment for cyclists and pedestrians
- disabled access
- public transport links serving the site
- existing facilities for the site and area.

The types of building occupants and users whose needs a Travel Plan must consider include, where appropriate:
- staff (for commuting journeys and business travel)
- pupils and students
- visitors
- patients
- customers
- personnel who make deliveries and collections to and from the development
- contractors and service providers who will work regularly in the development.

The Travel Plan has to include measures that can be incorporated into the design to assist in minimising car-based travel, which could include:
- parking priority for car sharing
- dedicated, convenient and safe cycle storage and changing facilities
- improved lighting to pedestrian and public transport waiting areas
- improving existing bus services on larger developments
- restricting or charging for car parking

→

- providing information on public transport and car sharing in a prominent place within the building
- pedestrian and cycle-friendly access
- taxi drop-off points and waiting areas
- locating rural buildings so that transport generated by the development can also serve the local community
- control of deliveries to and from the site.

If the building occupier is known, they must confirm that they will implement and support the Travel Plan.

INNOVATION CREDITS: None

BUILDING-TYPE VARIATIONS: None

CONSEQUENTIAL IMPACTS ON DESIGN/TIPS: Appointing a highway engineer will make it easier to undertake site-specific transport surveys and produce a site-specific Travel Plan.
Some of the above design options can also result in additional credits under other Issues, such as:

- *Tra02: Cyclist facilities*
- *Hea06: Safety and security* (*Safe access* criterion).

EVIDENCE TO BE PROVIDED FOR DESIGN STAGE ASSESSMENT:

- A copy of the Travel Plan.
- A copy of the site-specific transport survey or assessment.
- Copies of design drawings showing how the measures recommended by the Travel Plan are incorporated or a letter from the client confirming that these measures will be implemented.

EVIDENCE TO BE PROVIDED FOR POST-CONSTRUCTION STAGE ASSESSMENT: As at the design stage, updated to show the as-constructed status.

IMPLICATION FOR SHELL-ONLY DEVELOPMENTS: None. Where the building occupier is unknown, a Travel Plan that addresses the issues typically generated by that type of building is still required for the credit to be awarded.

3.11 Appointing a specialist commissioning manager

If the appointed service engineer does not have the necessary expertise, the client will have to appoint a specialist commissioning manager for the credit detailed below to be awarded.

Man01: *Sustainable procurement* (second part of *Construction and handover* criterion)

CREDITS AVAILABLE	INNOVATION CREDITS
1	0

Although the principal requirements of this criterion are described earlier in this chapter, in section 3.3, the client may be required to appoint a specialist commissioning manager during the RIBA Design Stages C–E to provide:

- commissioning advice which may affect the design
- commissioning management advice which may influence the proposed construction programme and commissioning processes
- advice on the type of commissioning, testing, handover and post-handover procedures required.

3.12 Appointing a BREEAM Accredited Professional (AP)

Up to **three credits** can be awarded in relation to the *Man01: Sustainable procurement* Issue, contributing over 1.5 per cent to the final BREEAM score, if the client appoints a BREEAM AP at the right time.

Man01: *Sustainable procurement* (three parts of the *Project brief and design* criterion)

CREDITS AVAILABLE	INNOVATION CREDITS
3	0

The aim of this Issue criterion is to assist in the delivery of functional and sustainably designed buildings by utilising the expertise of a BREEAM AP.

→

Man01: Sustainable procurement (three parts of the *Project brief and design* criterion) (continued)

PREREQUISITES: A BREEAM AP must be appointed at the appropriate time.

MINIMUM STANDARDS:
- For BREEAM ratings Pass, Good, Very Good and Excellent – **one credit** from any of the criteria in this Issue, including one of the three available for these parts of this criterion.
- For BREEAM Outstanding rating – **two credits** from any of the criteria in this Issue, including these two, of the three available for these parts of this criterion.

PERFORMANCE STANDARD REQUIRED: The **first credit** can be awarded if:
- the AP is appointed early in RIBA Stage C (Concept Design) to assist in establishing a BREEAM rating target and the Issues that have to be considered
- the client or design team agree to the BREEAM rating target and which Issues should be considered before the end of RIBA Stage C (Concept Design)
- the AP provides evidence of how this will be achieved to the Assessor for the BREEAM design stage assessment.

A **second credit** can be awarded if the AP is appointed to:
- attend key design team meetings during RIBA Preparation Stage B up to the end of RIBA Design Stage E
- monitor progress against the defined BREEAM targets with regular written reports to the client or design team.

A **third credit** can be awarded if the AP is appointed to:
- attend key meetings from the start of RIBA Stage F (Production Information) up to the end of RIBA Stage K (Construction to Practical Completion)
- monitor and report progress against the defined BREEAM targets with regular written reports to the client or design team
- confirm that the agreed BREEAM targets form part of the contract requirements
- confirm that the target is achieved in a report submitted to the Assessor for the BREEAM post-construction stage assessment.

INNOVATION CREDITS: None

BUILDING-TYPE VARIATIONS: None

CONSEQUENTIAL IMPACTS ON DESIGN/TIPS: The appointed AP and appointed Assessor can be the same person or organisation, although the fee incurred will reflect the additional workload for this dual role. For clarity, it is best if the AP and Assessor are different people even if they work for the same organisation.
A list of registered APs is available at the *GreenBookLive* website.[41]

EVIDENCE TO BE PROVIDED FOR DESIGN STAGE ASSESSMENT:
- The letter confirming the appointment of the AP
plus
- contract specification clauses or the contract programme confirming the key work stages of the development

→

> *Man01: Sustainable procurement* (three parts of the *Project brief and design* criterion) (continued)
>
> - meeting minutes, notes, correspondence or schedules demonstrating the AP's regular attendance and action on Issues.
> - the AP's progress reports.
>
> **EVIDENCE TO BE PROVIDED FOR POST-CONSTRUCTION STAGE ASSESSMENT:** As for the design stage **plus** the final post-construction AP reports.
>
> **IMPLICATION FOR SHELL-ONLY DEVELOPMENTS:** None

3.13 Overall impact of good design and specification

Credits awarded in relation to the Issues described in this chapter can add up to around 60 per cent of the total BREEAM score (see Table 3.5) from around three-quarters of the Issues, or part Issues, available. This would be sufficient in itself to achieve a BREEAM Very Good rating. While it is unlikely that all of the potential credits considered would be awarded, this table shows the contribution that this set of Issues can make towards the overall score and the importance of agreeing a good design and specification at the earliest opportunity. It should not be forgotten, however, that the remaining Issues can still contribute one-third of the final score. As will be seen in Chapter 4, the remaining Issues can prove more complex and their credits more difficult to achieve.

TABLE 3.5: Summary of potential value to BREEAM score of Issues discussed in Chapter 3

	Commercial buildings		Non-housing buildings							
	Offices	Retail	Industrial	Educational (schools)	Educational (higher education)	Healthcare	Prisons	Courts	Multi-residential buildings	Other buildings
Overall % value of the site towards the overall BREEAM score from Table 3.1	9.46	11.24	9.59	10.51	10.06	10.49	10.24	11.24	10.14	10.06
Overall % value of good design and specification towards the overall BREEAM score from Table 3.2	27.49	25.68	27.06	25.74	24.37	24.94	27.52	25.71	25.34	24.76
Overall % value of environmentally friendly construction activities towards the overall BREEAM score from Table 3.3	10.29	11.00	11.00	11.00	11.00	11.00	11.00	11.00	11.00	11.00
Overall % value of the client appointing specialist consultants towards the overall BREEAM score from Table 3.4	16.65	18.28	16.71	18.17	17.08	17.42	19.09	18.43	18.26	17.19
Total % value towards the overall BREEAM score from Issues discussed in Chapter 3*	60.79	63.10	61.26	62.32	59.41	60.75	64.75	63.28	61.64	59.91

* Adjusted for some credits appearing in more than one section of this chapter

References

1   *BREEAM New Construction: Non-Domestic Buildings – Technical Manual*, see at:
    www.breeam.org/BREEAM2011SchemeDocument/

2   The Greater London public transport accessibility map is available at:
    www.london.gov.uk/thelondonplan/maps-diagrams/map-2a-03.jsp

3   Transport for London's Planning Information Database, which can generate an AI for a site, is available at:
    http://webpid.elgin.gov.uk/

4   Planning Policy Guidance 3 (PPG3): Housing (2000) has now been cancelled and is no longer available
    for download.

5   For information in relation to nature sites, see the following:
    www.natureonthemap.naturalengland.org.uk/
    http://magic.defra.gov.uk/
    www.naturalengland.org.uk/ourwork/conservation/designatedareas/ramsars/default.aspx

6   Planning Policy Statement 25: Development and Flood Risk is available at:
    www.communities.gov.uk/publications/planningandbuilding/pps25floodrisk

7   Environment Agency Flood Maps are available online through:
    www.environment-agency.gov.uk/homeandleisure/floods/default.aspx

8   Scottish Environment Protection Agency Flood Maps are available at: www.sepa.org.uk/flooding/flood_map.aspx

9   *Creating Excellent Buildings: A Guide for Clients* (2010), Commission for Architecture and the Built Environment,
    available at:
    http://webarchive.nationalarchives.gov.uk/20110118095356/http://www.cabe.org.uk/buildings/downloads
    To see the web version of the section covering 'Defining the Outline Brief' go to: http://webarchive.
    nationalarchives.gov.uk/20110118095356/http://www.cabe.org.uk/buildings/defining-the-outline-brief

10 *Architect's Job Book* 8th edition (2008), RIBA Publishing, London

11 *Design and Access Statements: How to Write, Read and Use Them* (2007), Commission for Architecture and the
    Built Environment, available at: http://webarchive.nationalarchives.gov.uk/20110118095356/http://www.cabe.org.
    uk/files/design-and-access-statements.pdf

12 BS8206: *Lighting for Buildings – Part 2: Code of Practice for Daylighting* (2008), British Standards Institute, London

13 For Sustrans technical guidance, see: www.sustrans.org.uk/resources/design-and-construction/technical-guidelines

14 For the National Cycle Network Design and Construction Checklist, see:
    www.sustrans.org.uk/assets/files/guidelines/appendix.pdf

15 BS5489 *Part 1: Code of practice for the design of road lighting. Lighting of roads and public amenity areas* (2003),
    British Standards Institute, London

16 Secured by Design website: www.securedbydesign.com

17 For Safer Parking documents, see: www.britishparking.co.uk/Documents-Guidelines-for-the-Safer-Parking-Scheme

18 The *Green Guide to Specification* is available at: www.bre.co.uk/greenguide/podpage.jsp?id=2126. This can be
    accessed by anybody if they first register, by selecting:
    - a building type (e.g. commercial which includes office, retail and industrial buildings)
    - a main building element (e.g. external wall construction)
    - an individual element type that forms part of the chosen main building element (e.g. rendered or fairfaced
      blockwork cavity wall) and possibly another sub-element layer
    - a generic building element description with a Green Guide rating from A+ to E, which links to a detailed
      breakdown of its environmental impacts (including a 60-year $kgCO_2$ equivalent figure which is required for
      calculating how many points can be achieved).

    However, this can sometimes seem to be a long-winded process before the descriptions of the building elements
    are eventually reached.

19 Health Technical Memorandum 07-1: Safe Management of Healthcare Waste available at:
    www.dh.gov.uk/en/Publicationsandstatistics/Publications/PublicationsPolicyAndGuidance/DH_063274

20 *Metric Handbook – Planning and Design Date* 3rd edition (2008), David Littlefield (ed.), Architectural Press, Oxford

21 For BSRIA Soft Landings Framework, see: www.bsria.co.uk/services/design/soft-landings/

22 Pollock, R., McNair, D., McGuire, B. and Cunningham, C. (2008) *Design Lighting for People with Dementia*,
    Dementia Services Development Centre, University of Stirling

23 Carbon Trust's *Guide CTG002: Heating Control*, available at:
    www.carbontrust.co.uk/publications/pages/publicationdetail.aspx?id=CTG002

24 *ISO 14044:2006 Environmental Management Life Cycle Assessment – Requirements and Guidelines*

25 Environment Agency: *Pollution Prevention Guidelines 3*, see:
    http://publications.environment-agency.gov.uk/PDF/PMHO0406BIYL-E-E.pdf

26 Environment Agency: *Pollution Prevention Pays – Getting Your Site Right*, see:
    http://publications.environment-agency.gov.uk/PDF/PMHO0104BHQI-E-E.pdf

27 See UK Thermography Association at: www.ukta.org/

28 Considerate Constructors Scheme website, see: www.ccscheme.org.uk/

29 UK Government's Timber Procurement Policy, see: www.cpet.org.uk/uk-government-timber-procurement-policy

30 BS EN ISO 14001 (2004): *Environmental management systems. Requirements with guidance for use*

31 BS8555 (2003): *Environmental management systems. Guide to the phased implementation of an environmental
    management system including the use of environmental performance evaluation*

32 Environment Agency: *Building a Better Environment: A Guide for Developers*, see:
    www.environment-agency.gov.uk/business/sectors/32695.aspx

33 Strategic Forum's reports on reducing energy and water consumption can be found at:
    www.strategicforum.org.uk/Sustain.shtml

34 Construction Resource and Waste Platform, see: http://conwaste.aeastaging.co.uk/conwaste/
    WRAP Construction website, see: www.wrap.org.uk/construction/index.html

35 BRE SMARTWaste Scheme, see: www.smartwaste.co.uk/

36 Natural History Museum – Postcode Plant Database, see:
    www.nhm.ac.uk/nature-online/life/plants-fungi/postcode-plants/index.html

37 Williams, Dr C. (2010) *Biodiversity for Low and Zero Carbon Buildings: A Technical Guide for New Build*,
    RIBA Publishing

38 The Association of Noise Consultants' *Schools Testing Good Practice Guide*, see:
    www.association-of-noise-consultants.co.uk/index.php?*p=schools

39 Robust Details Limited, see: www.robustdetails.com/

40 BS EN ISO/IEC 17024 (2003): *Conformity Assessment. General requirements for bodies operating certification of
    persons*

41 For a list of BREEAM Accredited Professionals see *GreenBookLive* website at:
    www.greenbooklive.com/search/scheme.jsp?id=172

chapter four
Difficult BREEM Issues

This chapter examines those Issues that have not yet been considered in detail. The design team and client must give these Issues greater consideration because they:

- are more complex in terms of how credits are awarded and where a best practice design is required
- are difficult to achieve in certain building types
- require the client to instruct the design team to undertake additional activities outside what many would consider their normal terms of appointment
- are building-type specific.

There are around 20 Issues, or criteria within Issues, that fall into the above categories (see Table 4.1) and they can account for around 40 per cent of a final BREEAM score. So it is important to understand how credits can be awarded for these Issues and criteria.

4.1 Issues with complex scoring and where best practice design is required

The eight complete Issues and part of one Issue criterion described below all involve some complexity in assessing the number of credits that can be awarded. This complexity lies either in the way the credits are calculated or in the level of activity required of the design team to obtain the necessary evidence for the Assessor. They may also require best practice design solutions to be applied before credits can be awarded. These credits can contribute around 30 per cent of a final BREEAM score (see Table 4.2). Half of this potential comes from just one Issue, *Ene01: Reduction of CO$_2$ emissions*. In reality, it is unlikely that all these credits will be awarded, except in very well-designed, sustainable buildings. Over 8 per cent of a final BREEAM score comes from two Issues in the Materials Category, although maximising these credits may also present difficulties.

TABLE 4.1: The value of the more difficult Issues

	Commercial buildings		Non-housing buildings							
	Offices	Retail	Industrial	Educational (schools)	Educational (higher education)	Healthcare	Prisons	Courts	Multi-residential buildings	Other buildings
Management Category										
Man04: Stakeholder participation (Consultation criterion)	1	1	1	1	1	1	1	1	1	1
Man04: Stakeholder participation (Post-occupancy evaluation/information dissemination criterion)	1	1	1	1	1	1	1	1	1	1
Man05: Life-cycle cost and service life planning	3	3	3	3	3	3	3	3	3	3
Weighted % value of the above credits to the final BREEAM score	2.73	2.73	2.73	2.73	2.73	2.73	2.73	2.73	2.73	2.73
Health and Wellbeing Category	15% weighting towards BREEAM score									
Hea01: Visual comfort (Daylighting criterion)	1	2	1	1	2	2	1	1	1	1
Hea01: Visual comfort (Visual arts criterion)	0	0	0	0	0	1	0	0	0	0
Hea02: Indoor air quality (part of Minimising sources of air pollution criterion)	2	2	2	2	2	2	2	2	2	2
Hea02: Indoor air quality (Potential for natural ventilation criterion)	1	1	1	1	1	1	0	1	1	1
Hea02: Indoor air quality (Laboratory fume cupboards criterion)	0	0	0	1	1	1	0	0	0	1
Weighted % value of the above credits to the final BREEAM score	4.29	5.00	4.29	4.41	5.29	5.83	3.21	4.29	3.75	4.69
Energy Category										
Ene01: Reduction of CO_2 emissions	15	15	15	15	15	15	15	15	15	15
Ene05: Energy-efficient cold storage	0	3	3	0	3	3	0	0	0	3
Ene07: Energy-efficient laboratory systems	0	0	0	1	5	0	0	0	0	5
Ene08: Energy-efficient equipment	2	2	2	2	2	2	2	2	2	2
Weighted % value of the above credits to the final BREEAM score	11.96	12.67	12.67	12.21	13.57	12.67	12.42	12.42	11.96	13.57
Transport Category										
Tra03: Cyclist facilities	2	2	2	2	2	2	1	2	1	2
Tra04: Maximum car parking capacity	2	0	2	0	2	1	0	0	2	2
Weighted % value of the above credits to the final BREEAM score	3.78	2.00	3.78	2.00	3.45	2.80	2.00	2.00	3.78	3.45

	Commercial buildings		Non-housing buildings							
	Offices	Retail	Industrial	Educational (schools)	Educational (higher education)	Healthcare	Prisons	Courts	Multi-residential buildings	Other buildings
Water Category										
Wat01: Water consumption	5	5	5	5	5	5	5	5	5	5
Wat04: Water-efficient equipment	1	1	1	1	1	1	1	1	1	1
Weighted % value of the above credits to the final BREEAM score	4.00	4.00	4.00	4.00	4.00	4.00	4.00	4.00	4.00	4.00
Materials Category										
Mat01: Life-cycle impacts	5	5	2	6	6	6	4	6	6	6
Mat03: Responsible sourcing of materials	3	3	3	3	3	3	3	3	3	3
Weighted % value of the above credits to the final BREEAM score	8.33	8.33	6.94	8.65	8.65	8.65	7.95	8.65	8.65	8.65
Waste Category										
Wst02: Recycled aggregates	1	1	1	1	1	1	1	1	1	1
Weighted % value of the above credits to the final BREEAM score	1.07	1.25	1.25	1.25	1.25	1.25	1.25	1.25	1.25	1.25
Land Use and Ecology Category	No Issues in this category are considered in Chapter 4									
Pollution Category	10% weighting towards BREEAM score									
Pol01: Impact of refrigerants	3	3	3	3	3	3	3	3	3	3
Pol03: Surface water run-off (Surface water run-off criterion)	2	2	2	2	2	2	2	2	2	2
Weighted % value of the above credits to the final BREEAM score	3.85	3.85	4.17	3.85	3.85	3.85	3.85	3.85	3.85	3.85
Overall % value of Issues considered in Chapter 4 towards the overall BREEAM score	38.93	38.57	38.57	37.85	41.55	40.53	35.17	37.94	37.72	40.94

TABLE 4.2: Issues where scoring is complex and best practice design is required

	Commercial buildings		Non-housing buildings						Multi-residential buildings	Other buildings
	Offices	Retail	Industrial	Educational (schools)	Educational (higher education)	Healthcare	Prisons	Courts		
Management Category										
Man05: Life-cycle cost and service life planning	3	3	3	3	3	3	3	3	3	3
Weighted % value of the above credits to the final BREEAM score	1.64	1.64	1.64	1.64	1.64	1.64	1.64	1.64	1.64	1.64
Health and Wellbeing Category	15% weighting towards BREEAM score									
Hea02: Indoor air quality (part of Minimising sources of air pollution criterion)	2	2	2	2	2	2	2	2	2	2
Weighted % value of the above credits to the final BREEAM score	2.14	2.00	2.14	1.76	1.76	1.67	2.14	2.14	1.88	1.88
Energy Category										
Ene01: Reduction of CO_2 emissions	15	15	15	15	15	15	15	15	15	15
Weighted % value of the above credits to the final BREEAM score	10.56	9.50	9.50	10.18	8.14	9.50	10.96	10.96	10.56	8.14
Transport Category										
Tra03: Cyclist facilities	2	2	2	2	2	2	1	2	1	2
Weighted % value of the above credits to the final BREEAM score	1.78	1.78	1.78	2.29	1.45	1.60	2.00	1.78	0.89	1.45
Water Category										
Wat01: Water consumption	5	5	5	5	5	5	5	5	5	5
Wat04: Water-efficient equipment	1	1	1	1	1	1	1	1	1	1
Weighted % value of the above credits to the final BREEAM score	4.00	4.00	4.00	4.00	4.00	4.00	4.00	4.00	4.00	4.00
Materials Category										
Mat01: Life-cycle impacts	5	5	2	6	6	6	4	6	6	6
Mat03: Responsible sourcing of materials	3	3	3	3	3	3	3	3	3	3
Weighted % value of the above credits to the final BREEAM score	8.33	8.33	6.94	8.65	8.65	8.65	7.95	8.65	8.65	8.65
Waste Category										
Wst02: Recycled aggregates	1	1	1	1	1	1	1	1	1	1
Weighted % value of the above credits to the final BREEAM score	1.07	1.25	1.25	1.25	1.25	1.25	1.25	1.25	1.25	1.25
Land Use and Ecology Category	No Issues in this category are considered in Chapter 4									
Pollution Category	10% weighting towards BREEAM score									
Pol01: Impact of refrigerants	3	3	3	3	3	3	3	3	3	3
Weighted % value of the above credits to the final BREEAM score	2.31	2.31	2.50	2.31	2.31	2.31	2.31	2.31	2.31	2.31
Overall % value of Issues considered in Chapter 4 towards the overall BREEAM score	31.83	30.81	29.75	32.08	29.21	30.61	32.25	32.73	31.17	29.32

Man05: Life-cycle cost and service life planning

CREDITS AVAILABLE

3

INNOVATION CREDITS

0

The aim of this Issue criterion is to encourage the use of life-cycle costing and service life planning in the design of buildings.

PREREQUISITES: None

MINIMUM STANDARDS: None

PERFORMANCE STANDARD REQUIRED: One credit can be awarded when:
- a life-cycle cost analysis is carried out on the proposed feasibility design during RIBA Design Stages C (Concept) or D (Design Development)
- a service life planning appraisal is completed during the feasibility stage.

The life-cycle cost analysis must:
- meet the requirements of PD156865 (2008) *Standardized Method of Life Cycle Costing for Construction Procurement: A Supplement to BS ISO 15686 (2008) Buildings and Constructed Assets – Service Life Planning – Part 5: Life Cycle Costing*
- analyse a 60-year period, including
    - construction
    - operation (covering utilities, cleaning and management costs as a minimum)
    - planned maintenance
    - replacement and repair costs.

The service life planning appraisal has to:
- comply with the service life principles set out in BS ISO 15686 (2008) *Buildings and Constructed Assets – Service Life Planning – Part 1: General Principles*
- cover the service life estimates and maintenance implications of different design options.

Two credits can be awarded where, in addition to achieving the above performance standards, the following requirements are met:
- The life-cycle cost analysis demonstrates that at least two of the following building elements, which are of critical value to the building (in terms of costs, maintenance burden and volume or area), have been analysed at a strategic and system level as set out in Figure 6 of BS ISO 15686: Part 5:
    - envelope (cladding, windows and/or roofing)
    - services (heat source, cooling source and/or controls)
    - finishes (walls, floors and/or ceilings)
    - external spaces.
- The two options, referred to above, must meet the building's performance criteria **and** the lowest discounted life-cycle cost over the assessment period **and** achieve at least one of the following:
    - lower the building's energy consumption over its operational life span
    - reduce maintenance requirements and frequency

→

- extend service lives of systems and/or the building fabric, resulting in fewer replacements
- improve dismantling and recycling or reuse of building components.

Three credits can be awarded where, in addition to meeting all of the above:

- the life-cycle cost analysis is updated during RIBA Design Stage D (Design Development) or E (Technical Design)
- results of the study are incorporated into the constructed building and shown in the construction specification and drawings
- a maintenance strategy is developed, informed by the life-cycle cost analysis, that details:
  - the extent to which maintenance has been designed out and safe, efficient and cost-effective operation and maintenance procedures incorporated in the systems
  - how the removal or replacement of major plant is facilitated by the design
  - a Management Plan for the landscaping.

INNOVATION CREDITS: None

BUILDING-TYPE VARIATIONS: For schools and other educational buildings:

- storage space must meet the requirements of either Building Bulletins 98 or 99[1]
- storage space must be evenly distributed over a site or building and, as a minimum, provided on each floor.

For court buildings, the Department of Constitutional Affairs may have to be consulted during the process. Seek advice from BRE in this instance.

CONSEQUENTIAL IMPACTS ON DESIGN/TIPS: BREEAM requires a 60-year study period in relation to this Issue, to align with the *Green Guide to Specification*. The Green Guide uses a 60-year period for quantifying the environmental impacts of building specifications and their replacement components. It can be difficult to obtain reliable information about the durability of building components. One possible source is a product's British Board of Agrément Certificate.[2] BS7543 (2003): *Guide to durability of buildings and building elements, products and components* offers generic advice on design lives.

It should also be noted that undertaking a BREEAM Life Cycle Cost will attract additional fees.

EVIDENCE TO BE PROVIDED FOR DESIGN STAGE ASSESSMENT: For **the first credit**:

- the feasibility stage life-cycle cost analysis report
- the feasibility service life planning appraisal.

For the **second credit**, the evidence listed above, **plus**:

- details of the alternative options considered and benefits of selected options
- confirmation that the selected options are of critical value.

For the **third credit**, the evidence listed above, **plus**:

- design drawings or contract specification clauses requiring the implementation of the preferred latest life-cycle cost analysis options
- a copy of the maintenance strategy and/or a letter from the client committing to providing one
- evidence of how the maintenance strategy was informed by the life-cycle cost analysis.

→

Man05: Life-cycle cost and service life planning (continued)

EVIDENCE TO BE PROVIDED FOR POST-CONSTRUCTION STAGE ASSESSMENT: As for the design stage, updated to show the as-constructed status, **plus**:

- for **two credits**, evidence that the preferred options selected at the design stage have been implemented
- for **three credits**, as-constructed drawings confirming that strategies recommended at the design stage have been implemented.

IMPLICATION FOR SHELL-ONLY DEVELOPMENTS: If services and finishes are not provided as part of the shell works, they can be excluded from the life-cycle cost analysis. If the shell works exclude services and finishes, and there are no external spaces, elements within the building's envelope must meet the required standards for the second credit to be awarded.

Hea02: Indoor air quality (second and third parts of *Minimising sources of air pollution* criterion)

CREDITS AVAILABLE

2

INNOVATION CREDITS

0

The aim of these parts of this Issue criterion is to create healthy internal environments by minimising sources of internal air pollution. This is achieved by specifying materials and products which emit low levels of volatile organic compound (VOC) and formaldehyde.

PREREQUISITES: An Indoor Air Quality Plan must be produced. This is described in Chapter 3 in section 3.1 Measuring a site's impact on an Assessment.

MINIMUM STANDARDS: None

PERFORMANCE STANDARD REQUIRED: One credit can be awarded, for the second part of this criterion, where all decorative paints and varnishes specified or used are:

- tested for VOC emissions levels in accordance with BS EN 13300 (2001) or by another calculation technique which complies with the European Regulation on Classification, Labelling and Packaging of Substances and Mixtures[3] or the UK Chemicals (Hazard Information and Packing for Supply) Regulations (2009)[4]
- verified to comply with Phase 2 levels of VOC emissions contained in the Decorative Paint Directive 2004/42/CE[5]
- confirmed as fungus- and algae-resistant, as required by BS EN 13300 (2001)
- produced by an ISO 9001 certified manufacturing process (formulation and raw material mixing).

→

Hea02: Indoor air quality (second and third parts of Minimising sources of air pollution criterion) (continued)

Plus five of the following eight categories must achieve the testing requirements and VOC emission levels determined by the appropriate standard:

- **Wood panels** (including particleboard, fibreboard including medium density fibreboard (MDF), orientated strand board (OSB), cement-bonded particleboard, plywood, solid wood panel and acoustic board) must achieve Class E1 when tested for formaldehyde in accordance with BS EN 13986 (2004) and the absence of regulated wood preservatives, as defined by BS EN 13986 (2004), must be proved.
- **Timber structures** (glued laminated timber, etc.) must achieve Class E1 when tested for formaldehyde in accordance with BS EN 14080 (2005).
- **Wood flooring** (parquet flooring, etc.) must achieve Class E1 when tested for formaldehyde in accordance with BS EN 14342 (2005).
- **Resilient, textile and laminated floor covering** (vinyl, linoleum, cork and rubber, carpet, laminated wood flooring) must achieve Class E1 when tested for formaldehyde in accordance with BS EN 14041 (2004) and the absence of wood preservatives, as defined by BS EN 14041 (2004), must be proved.
- **Suspended ceiling tiles** must achieve Class E1 when tested for formaldehyde in accordance with BS EN 13964 (2004) and contain no asbestos.
- **Flooring adhesives (and adhesives for rigid wall coverings)** the absence of carcinogenic or sensitising volatile substances must be proved by testing to BS EN 13999 – Part 1 (2007).
- **Wall-coverings (wallpapers, wall vinyls and plastic wall coverings)** formaldehyde and vinyl chloride monomer (VCM) release is low when tested to BS EN 12149 (1998) and in accordance with BS ENs 233 (1999), 234 (1997), 259 (2001) and 266 (1992).
- **Adhesives for hanging flexible wall coverings** – should contain no harmful substances and any preservatives should be of minimum toxicity in accordance with BS 3046 (1981).

Where there are five or fewer of these products present in a building, all of them must meet the required standards for the credit to be awarded.

One credit can be awarded, for the third part of this criterion, where:

- post-construction formaldehyde concentration levels are measured, prior to occupancy, at less than 100 µg/m^3 over 30 minutes
- post-construction total VOC concentration levels are measured, prior to occupancy, at less than 300 µg/m^3 over eight hours
- if measurements show post-construction formaldehyde and total VOC concentration levels exceeding the above limits, it is confirmed that steps will be taken, in accordance with the Indoor Air Quality Plan, to reduce the levels to meet the limits
- the testing and measurement of the above is done in accordance with the requirements of: BS EN ISO 16000 – Part 4 (2004) in relation to the diffusive sampling of formaldehyde in the air; BS EN ISO 16000 – Part 6 in relation to VOCs in the air by active sampling; BS EN 16017 – Part 2 (2003) in relation to indoor, ambient and workplace air by passive sampling; and BS EN ISO 16000 – Part 3 (2001) in relation to formaldehyde and other carbonyls in the air by pumped sampling

and

- the results of the above measurements are reported.

→

Hea02: Indoor air quality (second and third parts of *Minimising sources of air pollution* criterion) (continued)

INNOVATION CREDITS: None

BUILDING-TYPE VARIATIONS: None

CONSEQUENTIAL IMPACTS ON DESIGN/TIPS: The number of products likely to fall within this criterion is large, and considerable effort is needed on the part of the design team to obtain the relevant information for even the first of the above credits to be awarded. Failure to obtain the necessary information for one product could jeopardise the award of the entire credit. Certain products are excluded from some of the above requirements:

- furniture, such as desks, shelving, etc., does not have to meet the testing requirements
- if manufacturers make a written declaration that their products do not contain formaldehyde, those products achieve formaldehyde Class E1 without testing.

BRE Digest 464 Parts 1 and 2 offer advice and guidance on the sources of emissions from materials and assessing their impact.

EVIDENCE TO BE PROVIDED FOR DESIGN STAGE ASSESSMENT: For the **first credit**:

- the Indoor Air Quality Plan, as described in Chapter 3, section 3.1 on *Hea 02: Indoor air quality*
- contract specification clauses confirming testing standards and emission levels required for products.

For the **second credit**:

- the Indoor Air Quality Plan, as described in Chapter 3, section 3.1 on *Hea 02: Indoor air quality*
- contract specification clauses confirming a commitment to undertake post-construction testing and achieve required emission levels.

EVIDENCE TO BE PROVIDED FOR POST-CONSTRUCTION STAGE ASSESSMENT: As for the design stage, updated to show the as-constructed status, **plus** for the **first credit**:

- manufacturers' letters or literature confirming testing regimes and emission levels.

For the **second credit**:

- the Indoor Air Quality Plan, as described in Chapter 3, section 3.1 on *Hea 02: Indoor air quality*
- a copy of the testing results from the post-construction measurements at the post-construction stage assessment.

IMPLICATION FOR SHELL-ONLY DEVELOPMENTS: If any of the materials or products referred to in these parts of this Issue's criterion are to be part of a tenant's fit-out works, any of the Options 1, 2 or 3 (described in Chapter 2, section 2.11) can be used to assess compliance with the required performance standards.

Ene01: Reduction of CO_2 emissions

CREDITS AVAILABLE

15

INNOVATION CREDITS

up to 5

The aim of this Issue is to minimise operational energy consumption and CO_2 emissions through good building design.

PREREQUISITES: None

MINIMUM STANDARDS:
- For BREEAM Excellent – **six credits**
- For BREEAM Outstanding – **ten credits**.

PERFORMANCE STANDARD REQUIRED: The process for assessing this Issue under BREEAM 2011 has changed significantly from that used in the BREEAM 2008 Schemes. This has been necessary due to changes, in 2010, to Part L2A of the Building Regulations. Under the new Regulations, employing the previous BREEAM method of simply comparing a building's Carbon Index (taken from the Energy Performance Certificate Rating calculation used for England, Wales and Northern Ireland), with set benchmarks, could result in the paradox of more credits being awarded to certain buildings which actually have higher CO_2 emissions than others. This is because the new Regulations aim to achieve a 25 per cent aggregate reduction in CO_2 emissions across all non-domestic building types. However, improvements for different building types vary, as can be seen in Table 4.3.

TABLE 4.3: Percentage CO_2 reductions for various Building Regulations Part L2A compliant non-domestic building types

Building type	Percentage reduction for compliant building
Shallow plan heated office building	–22
Shallow plan air-conditioned office building	–40
Deep plan air-conditioned office building	–26
Warehouse	–34
Hotel	–16
Retail unit	–21
Supermarket	–26
School	–27

Source: Table 7 – *Implementation Stage Impact Assessment of Revisions to Parts F and L of the Building Regulations from 2010*, Department for Communities and Local Government (March 2010).
Available at: www.communities.gov.uk/publications/planningandbuilding/partlf2010ia

BRE has, therefore, adopted a new approach which requires a building's Energy Performance Ratio for New Construction (EPR_{NC}) to be established if credits are to be awarded. This is based on the following

→

benchmark outputs from a National Calculation Methodology software analysis (Simplified Building Energy Model (SBEM) or other approved software), undertaken by an accredited energy assessor:

- Energy demand ($EPR_{NCDemand}$) – the building's actual energy demand for heating and cooling as a proportion of the notional building's heating and cooling energy demand (in MJ/m^2).
- Energy consumption ($EPR_{NCConsumption}$) – the building's actual energy consumption as a proportion of the notional building's energy consumption (in kWh/m^2).
- CO$_2$ emissions (EPR_{NCCO_2}) – the building's Building Emission Rate (BER) as a proportion of the Target Emission Rate (in kgCO$_2$/m^2).

There are four steps in determining a building's EPR_{NC} figure:

- **Stage 1**: a building's actual performance, expressed as a percentage of its 2010 Building Regulations' notional building performance, is determined for its energy demand ($EPR_{NCDemand}$), energy consumption ($EPR_{NCConsumption}$) and CO$_2$ emissions (EPR_{NCCO_2}) using the *Ene01* calculator.
- **Stage 2**: each of the percentages from Stage 1 is then translated into a building's EPR_{NC} expressed as a value between zero and one, based on where it lies within the range of building stock modelled by BRE. This is done automatically by the *Ene01* calculator.
- **Stage 3**: the ratios from Stage 2 are then multiplied by the following weightings, again using the *Ene01* calculator, to reflect the degree of influence the designer has over a building's performance measured against each parameter. The permitted maximum contribution that each parameter can make towards the overall EPR_{NC} figure is:
  - energy demand ($EPR_{NCDemand}$) – 0.28
  - energy consumption ($EPR_{NCConsumption}$) – 0.34
  - CO$_2$ emissions (EPR_{NCCO_2}) – 0.38.
- **Stage 4**: The weighted ratios from Stage 3 are then totalled to give an overall EPR_{NC}.

A building's overall EPR_{NC} is then compared with the benchmarks given in Table 6.1 in the online *Technical Manual*,[6] to establish the number of credits that can be awarded, which are:

- **one credit** if a building's EPR_{NC} is 0.05
- for each 0.1 increment in the EPR_{NC} an additional credit can be awarded, **up to six credits**
- then, for each 0.04 increment in the EPR_{NC} an additional credit can be awarded, **up to nine credits**
- **ten credits** are awarded for an EPR_{NC} of 0.72
- **11 credits** for an EPR_{NC} of 0.75
- then an additional credit is awarded for each 0.04 increment, **up to 14 credits**
- **15 credits** are awarded for an EPR_{NC} of 0.90.

Low- and zero-carbon energy-generating technologies considered in relation to this Issue can be installed:

either

- on site

or

- near to the site where a private wire arrangement is in place. If any energy generated off site is fed directly to the building by a dedicated power supply network and the energy generated is surplus to the demand of the building at the time of supply, it can be fed back into the national electricity grid.

→

It might be possible to use off-site low- and zero-carbon energy-generating technologies via accredited external renewable energy suppliers but the proposed arrangement for their use must be agreed with BRE, since generic mechanisms for accrediting their use are not currently recognised.

INNOVATION CREDITS: Innovation credits can be awarded for achieving the following exemplar levels of performance:
- **Five credits** where the building is carbon negative in terms of:
    - its total operational energy (i.e. regulated and unregulated energy) consumption
    - being a net exporter of zero-carbon energy.

The building has to generate more energy from renewable or carbon-neutral energy generation technologies than it needs to meet its own regulated and unregulated energy use (that is, any energy use not covered by the Building Regulations, such as energy for office equipment, appliances, cooking, lifts, etc.).

Or
- **Up to four credits** can be awarded where a building's EPR_{NC} is equal to or less than 0.90, there are net CO_2 emissions from space heating or cooling, water heating, ventilation and lighting **and** a percentage of its regulated operational energy consumption is provided by carbon-neutral on-site, near-site or accredited external sources of energy generation,

for
    - **one additional credit** can be awarded where this percentage is 10 per cent
    - **two credits** where it is 20 per cent
    - **three credits** for 50 per cent
    - **four credits** for 80 per cent.

BUILDING-TYPE VARIATIONS: For self-contained dwellings in multi-residential buildings, two sets of energy performance data may be required: one set from a Standard Assessment Procedure (SAP) calculation[7] for the dwellings and one from a SBEM calculation for any for non-domestic areas. Both sets of information must then be inserted into the BREEAM *Ene01* calculator to determine the number of credits to be awarded.

CONSEQUENTIAL IMPACTS ON DESIGN/TIPS: The benchmarks that make up a building's EPR_{NC} are influenced by the following:
- Energy demand ($EPR_{NCDemand}$) – the design and form of a building contribute by reducing fabric heat loss, minimising air leakage, reducing solar gains from excessive glazing, etc.
- Energy consumption ($EPR_{NCConsumption}$) – the type and efficiency of the building services contribute by using highly efficient boilers and lighting and reducing consumption through controls, etc.
- CO_2 emissions (EPR_{NCCO_2}) – the type of fuel used by building services contributes, especially if low- or zero-carbon energy-generating technologies are used.

In order to maximise the credits from this Issue, designers must adopt an energy hierarchy approach to the design:
- First, reducing energy demand as far as possible through architectural passive measures appropriate to the local climate, site constraints and building use.

→

- Second, reducing energy consumption through the careful choice of plant and equipment.
- Finally, only when demand has been reduced as far as possible should low-carbon and zero-carbon renewable energy technologies, appropriate for the required energy profile and location, be considered in order to reduce the building's CO_2 emissions further.

The BREEAM online *Technical Manual*[6] states that, for any credits to be awarded, a building must perform better than a Building Regulations compliant building. It also suggests the level of improvement required to Building Regulations compliant buildings for the following credits to be awarded:

- For **one credit**, a building's BER has to be 5 per cent lower than its Target Emission Rate (TER), even if demand and consumption are no better than those of the notional building. Alternatively, a 5 per cent improvement in a building's energy demand or energy consumption will also result in a single credit, even if the improvement of the BER over the TER is less than 5 per cent.
- The minimum EPR_{NC} required to achieve the **six credits** needed for a BREEAM Excellent rating is 0.55, which will require an EPR_{NCCO_2} of 0.22, equating to a building's BER showing a 25 per cent improvement on its TER.
- The minimum EPR_{NC} required to achieve the **ten credits** needed for a BREEAM Outstanding rating is 0.72, which will require a EPR_{NCCO_2} of 0.30, equating to a building's BER showing a 40 per cent improvement on its TER.
- The maximum number of **15 credits**, in relation to regulated energy, can only be awarded to a net zero-carbon building with an EPR_{NC} of 0.90, which will require an EPR_{NCCO_2} of 0.38, equating to a building's BER showing a 100 per cent improvement on its TER.

EVIDENCE TO BE PROVIDED FOR DESIGN STAGE ASSESSMENT: To determine a building's EPR_{NC} and the number of credits available:

- a copy of the Building Regulations Part L (BRUKL) Output Document produced by an accredited energy assessor using an approved form of software.

For the **Innovation credits** associated with the exemplar levels of performance, the following additional information is required:

- A report, calculations, etc. from manufacturers, suppliers or service engineers confirming the source and quantity of carbon-neutral energy generation for the building, and a calculation estimating the energy consumption of any unregulated energy and of any exported energy surplus.
- Written confirmation from the client that any surplus carbon-neutral energy generated and exported to the grid will not be used to claim Renewable Obligations Certificates (ROCs).

EVIDENCE TO BE PROVIDED FOR POST-CONSTRUCTION STAGE ASSESSMENT: To determine a building's EPR_{NC}, the same as at the design stage, but updated to show the as-constructed status.

IMPLICATION FOR SHELL-ONLY DEVELOPMENTS: When calculating the energy performance for a shell and core building, the most intensive heating, ventilation, air conditioning and lighting efficiencies permissible for a fit-out under the Building Regulations have to be assumed in determining the number of credits to be awarded, unless performance specification levels are confirmed with a tenant within a legally enforceable Green Lease Agreement.

Green Building Guides **cannot** be used in relation to this Issue.

Tra03: Cyclist facilities

CREDITS AVAILABLE

1 or 2
(depending on building type)

INNOVATION CREDITS

0

The aim of this Issue criterion is to encourage building users to cycle by providing adequate facilities for cyclists.

PREREQUISITES: None relating to cycle storage, but credits relating to cyclist facilities are only awarded if sufficient cycle storage is provided.

MINIMUM STANDARDS: None

PERFORMANCE STANDARD REQUIRED: The detailed requirements regarding the number of cycle storage spaces and cyclist facilities required for the award of credits can be summarised as follows (but check the online *Technical Manual*[6] for details):

- Pre-school:
    - for **one credit** – one cycle space per ten staff
    - for **two credits** – required cycle storage
  plus
    - two compliant cyclist facilities.
- Primary schools:
    - for **one credit** – five cycle spaces per form or class in year group
    - for **two credits** – required cycle storage
  plus
    - two compliant cyclist facilities.
- Secondary schools and sixth-form colleges:
    - for **one credit** – one cycle space per ten staff and pupils
    - for **two credits** – required cycle storage
  plus
    - two compliant cyclist facilities.
- Further and higher education buildings:
    - for **one credit** – one cycle space per ten staff and students
    - for **two credits** – required cycle storage
  plus
    - two compliant cyclist facilities.
- Offices and industrial buildings:
    - for **one credit** – one cycle space per ten building occupants
    - for **two credits** – required cycle storage
  plus
    - two compliant cyclist facilities.

→

- Retail buildings – shopping centres and retail parks:
    - for **one credit** – one cycle space per ten staff

  plus
    - one cycle space per 20 public car-parking spaces (with a minimum of ten and a maximum of 50 spaces)
    - for **two credits** – required cycle storage

  plus
    - two compliant cyclist facilities for staff only.
- Individual retail units:
    - for **one credit** – ten cycle spaces per unit
    - for **two credits** – required cycle storage

  plus
    - two compliant cyclist facilities.
- Healthcare buildings:
    - for **one credit** – one cycle space per ten staff

  plus
    - one cycle space per two consulting rooms or ten beds
    - for **two credits** – required cycle storage

  plus
    - two compliant cyclist facilities for staff only.
- Law courts:
    - for **one credit** – one cycle space per ten staff

  plus
    - one cycle space per ten building visitors
    - for **two credits** – required cycle storage

  plus
    - two compliant cyclist facilities for staff only.
- Prison establishment located building:
    - for **one credit** – one cycle space per ten staff

  plus
    - two compliant cyclist facilities.
- Multi-residential buildings – student residences and key worker accommodation:
    - for **one credit** – one cycle space per ten staff

  plus
    - one cycle space per two residents.
- Multi-residential buildings – sheltered housing, care homes and supported housing for the disabled:
    - for **one credit** – one cycle space per ten staff

  plus
    - two compliant cyclist facilities for staff, and
    - one wheelchair or electric buggy storage space per ten residents.
- Other buildings predominantly occupied by staff with occasional business-related visitors:
    - for **one credit** – one cycle space per ten building occupants
    - for **two credits** – required cycle storage

  →

plus
  – two compliant cyclist facilities.
- Other buildings – occupied by a core of staff with a larger number of consistently frequent visitors:
  – for **one credit** – one cycle space per ten staff

plus
  – one cycle space per ten visitors or beds
  – for **two credits** – required cycle storage

plus
  – two compliant cyclist facilities for staff only.
- Other buildings – occupied by a core of staff with a larger number of consistently frequent visitors but located rurally:
  – for **one credit** – one cycle space per 20 staff

plus
  – two compliant cyclist facilities for staff only
  – for **one credit** – one cycle space per 20 visitors or beds.
- Other buildings – transport hubs:
  – for **one credit** – one cycle space per ten staff
  – for **one credit** – one cycle space per ten public users.
- Other buildings – MOD non-residential buildings:
  – for **one credit** – one cycle space per ten living-out personnel
  – for **two credits** – required cycle storage

plus
  – two compliant cyclist facilities.
- Other buildings – MOD residential buildings:
  – **one credit** – one cycle space per two residents.

Compliant cycle storage requires the following provisions:
- One storage space per unit of measure (i.e. number of staff or other user groups) as defined above with a minimum of four spaces.
- For up to 500 users, one space per ten users; between 500 and 1,000 users, one space per 15 users; and over 1,000 users, one space per 20 users.
- A permanent structure with a roof to protect from the weather.
- To be located within view of, or overlooked by, an occupied building or main access road.
- The majority of the cycle storage must be within 50 m of the building entrance. However, if site constraints dictate that it can be only within 100 m, this might be accepted if supporting evidence is provided.
- Lighting must achieve the performance standards set out in *Hea01: Visual comfort*, controlled to avoid out-of-hours use or operation during daylight hours.
- Cycle storage racks which allow the cycle's frame and wheels to be securely locked to them. Alternatively, cycle storage can be located in a locked enclosure or room, but this must be equipped with CCTV surveillance, which imposes a maintenance and management burden.
- Distances between cycle racks must be as indicated in the *Metric Handbook*[8] for easy storage and removal of cycles.

→

- The minimum distance between cycle storage racks and obstructions or walls is 300 mm for single-sided storage and 900 mm for double-sided storage.

If it is not possible to confirm the number of building occupants:

either

- use the default occupancy rates given in Table 7-1 in relation to *Tra04: Maximum car parking capacity*

or

- quote examples of similar sized buildings.

There is a choice of three types of cyclist facilities:

- showers
- changing facilities and lockers
- drying space for clothes.

Compliant showers must have:

- one shower per ten cycle storage spaces with a minimum of one shower, though showers do not need to be dedicated for cyclist use only
- provision for both male and female cyclists by providing either separate showers or a single shower cubicle with changing space for mixed use.

Additional requirements for schools are described in the online *Technical Manual*.[6]

Compliant changing facilities and lockers must:

- be appropriately sized for the numbers using them (this is left to the judgement of the Assessor so any proposals should be based on a recognised standard, such as the *Metric Handbook*,[8] and discussed with the Assessor)
- provide adequate space to store clothes and equipment while cyclists change and shower
- have a number of lockers equal to the number of cycle spaces provided, for both male and female cyclists, adjacent to changing rooms.

Note that toilet and shower cubicles cannot be counted as changing facilities.

Compliant drying space for clothes must:

- be designed and designated as a drying space
- be adequately heated and ventilated to comply with Part F of the Building Regulations.

Plant rooms cannot be used as drying spaces

Compliant wheelchair and buggy storage facilities must have:

- charging points for at least two electric buggies provided within the storage space
- easy access from inside and outside the building and must be secure
- direct access to the inside of the building
- lighting that meets the criteria of *Hea01: Visual comfort*.

INNOVATION CREDITS: None

BUILDING-TYPE VARIATIONS: Where self-contained dwellings in multi-residential buildings are assessed using the Code for Sustainable Homes (CSH), the requirements of CSH Issue Ene 8 must be achieved for any BREEAM credits to be awarded.

→

CONSEQUENTIAL IMPACTS ON DESIGN/TIPS: For buildings with large numbers of staff or visitors the required number of cycle spaces can be reduced using a sliding scale. If the cycle provision is for one cycle space per ten staff or visitors, this is used for up to 500 users, then:

- between 500 and 1,000 the requirement is one cycle space per 15 users
- over 1,000, one cycle space per 20 users.

The cycle storage provision can be halved:

- for sites where at least 50 per cent of the credits have been awarded in relation to *Tra01: Public transport accessibility*
- for sites in rural locations where the average building user's commuting distance is more than ten miles, including sites in villages, greenfield sites or small urban areas with populations of under 3,000.

In both cases this will also reduce the requirement for compliant showers, etc. However, the two 50 per cent reductions cannot be added together.

EVIDENCE TO BE PROVIDED FOR DESIGN STAGE ASSESSMENT: Design drawings and/or contract specification clauses confirming provision

plus (if relevant):

- the location and size of wheelchair and buggy storage
- the location and number of charging points
- assumptions and calculations used to determine the number of public users.

EVIDENCE TO BE PROVIDED FOR POST-CONSTRUCTION STAGE ASSESSMENT: As for the design stage, updated to show the as-constructed status.

IMPLICATION FOR SHELL-ONLY DEVELOPMENTS: None

Wat01: Water consumption

CREDITS AVAILABLE

5

INNOVATION CREDITS

1

The aim of this Issue is to reduce the consumption of potable water for sanitary use in buildings.

PREREQUISITES: None

MINIMUM STANDARDS:

- For a BREEAM Good, Very Good or Excellent rating – **one credit**.
- For a BREEAM Outstanding rating – **two credits**.

→

PERFORMANCE STANDARD REQUIRED: Where a building's water consumption is reduced in comparison with a notional baseline consumption level for a particular building type, the following credits can be awarded:

- for a 12.5 per cent reduction – **one credit**
- for a 25 per cent reduction – **two credits**
- for a 40 per cent reduction – **three credits**
- for a 50 per cent reduction – **four credits**
- for a 55 per cent reduction – **five credits**.

Credits are calculated by the Assessor using the *Wat01* calculator using net water consumption figures provided by the design team or contractor for the following:

- WCs – actual maximum or, where a dual flush cistern is specified, the effective volume in litres per use. The effective volume for a dual flush cistern is calculated as the ratio of one full flush for every three reduced volume flushes. So the effective volume of a 6/4 litre dual flush cistern is 4.5 litres per use.
- Urinals – flush volume in litres per user for a single use flush urinal. For cistern-fed urinals the flushing frequency per hour and cistern capacity in litres must be provided.
- Taps – flush rate for each tap type must be provided, including any reduction achieved by any flow restrictor at full flow rate in litres per minute, at a pressure of 3.0±0.2 bar/0.3±0.02 MPa if they are high pressure (Type 1) taps or at 0.1±0.02 bar/0.01±0.002 MPa if they are low pressure (Type 2) taps, as defined by BS EN 200: *Sanitary tapware: Single taps and combination taps for water supply systems of type 1 and type 2: General technical specification* (2008).
- Showers – flow rate for each shower type at the outlet, when using cold water, in litres per minute at a pressure of 3.0±0.2 bar/0.3±0.02 MPa if they are high pressure (Type 1) supply systems or at a dynamic pressure of 0.1±0.05 bar/0.01±0.005 MPa if they are low pressure (Type 2) supply systems, as defined by BS EN 1112: *Sanitary tapware: Shower outlets for sanitary tapware for water supply systems type 1 and type 2. General technical specification* (2008).
- Kitchen taps – maximum flow rate in litres per minute.
- Baths – capacity up to the overflow level in litres. The *Wat01* calculator will then assume 40 per cent of this for the water consumption calculation and flow rates for any taps on the bath are not required.
- Dishwashers – for domestic situations, litres per cycle, and for non-domestic situations, litres per rack.
- Washing machines – for domestic situations, litres per use, and for non-domestic situations, litres per kilogram of washing.
- Waste disposal units – flow rate in litres per minute.

Additionally, the water consumption of a building can be reduced through the use of either a rainwater harvesting or greywater system for flushing WCs and/or urinals as follows:

- Rainwater harvesting system – to be specified and installed to BS8515: *Rainwater Harvesting System – Code of Practice* (2009). Its capacity to reduce the water consumption is based on a calculation either using the *intermediate approach* in this standard (which will require the area of the collection zone, yield co-efficient for the system, hydraulic filter efficiency and the appropriate rainfall for the site in mm per year) or the *detailed approach* using the daily rainfall collection figure in litres.

→

- Greywater system – to be specified to BS8525: *Greywater System – Part 1: Code of Practice* (2010). Capacity to reduce water consumption is based on a calculation from this standard using manufacturers' data and the percentage volume of waste water collected from wash-hand basins, showers, kitchen basins, baths, dishwashers, washing machines and other appropriate sources of waste water.
- Water consumption should be reduced first, prior to considering the use of either a rainwater harvesting or greywater system if either **four** or **five credits**, or an **Innovation credit**, are targeted for award. The rainwater harvesting and/or greywater systems must, in themselves, provide water for reuse that is equivalent to a 25 per cent reduction on the notional baseline consumption level for a particular building type.
- Water from either a rainwater harvesting or greywater system could also be used to offset mains water usage for other consistent non-potable water demand within a building, such as a laundry. It is advisable to seek advice from the Assessor in these instances.

If the building being assessed is a mixed-use development, the overall building's total water consumption performance is determined by a separate assessment for each area of different uses or building types from which the Assessor will calculate an overall reduction level.

In some instances, the proposed building use may not be covered by the *Wat01* calculator, in which case the Assessor will contact BRE to agree an appropriate methodology for calculating the building's water consumption. Where a building, or an extension to a building, does not contain any water-consuming equipment, the facilities that are most likely to be used by the building users must be assessed, applying the criteria of this Issue.

INNOVATION CREDITS: One Innovation credit can be awarded if the exemplar performance standard is achieved for a 65 per cent reduction when compared with a notional baseline consumption level for a particular building type.

BUILDING-TYPE VARIATIONS:
- For healthcare buildings, in addition to meeting an overall percentage in water consumption, each bath must also be fitted with a device which automatically stops the flow from taps once the bath's maximum capacity is reached. The flushing control for each WC and urinal must also be suitable for operation by patients with frail or infirm hands or activated by electronic sensors. Water-consuming equipment in clinical areas, such as scrub facilities, can be excluded from the calculations.
- For prison buildings, in addition to meeting an overall percentage in water consumption, where sanitary fittings are specified in cells, a volume controller, which will turn off the water supply once the maximum preset volume has been reached within a defined period, must be attached to each fitting or to the water supply to each cell.
- For multi-residential buildings, where self-contained dwellings are assessed using the Code for Sustainable Homes (CSH), any credits awarded for CSH Issue Wat 1 **cannot** be applied directly to a BREEAM 2011 Assessment.

→

CONSEQUENTIAL IMPACTS ON DESIGN/TIPS: The online *Technical Manual*[6] suggests the typical water efficiency levels that different pieces of water-consuming equipment have to achieve in relation to the number of credits that can be awarded. This information is summarised in Table 4.4. These figures are indicative only and the consumption figures obtained for each specified item should be checked with the Assessor using the *Wat01* calculator to ensure that the credits being targeted can be awarded before the contract specification is finalised and components ordered.

TABLE 4.4: *Wat01: Water consumption* – typical water efficiency levels for the award of credits, © BRE Global Ltd 2011

Component	Unit of measure	For 1 credit to be awarded	For 2 credits to be awarded	For 3 credits to be awarded	For 4 credits to be awarded	For 5 credits to be awarded
WCs	Effective flush volume (litres)	5.00	4.50	4.00	3.75	3.00
Wash-hand basin taps	Volume (litres/minute)	9.00	7.50	4.50	3.75	3.00
Showers	Volume (litres/minute)	10.00	8.00	6.00	4.00	3.50
Baths	Volume (litres)	180.00	160.00	140.00	120.00	100.00
Single urinal	Volume (litres/bowl/hour)	8.00	4.00	2.00	1.00	0.00
Two or more urinals	Volume (litres/bowl/hour)	6.00	3.00	1.50	0.75	0.00
Kitchen taps	Volume (litres/minute)	10.00	7.50	5.00	5.00	5.00
Kitchen taps in restaurants (pre-rinse nozzles)	Volume (litres/minute)	9.00	8.30	7.30	6.30	6.00
Domestic-sized dishwashers	Volume (litres/cycle)	13.00	13.00	12.00	11.00	10.00
Commercial dishwashers	Volume (litres/rack)	7.00	6.00	5.00	4.00	3.00
Domestic-sized washing machines	Volume (litres/use)	60.00	50.00	40.00	35.00	30.00
Commercial/industrial-sized washing machines	Volume (litres/kg)	12.00	10.00	7.50	5.00	4.50
Waste disposal unit	Volume (litres/minute)	17.00	Not specified	Not specified	Not specified	Not specified

→

EVIDENCE TO BE PROVIDED FOR DESIGN STAGE ASSESSMENT:

- Specification clauses confirming technical requirements for all sanitary fittings and rainwater harvesting or greywater systems.
- Manufacturers' data sheets confirming the capacity of the sanitary fittings specified or installed.
- A copy of the instruction to or a letter from the client or principal contractor confirming that sufficient information will be provided to allow the *Wat01* calculations to be completed.

Where documentary information is not available at this stage, the client must forward a copy of the written instruction to the main contractor and/or suppliers to provide sufficient information to complete the water calculations.

EVIDENCE TO BE PROVIDED FOR POST-CONSTRUCTION STAGE ASSESSMENT:
Either

- a completed *Wat01* calculation supported by manufacturers' literature confirming consumption figures
- written confirmation from the client that fittings specified at the design stage have been installed, supported by a BREEAM Assessor site inspection or photographic evidence confirming a compliant installation
- where only a letter of commitment has been provided at the design stage, revised calculations and detailed evidence as required at the design stage

or

- where installed sanitary fittings differ from those proposed at the design stage, a revised *Wat01* calculation is undertaken, supported by manufacturers' literature confirming water consumption figures and revised calculations for rainwater harvesting or greywater systems, if necessary.

IMPLICATION FOR SHELL-ONLY DEVELOPMENTS: If a water supply is provided to tenanted areas but sanitary fittings are to be specified and fitted by the tenant, one of the Options 1, 2 or 3 (described in Chapter 2, section 2.11) can be used to assess compliance with the required performance standards.

Wat04: Water-efficient equipment

CREDITS AVAILABLE

1

INNOVATION CREDITS

0

The aim of this Issue criterion is to reduce unregulated water consumption by the procurement of water-efficient equipment.

PREREQUISITES: None

→

MINIMUM STANDARDS: None

PERFORMANCE STANDARD REQUIRED: One credit can be awarded where the irrigation method for both internal and external planting is one of the following:

- Drip-feed sub-surface zoned irrigation incorporating soil-moisture sensors to provide variable levels of irrigation (a *rainstat* must also be installed to prevent automatic irrigation to external planting during periods of rainfall).
- Water from a rainwater harvesting and/or greywater system with storage sized to suit the area of soft landscaping.
- External planting that relies solely on precipitation all year round.
- Specified planting of species that thrive in hot and dry conditions.
- Manual watering where no dedicated, mains-fed irrigation system (including pop-up sprinklers and hoses) is provided.

Plus, where a vehicle-wash facility is specified, it must be either a full or partial water-reclaim unit containing one or more of the following items, provided by a product listed on the Enhanced Capital Allowances Water Technology List:[9]

- a Hydro-cyclone
- a sand or activated filter
- a sump tank
- three chamber interceptors
- a cartridge or bag filter.

If there is no planting or vehicle wash in a particular development, this Issue will not be assessed.

INNOVATION CREDITS: None

BUILDING-TYPE VARIATIONS: Where self-contained dwellings in multi-residential buildings are assessed using the Code for Sustainable Homes (CSH), and the requirements of CSH Issue Wat 4 are achieved, this BREEAM credit can be awarded, provided that the external water collection facility provides sufficient storage volume for all the buildings.

CONSEQUENTIAL IMPACTS ON DESIGN/TIPS: It is important that the architect works closely with the landscape architect and service engineer so that they are aware of the requirements of this Issue. The products listed on the Enhanced Capital Allowances Water Technology List[9] must be checked prior to specifying the vehicle-wash facility.

EVIDENCE TO BE PROVIDED FOR DESIGN STAGE ASSESSMENT:

- Documents detailing the proposed internal and/or external planting and the irrigation strategy.
- Drawings and specification clauses confirming the planting and irrigation or vehicle-wash system proposed.

And/or

- manufacturers' product details.

→

EVIDENCE TO BE PROVIDED FOR POST-CONSTRUCTION STAGE ASSESSMENT:

- As-constructed drawings or specification confirming internal and external planting and irrigation or vehicle-wash system.
- Manufacturer's product details of the system installed.

IMPLICATION FOR SHELL-ONLY DEVELOPMENTS: None

Mat01: Life-cycle impacts

CREDITS AVAILABLE

2, 4, 5 or 6
(depending on building type)

INNOVATION CREDITS

1

The aim of this Issue is to encourage the use of construction materials with low environmental impact over the full life cycle of a building.

PREREQUISITES: None

MINIMUM STANDARDS: None

PERFORMANCE STANDARD REQUIRED: Credits will be awarded in relation to the environmental life-cycle impact of the following main building elements:

- external walls
- windows
- roofs
- upper floor construction
- internal walls
- floor finishes and coverings.

Not all of the above building elements are assessed for every building type, so the number of credits that can be awarded varies between building types, as follows:

- industrial buildings – **up to two credits**
- prison buildings – **up to four credits**
- office and retail buildings – **up to five credits**
- education, healthcare buildings, courts, multi-residential buildings and other building types – **up to six credits**.

The environmental life-cycle impacts of main building elements are expressed by the following:

- Their Green Guide rating: a generic rating can be obtained from the BRE's *Green Guide to Specification* website.[10]

→

- A bespoke Green Guide rating, which the Assessor can obtain by completing the online Green Guide calculator or by submitting a bespoke Green Guide query pro-forma to BRE. A detailed specification and detailed drawings of the element must be submitted for BRE to provide the rating.
- An independently verified third party Environmental Product Declaration (EPD), produced in accordance with the requirements of the BS ISO 14020 series. Where a product within a building element has an EPD, its impact can be assessed by inserting its details into a request for a bespoke Green Guide rating. The extent of the EPD should also be considered. If it covers the whole life cycle of a product (i.e. cradle to grave), it is considered to be a Tier 1 EPD. If it only covers part of a product's life cycle (i.e. cradle to gate), it is considered a Tier 2 EPD. This information is inserted into the *Mat01* calculator.

Credits are awarded in relation to the points scored when the details of the specified building elements are inserted into the *Mat01* calculator.

The steps required to translate the environmental life-cycle impacts of building elements, as represented by their Green Guide rating,[10] into an overall performance score for a building's life-cycle impact, and the corresponding number of credits, are detailed below:

- **Step 1**: the Green Guide rating is translated into a number of points as indicated in the online *Technical Manual*[6] for use in the *Mat01* calculator, as follows:
  - A+ rating – 3.00 points
  - A rating – 2.00 points
  - B rating – 1.00 point
  - C rating – 0.5 points
  - D rating – 0.25 points
  - E rating – 0.0 points
- **Step 2**: the maximum number of points available for any building is the number of main building elements being assessed multiplied by three. For an office building, five main building elements are assessed, so the maximum number of points available is 15 (i.e. 5 × 3 = 15).
- **Step 3**: where a main building element (e.g. external walls) consists of a number of different specifications, an overall weighted points score is calculated according to the relative area and points scored for each element.
- **Step 4**: a weighted overall building performance is calculated by totalling the sum of each main building element area, multiplied by its weighted Green Guide score, divided by the total area of all of the main building elements.

INNOVATION CREDITS: One Innovation credit can be awarded in the following circumstances:
Either
- Where four or more main building elements are assessed, the overall building score is two points better that the score required for the maximum number of credits for that building type.

Or
- where fewer than four main building elements are assessed, the overall building score is at least one point better than the score required for the maximum number of credits for that building type.

→

BUILDING-TYPE VARIATIONS: The main building elements assessed by this Issue vary between different building types, as follows:

- industrial buildings – external walls and roof
- prison buildings – external walls, roof, upper floors and floor finishes and coverings
- office and retail buildings – external walls, windows, roofs, upper floors and floor finishes and coverings
- education, healthcare, courts, multi-residential and other building types – external walls, windows, roofs, upper floors, internal walls and floor finishes and coverings.

Not all of the building types for which a BREEAM Assessment can be carried out are indicated on the *Green Guide to Specification* web page. The online *Technical Manual*[6] provides additional guidance in relation to the following building types:

- Further or higher education buildings – use elements in the education section or, if the building use is closer to another building type (e.g. an office), use the appropriate section.
- Prison buildings – use the healthcare section for elements that might not be common in other building types. If the prison building is closer to another building type, select the appropriate section.
- Law courts – the education section may be most appropriate in this case.
- Multi-residential buildings – use the domestic section, unless it is a high-rise building (that is, over three storeys), in which case use the commercial section for external walls and windows, although the healthcare section might provide more appropriate guidance on floor finishes.
- Other building types – if there is any doubt about which section to use, the Assessor will seek advice from BRE.
- Common elements – the Green Guide ratings for external wall, landscaping and commercial windows are common to all building types.

CONSEQUENTIAL IMPACTS ON DESIGN/TIPS: The choice of materials for the major building elements clearly has a significant impact on the credits that can be awarded for this Issue. The architect should discuss this choice with the Assessor at the earliest possible stage so that a sample calculation using the *Mat01* calculator can be undertaken and, if any changes are required, they can be included as soon as possible.

Some building elements will have a greater influence than others on the score and the number of credits to be awarded. This is because the Green Guide rating levels vary for each building element due to the fact that their environmental impacts, measured by BRE's Ecopoints, also vary. Some building elements (such as external walls) have a larger number of Ecopoints than others (such as internal walls), making it crucial that they have a higher Green Guide rating score. For example, in multi-storey buildings it is often more critical that the upper floor construction specification has an A+ rated than that the windows do.

EVIDENCE TO BE PROVIDED FOR DESIGN STAGE ASSESSMENT:
- Drawings showing locations and areas of all the various building element specifications.
- Confirmation of the Green Guide rating and element number for each element specified **or** copies of an element's EPD **or** a copy of BRE's bespoke Green Guide rating **or** a copy of an Environmental Profile Certificate.

→

- Contract specification clauses providing a detailed description of each building element.

EVIDENCE TO BE PROVIDED FOR POST-CONSTRUCTION STAGE ASSESSMENT:
- Drawings showing locations and areas of all the various as-constructed building element specifications and highlighting any changes since the design stages.
- Confirmation of the as-constructed Green Guide rating.

IMPLICATION FOR SHELL-ONLY DEVELOPMENTS: Where floor finishes are not specified, one of the Options 1, 2 or 3 (described in Chapter 2, section 2.11) can be used to assess compliance with the required performance standards.

Mat03: Responsible sourcing of materials

CREDITS AVAILABLE

3

INNOVATION CREDITS

1

The aim of this Issue criterion is to encourage the specification of responsibly sourced key building materials and products.

PREREQUISITES: None

MINIMUM STANDARDS: For any BREEAM rating to be achieved, all timber specified and installed in a building must be sourced in accordance with the UK Government's Timber Procurement Policy. Details of this policy and the individual policies of the Scottish, Welsh and Northern Irish Governments can be found on the Central Point of Expertise for Timber Procurement website.[11] Government policy requires all timber and wood-derived products to be sourced only from one of the following:
Either
- independently verified legal and sustainable sources, such as those certified by the Programme for the Endorsement of Forest Certification (PEFC) or the Forest Stewardship Council (FSC). As an umbrella scheme, PEFC also endorses national schemes, such as the Canadian CSA and North American SFI schemes.

Or
- Forest Law Enforcement, Governance and Trade (FLEGT) licensed timber or equivalent sources, although at the time of writing no FLEGT licensed timber was available. For the latest position, consult the Central Point of Expertise for Timber Procurement website.[11]

Plus

→

- the timber must not be listed in the Convention on International Trade in Endangered Species (CITES) agreement as species threatened with extinction (Appendix I), or as species in which trade must be controlled to avoid utilisation incompatible with their survival (Appendix II). The Convention applies to species that are protected in at least one country, which has asked other CITES parties for assistance in controlling trade in that timber species (Appendix III).[12]

PERFORMANCE STANDARD REQUIRED: The number of credits available is determined by assessing the rigour of the process involved in responsibly sourcing the products or materials within a range of building elements. The points scored are given as a percentage of the possible maximum score, as follows:

- **one credit** – where 18 per cent of the available points are achieved
- **two credits** – where 36 per cent of the available points are achieved
- **three credits** – where 54 per cent of the available points are achieved.

A maximum of 4.0 points can be scored for each of the following building elements, if present, within a building:

- structural frame
- ground floor
- upper floors
- roof
- external walls
- internal walls
- foundations or substructure
- fittings, including staircases, windows (frame and glazing units), doors (internal and external), floor finishes and any other significant fittings
- hard landscaping, including materials for surfacing (and sub-bases) external pedestrian areas and lightly and heavily trafficked areas. Where the area of hard landscaping is smaller than the gross floor area of the building, it is excluded from the assessment.

The number of points that can be scored will vary depending on the number of building elements being assessed. So, if all of the nine building elements listed above are present, the maximum number of points available would be 36, i.e.

$$9 \times 4 = 36 \text{ points}$$

So, in this case, for **one credit** to be awarded, 6.5 points would have to be achieved, i.e.

$$36 \times 18\% (0.18) = 6.5 \text{ points} = \textbf{one credit}$$

Plus, to achieve any points in a given building element at least 80 per cent of that element must comprise materials that are responsibly sourced and fall within Tier Levels 1 to 7, as described below.

The range of materials that must be assessed within a building element, and the key processes and key supply chain processes that must be assessed in relation to a material, are as follows:

- Bricks (including clay tiles, clay pavers and other ceramic products):
    - key process – product manufacture
    - key supply chain processes – clay extraction.

→

Mat03: Responsible sourcing of materials (continued)

- Resin-based composites and materials (including GRP and polymeric renders):
  - key process – composite product manufacture
  - key supply chain processes – glass fibre production (or other principal matrix materials) and polymer production.
- In-situ concrete (including ready mix, cementitious mortars and renders):
  - key process – ready mix concrete plant
  - key supply chain processes – cement production and aggregate extraction and production.
- Pre-cast concrete and other concrete products (including blocks, cladding, pre-cast flooring, pavers, concrete or cementitious roof tiles):
  - key process – concrete product manufacture
  - key supply chain processes – cement production and aggregate extraction and production.
- Glass:
  - key process – glass production
  - key supply chain processes – sand extraction and soda ash production or extraction.
- Plastic and rubbers (including EPDM, TPO, PVC and VET roofing and other membranes and polymeric renders):
  - key process – plastic and rubber product manufacture
  - key supply chain process – main polymer production.
- Metals (steel, aluminium, etc.):
  - key process – metal production manufacture for steel section or cladding, etc.
  - key supply chain processes – for steel: electric arc furnace or basic oxygen furnace process; for aluminium: ingot production; for copper: ingot or cathode production.
- Dressed or building stone (including slate):
  - key process – stone product manufacture
  - key supply chain process – stone extraction.
- Stone and gravel:
  - key process – product manufacture
  - key supply chain processes – one or two inputs with significant production or extraction impacts have to be identified.
- Timber, wood-based composite and panels (including glulam, plywood, OSB, MDF, chipboard and cement-bonded particle board):
  - key process – timber from certified sources
  - key supply chain process – timber production from certified sources.
- Cement-bonded particle board:
  - key process – production manufacture and timber production from certified sources
  - key supply chain processes – cement production and timber production from certified sources.
- Plasterboard and plaster:
  - key process – plasterboard or plaster manufacture
  - key supply chain processes – gypsum extraction, synthetic gypsum (from flue gas desulphurisation) by default (recycled content).

→

- Bituminous materials (including roofing membranes and asphalt):
  - key process – product manufacture
  - key supply chain processes – bitumen production, aggregate extraction and production.
- Other mineral-based materials (including fibre cement and calcium silicate products):
  - key process – product manufacture
  - key supply chain processes – cement production, lime production, other mineral extraction and production.
- Products with 100 per cent recycled content:
  - key process – product manufacture
  - key supply chain processes – recycled input by default.
- Products with lower percentage of recycled content:
  - key process – product manufacture
  - key supply chain processes – supply chain processes for any virgin material in the product type above, recycled input by default.

For other materials forming part of the building elements being assessed which are not described above, ask your BREEAM Assessor to confirm the relevant key process and supply chain process(es) with BRE. Insulation materials, fixings, adhesives and additives are excluded from the assessment of this Issue.

BREEAM has allocated a Tier Level, ranging from 1 to 7, to the various responsible sourcing certification schemes used to assess a material's key process and key supply chain processes. The levels are intended to represent the rigour of the certification scheme in terms of BREEAM's responsible sourcing criteria. The following certification schemes are recognised by BREEAM:

- BRE Global BES60001 product certification,[13] for certification level or scope:
  - Excellent – Tier Level 2
  - Very Good – Tier Level 3
  - Good – Tier Level 4
  - Pass – Tier Level 5.
- BRE Global BES60001 standard certification,[13] for certification level or scope:
  - Excellent – Tier Level 2
  - Very Good – Tier Level 3
  - Good – Tier Level 4
  - Pass – Tier Level 5.
- Canadian Standards Association's (CSA) Chain of Custody certification – Tier Level 3.
- Certified Environmental Management System for key process and supply chain extraction process – Tier Level 6.
- Certified Environmental Management System for the key process only – Tier Level 7.
- Forest Stewardship Council's (FSC) Chain of Custody certification – Tier Level 3.
- Green Dragon Environmental Standard for Level 4 or above – Tier Level 7.
- Recycled materials, with a certified EMS for the key process – Tier Level 6.
- Reused materials – Tier Level 3.
- Malaysian Timber Certification Council's (MTCC) Chain of Custody certification – Tier Level 6.
- Programme for the Endorsement of Forest Certification (PEFC) Chain of Custody certification – Tier Level 3.

→

- Sustainable Forestry Initiative Chain of Custody certification – Tier Level 3.
- Société Général de Surveillance's (SGS) Timber Legality and Traceability Scheme verification – Tier Level 6.
- Rainforest Alliance's Verification of Legal Origin and Compliance Scheme – Tier Level 6.

The points awarded for each Tier Level are:

- Tier Level 1 – 4.0 points
- Tier Level 2 – 3.5 points
- Tier Level 3 – 3.0 points
- Tier Level 4 – 2.5 points
- Tier Level 5 – 1.5 points
- Tier Level 6 – 1.0 points
- Tier Level 7 – 0 points.

Where a building element is made up of several materials, each material has to be considered separately and a relative proportion of points awarded for its use as follows:

1 Establish the percentage of each applicable material in relation to the overall building element (e.g. bricks make up 60 per cent of an external wall).

2 Determine the Tier Level of each applicable material and the points applicable to that Tier Level (i.e. a Tier Level 3 material will score 3.0 points).

3 Establish the percentage of each responsibly sourced material in relation to the overall contribution of the responsibly sourced materials (e.g. if 85 per cent of an external wall comprises responsibly sourced materials, then the bricks contribute 70.5 per cent to the responsible sourcing of this element, $60/85 \times 100$. The points achieved by the bricks are 2.12 points, 3×70.5 per cent).

4 The adjusted points for each responsibly sourced material are then totalled to establish the points scored for that building element.

In addition to consisting of several materials, a building element may also incorporate a number of different specifications. In this case, the above process should be repeated for each specification as follows:

- Establish the percentage of each applicable material, both in relation to each building element specification and in relation to the overall building element.
- Determine the Tier Level of each applicable material and the points applicable to that Tier Level.
- Establish the percentage of each responsibly sourced material in relation to its overall contribution to the whole building element and calculate the adjusted points scored for each applicable material in each specification.
- Total the adjusted points for each responsibly sourced material within a building element to establish the points scored for that building element.

The percentage breakdown of materials within a building element is determined:

either

- where a specification matches a Green Guide rated element specification, by use of the BRE online Responsible Sourcing calculator, available to BREEAM Assessors on their Extranet site

or

- by use of an applicable materials breakdown provided by the design team giving a volume or percentage for each material in the building element.

→

Timber volumes in window and door components can be established by obtaining the following manufacturers' product data:

- Timber windows: for fixed lights multiply the total length of the window frame by 0.00653 and for opening lights multiply the total length of the frame by 0.01089 to establish a volume.
- Timber flush doors: multiply the face areas of all the doors by 0.02187 to establish a volume for the door leafs and frames.

INNOVATION CREDITS: One Innovation credit can be awarded where 70 per cent of the available responsible sourcing points are achieved.

BUILDING-TYPE VARIATIONS: In industrial buildings, fittings can be excluded from the range of building elements to be assessed.

CONSEQUENTIAL IMPACTS ON DESIGN/TIPS: This can be one of the most complex Issues to assess, making it very difficult to gauge how many credits can be awarded at an early stage in the BREEAM process. It is, therefore, important to establish as early in the design process as possible that responsible sourcing data is available from potential suppliers of products that may be specified. Unfortunately, it is often very difficult to obtain the appropriate information from manufacturers' websites.

The *GreenBookLive* website provides a list of manufacturers whose processes have been assessed using BES60001.[13] Currently, this is limited mainly to manufacturers of concrete or brick-related products and steel reinforcement, etc. BRE Global also certifies a limited number of manufactures' ISO 14001 environmental management schemes. A list of these is available on the *GreenBookLive* website.

The design team must be prepared to put considerable effort into tracking down the information required by the Assessor.

EVIDENCE TO BE PROVIDED FOR DESIGN STAGE ASSESSMENT:
- Copies of design plans and details of the materials specified for each building element.
- Copies of relevant responsible source certificates for the applicable materials within the building elements, or the relevant contract specification clause or a letter of commitment from the design team that the applicable products will be responsibly sourced from suppliers capable of providing certification appropriate to the level required for the Tier Level claimed.
- A copy of the completed output from the *Mat03* calculator.

If any recycled materials are proposed, the design team must provide:
- a report from the design team confirming the use of recycled materials in relation to building elements and applicable materials
- a letter of intent to use suppliers that can provide the required certification for their recycling processes.

→

In relation to the procurement of timber and wood-derived products, the following must be provided:

Either

- Written confirmation from the supplier(s) of the timber products that all the timber to be used is sourced in compliance with the UK Government's Timber Procurement Policy for legal and sustainable sourcing.

Or

- copies of actual Chain of Custody evidence meeting the Central Point of Expertise for Timber Procurement requirements.

Or

- a letter of intent from the design team confirming that all timber will be procured in accordance with the above.

In relation to the Green Dragon Environmental Standard, the following must be provided:

- Written confirmation from the proposed supplier of a product or material that the Green Dragon Environmental Standard has been completed up to and including Tier Level 4, as indicated on the Green Dragon Environmental Standard Certificate. This certificate should be dated within one year of the date of the last purchase made from the company, although for smaller companies with low environmental impacts a renewal date within two years would be acceptable.

In relation to suppliers who are classed as small or medium-sized companies (i.e. those with turnovers of no more than £5.6 million per year and with 50 employees or fewer, with Environmental Management Systems (EMS)), written confirmation should be obtained from the company that:

- the EMS complies with the requirements of BS8555 (2003)
- the EMS has completed Phase Audits one to four as outlined in BS8555 (2003)

and

- copies of independent certification of the above, where it exists, should be obtained.

EVIDENCE TO BE PROVIDED FOR POST-CONSTRUCTION STAGE ASSESSMENT: Essentially the same as for the design stage, except that the following must be provided:

- Written confirmation from the design team that evidence provided at the design stage regarding the use of materials in building elements is still applicable.
- Where the specification of materials has altered, evidence as required at the design stage for any replacement materials on as-constructed drawings, specification, etc.
- Copies of all relevant certificates of as-constructed materials, etc.
- A revised copy of the output from the *Mat03* calculator, updated for any new materials, etc.

IMPLICATION FOR SHELL-ONLY DEVELOPMENTS: Fittings, as described in the performance standards section of this criterion, can be excluded from the range of building elements to be assessed if they are not included in the base build.

Wst02: Recycled aggregates

CREDITS AVAILABLE

1

INNOVATION CREDITS

1

The aim of this Issue is to reduce the demand for virgin building materials and optimise material efficiency in the construction of buildings by encouraging the use of recycled and secondary aggregates.

PREREQUISITES: None

MINIMUM STANDARDS: None

PERFORMANCE STANDARD REQUIRED: One credit can be awarded where the total amount of recycled and/or secondary aggregates specified for the development is greater than 25 per cent (by weight or volume) of the total high-grade aggregates required.
Plus the minimum levels are achieved in relation to the following applications:

- Structural frames, floor slabs (including ground floor slabs), concrete road surfaces, building foundations – 25 per cent for each element.
- Bitumen or hydraulic bound base, binder and surface courses for paved areas and roads – 50 per cent.
- Pipe bedding – 50 per cent.
- Granular fill and capping – 75 per cent; for granular fill to be considered a high-grade aggregate it must conform to one of the classes described in the *Specification for Highway Works Series – 600 Earthworks*.
- Gravel landscaping – 100 per cent.

Recycled and secondary aggregates are defined as:
either

- recycled aggregate obtained from the site being developed
- recycled aggregate obtained from construction, demolition or excavation waste (including road planings) from a waste processing site within a 30 km radius of the site being developed

or

- secondary aggregate obtained from non-construction, post-consumer or post-industrial by-products. This includes china clay waste, slate overburden, pulverised fuel ash (PFA), ground granulated blast furnace slag (GGBFS), air-cooled blast furnace slag, steel slag, furnace bottom ash (FBA), incinerator bottom ash, foundry sands, recycled glass, recycled plastic, tyres, spent oil shale, colliery spoil and municipal solid waste treatment residues.

INNOVATION CREDITS: One Innovation credit can be awarded where the total amount of recycled and/or secondary aggregates specified is greater than 35 per cent (by weight or volume) of the total high-grade aggregate specified for the development, **plus** minimum levels are achieved in relation to the following applications:

- Structural frames, floor slabs (including ground floor slabs), concrete road surfaces, building foundations – 50 per cent for each element.

→

- Bitumen or hydraulic bound base, binder and surface courses for paved areas and roads – 75 per cent.
- Pipe bedding – 100 per cent.
- Granular fill and capping – 100 per cent.
- Gravel landscaping – 100 per cent.

BUILDING-TYPE VARIATIONS: None

CONSEQUENTIAL IMPACTS ON DESIGN/TIPS: The principal difficulties in achieving the requirements of this Issue are twofold:

- The calculation that the structural engineer must complete to demonstrate that the required performance standards are being achieved can involve significant work.
- Suitable recycled and/or secondary aggregates may not be available in the required quantities at the time stipulated in the construction programme, although the supply of recycled and/or secondary aggregates is increasing.

WRAP has set up *AggRegain*, a website that helps designers to source recycled and/or secondary aggregates.[14]

EVIDENCE TO BE PROVIDED FOR DESIGN STAGE ASSESSMENT:

- Copies of contract specification clauses requiring the use of recycled and/or secondary aggregates for each of the above applications.
- A calculation, usually carried out by the structural engineer, confirming the weight or volume of high-grade aggregate used for each of the above applications and a calculation confirming the percentage of recycled and/or secondary aggregates specified for use.
- Documentation confirming the source of the proposed recycled and/or secondary aggregates and confirmation that the amounts required can be sourced.

EVIDENCE TO BE PROVIDED FOR POST-CONSTRUCTION STAGE ASSESSMENT:

- Calculations detailing the weights or volumes and types of aggregates actually used in the construction works to demonstrate that the design intent was carried out.
- Copies of delivery notes, or letters of confirmation from suppliers, confirming the types and quantities of aggregate used on site during the construction.

IMPLICATION FOR SHELL-ONLY DEVELOPMENTS: None

Pol01: Impact of refrigerants

The aim of this Issue criterion is to reduce the level of greenhouse gas emissions arising from the leakage of refrigerants from buildings.

PREREQUISITES: None

MINIMUM STANDARDS: None

PERFORMANCE STANDARD REQUIRED: Three credits can be awarded if the building **does not** require the use of any refrigerants within the following installed systems:
- air conditioning and refrigeration systems
- comfort cooling
- cold storage (excluding domestic fridges and freezers)
- process-based cooling loads (e.g. server room systems).

Alternatively, if the building **does** require the use of refrigerants in these systems:
- **one credit** can be awarded where the systems using the refrigerants have a Direct Effect Life Cycle CO_2 equivalent emissions (DELC CO_{2e}) of ≤1,000 $kgCO_{2e}$ per kW cooling capacity
- **two credits** can be awarded where the systems using the refrigerants have DELC CO_{2e} of ≤100 $kgCO_{2e}$ per kW cooling capacity **or** the refrigerants have a Global Warming Potential (GWP) of ≤10. GWP is a measure of potential for global warming relative to one unit of carbon dioxide. A list of common refrigerants with a GWP of ≤10 is given in Table 12-1 in the online *Technical Manual.*[6]

DELC CO_{2e} is a measure of the refrigerant's effect on global warming and is calculated using the *Pol01* calculator by entering the following information:
- Global Warming Potential (GWP) of specified refrigerants
- total refrigerant charge (kg)
- cooling capacity of the system(s) (kW)
- sectoral release factors covering:
  - annual refrigerant leakage rate, as a percentage of the refrigerant charge – typical rates for average annual leakage are given in Table 12-2 in the online *Technical Manual*[6]
  - annual purge release factor, as a percentage of the refrigerant charge
  - annual service release factor, as a percentage of the refrigerant charge
  - probability factors for catastrophic system failure (as a percentage)
  - recovery efficiency, as a percentage of the refrigerant charge.

One further credit can be awarded for buildings with systems using refrigerants in the following circumstances:
- The systems are contained in a moderately airtight enclosure (one that produces a draught or significant fresh air ingress), or a mechanically ventilated plant room, and an automated refrigerant leak detection system covering high-risk parts of the plant (typically pipe connections

→

close to the compressor) or a refrigerant leakage or charge loss detection system (not based on measuring refrigerant in the air) is specified.

- An automatic shut down and pump down of refrigerant will occur on the detection of refrigerant leakage or charge loss. This can be to either a separate storage tank or into the heat exchanger if automatic isolation valves are fitted to contain the refrigerant once pumped down.
- The alarm threshold triggering the automatic pump down is set to a maximum level of 2,000 ppm (0.2 per cent).
- The proposed refrigerant leak detection system is included on the Enhanced Capital Allowances Energy Technology Products List.[9]

This credit is awarded by default for small multiple hermetic systems where the refrigerant charge is less than 5 kg.

There are also specific performance standards if certain types of refrigerants are proposed:

- CO_2 as refrigerant – the installation must comply with BS EN 378 (2008) and the Institute of Refrigeration's (IOR) *Carbon Dioxide as a Refrigerant Code of Practice*,[15] except for the criteria relating to the refrigerant recovery system.
- Ammonia as refrigerant – **one credit** can be awarded without the need for a recovery system if designed to BS EN 378 (2008) and the IOR's Ammonia Refrigeration Systems Code of Practice.[16]

INNOVATION CREDITS: None

BUILDING-TYPE VARIATIONS: For industrial buildings, this Issue will not be assessed if there are no offices and the operational areas are untreated.

CONSEQUENTIAL IMPACTS ON DESIGN/TIPS: If the building is designed to have no refrigerant-using building services, the credits can be awarded even for a shell-only development, provided that the tenant does not install refrigerant-using systems before the post-construction stage assessment is undertaken.

EVIDENCE TO BE PROVIDED FOR DESIGN STAGE ASSESSMENT:

- Documentary evidence confirming the absence of refrigerants in the building.
- A copy of the contract specification clauses or a letter from the service engineer confirming relevant refrigerant types and systems proposed.
- The information described above must be provided to allow the Assessor to complete the DELC CO_{2e} calculation using the *Pol01* calculator.

EVIDENCE TO BE PROVIDED FOR POST-CONSTRUCTION STAGE ASSESSMENT: As for the design stage, updated to show any design changes, confirmed by the provision of as-constructed drawings and specification.

IMPLICATION FOR SHELL-ONLY DEVELOPMENTS: If the building does contain refrigerant-using systems and the tenant is to be responsible for part or all of the refrigerant system, one of the Options 1, 2 or 3 (described in Chapter 2, section 2.11) can be used to assess compliance with the required performance standards.

4.2 Issues which are difficult to achieve in certain buildings

The parts of the three Issues described below and the credits available for them can be difficult to achieve in certain buildings. Table 4.5 shows that these Issues only generally contribute between three and four per cent towards a final BREEAM score. Although the issues they address are important, their limited impact can, unfortunately, make failure to achieved their performance standards less critical than in the case of credits from other Issues.

TABLE 4.5: Issues which are difficult to achieve in certain buildings

	Commercial buildings		Non-housing buildings							
	Offices	Retail	Industrial	Educational (schools)	Educational (higher education)	Healthcare	Prisons	Multi-residential buildings	Courts	Other buildings
Management Category	No Issues in this category are considered in Chapter 4									
Health and Wellbeing Category										
Hea01: Visual comfort (Daylighting criterion)	1	2	1	1	2	2	1	1	1	1
Hea02: Indoor air quality (Potential for natural ventilation criterion)	1	1	1	1	1	1	0	1	1	1
Weighted % value of the above credits to the final BREEAM score	2.14	3.00	2.14	1.76	2.65	2.50	1.07	2.14	1.88	1.88
Energy Category	No Issues in this category are considered in Chapter 4									
Transport Category	No Issues in this category are considered in Chapter 4									
Water Category	No Issues in this category are considered in Chapter 4									
Materials Category	No Issues in this category are considered in Chapter 4									
Waste Category	No Issues in this category are considered in Chapter 4									
Land Use and Ecology Category	No Issues in this category are considered in Chapter 4									
Pollution Category	10% weighting towards BREEAM score									
Pol03: Surface water run-off (Surface water run-off criterion)	2	2	2	2	2	2	2	2	2	2
Weighted % value of the above credits to the final BREEAM score	1.54	1.54	1.67	1.54	1.54	1.54	1.54	1.54	1.54	1.54
Overall % value of the Issues considered in Chapter 4 towards the overall BREEAM score	3.68	4.54	3.81	3.30	4.19	4.04	2.61	3.68	3.41	3.41

Hea01: Visual comfort (Daylighting criterion)

CREDITS AVAILABLE

1 or 2

(depending on building type)

INNOVATION CREDITS

1

The aim of this Issue criterion is to achieve best practice visual performance in buildings and improve comfort for the occupants through the provision of adequate levels of daylighting.

PREREQUISITES: All fluorescent and compact fluorescent lamps have to be fitted with high-frequency ballasts.

MINIMUM STANDARDS: For any BREEAM rating, all fluorescent and compact fluorescent lamps must be fitted with high-frequency ballasts.

PERFORMANCE STANDARD REQUIRED: The following *daylight factors* (DF) have to be achieved in the *relevant occupied spaces* of the building types described **plus** the additional standards indicated below:

- Pre-schools, schools and further education buildings:
  - **One credit** where 2 per cent DF is achieved over 80 per cent of the occupied spaces
  plus
  - the uniformity ratio **or** the sky view **and** room depth criteria described below are met.
- Higher education buildings:
  - **One credit** where 2 per cent DF is achieved over 60 per cent of the occupied spaces
  plus
  - the uniformity ratio **or** the sky view **and** room depth criteria are met.
  - **Two credits** where 2 per cent DF is achieved over 80 per cent of the occupied spaces
  plus
  - the uniformity ratio **or** the sky view **and** room depth criteria are met.
- Healthcare buildings:
  - **two credits** where 2 per cent DF is achieved over 80 per cent of the staff and public areas, **and**
  - 3 per cent DF is achieved over 80 per cent of the occupied patient areas (day rooms, wards, etc.) and consulting rooms.
- Multi-residential buildings:
  - **One credit** where 2 per cent DF is achieved over 80 per cent of kitchens, **and**
  - 1.5 per cent DF over 80 per cent of living rooms, dining rooms and studies, **and**
  - 2 per cent DF over 80 per cent of non-residential and communal occupied spaces
  plus
  - the uniformity ratio **or** the sky view **and** room depth criteria are met in non-residential and communal occupied spaces.
- Retail units:
  - **One credit** where point DF of 2 per cent or more is achieved over 35 per cent of sales

→

areas. It is best to use software to calculate and link all the points of the same daylight factor values with isolux contours.

- **One credit** where 2 per cent DF is achieved over 80 per cent of other occupied areas,

plus

- the uniformity ratio **or** the sky view **and** room depth criteria are met in other occupied areas only

- Offices, industrial, courts, prison and other building types:
  - **one credit** where 2 per cent DF is achieved over 80 per cent of occupied spaces in each of these building types.

  plus

  - the uniformity ratio **or** the sky view **and** room depth criteria are met

  except for

    1.5 per cent DF is achieved over 80 per cent of cells and custody cells (e.g. in prisons, courts, etc.)
  - 3 per cent DF is achieved over 80 per cent of the internal association and atrium areas (prison buildings only) and a uniformity ratio of at least 0.7 **or** a minimum point DF of 2.1 per cent is achieved
  - 3 per cent DF is achieved over 80 per cent of patient care spaces
  - 2 per cent DF is achieved over 80 per cent of teaching, lecture and seminar spaces and the uniformity ratio **or** the sky view **and** room depth criteria are met
  - a point DF of 2 per cent or more over 35 per cent of any retail spaces in these building types.

The additional performance standards over and above the DF levels that have to be achieved are listed below:

- **Uniformity ratio** – the ratio between lowest and highest calculated DFs must be at least 0.4, or there must be a minimum point DF of at least 0.8 per cent. In teaching spaces this uniformity ratio can be 0.3 as defined in *Building Bulletin 87: Guidelines for Environmental Design in Schools*. In spaces with glazed roofs a uniformity ratio of at least 0.7 must be achieved or a minimum point of DF of at least 1.4 per cent.
- **Sky view** – a direct view of the sky must be achieved from a desk height of 0.7 m in the 80 per cent of a room that complies with the average DF requirement.
- **Room depth criterion** – the room depth criterion is calculated from:

  $d/w + d/HW < 2/(1 - RB)$, where:

  d = room depth

  w = room width

  HW = window head height from floor level

  RB = the average reflectance of surfaces in the rear half of the rooms.

  For rooms lit by windows on two opposite sides, the maximum room depth that can be satisfactorily daylit is usually twice the limiting depth (d) for a room with windows in one wall. The room depth criterion cannot be used on rooms lit by rooflights, so daylight calculations should be carried out using appropriate software and Figure 2.36 in CIBSE *Lighting Guide LG10* used to determine the uniformity ratio.

'**Relevant occupied spaces**' in relation to this criterion are areas that are generally occupied continuously for 30 minutes or more. It is important to ensure that all the relevant occupied areas are considered and the daylighting performance standards achieved to avoid credits being lost. Even small

→

offices, meeting rooms, kitchens and catering areas can be counted as occupied. It is advisable to agree a list of relevant occupied areas with the Assessor as early as possible in the design process.

INNOVATION CREDITS: Innovation credits can be awarded for achieving the following exemplary levels of performance in relation to the specified building types:

- All multi-storey building types (except retail units): 3 per cent DF over 80 per cent of the occupied spaces **or**, where used, a minimum point DF of 1.2 per cent or 2.1 per cent for spaces with glazed roofs – **one credit**.
- All single-storey building types (except retail units): 4 per cent DF over 80 per cent of the occupied spaces **or**, where used, a minimum point DF of 1.6 per cent or 2.8 per cent for spaces with glazed roofs – **one credit**.
- Prison and court cells: 2 per cent DF over 80 per cent of the cell area – **one credit**.
- Prison, in addition to the above cell requirement, internal association and atrium areas: 5 per cent DF over 80 per cent of the area **plus** a uniformity ratio of at least 0.7 or a minimum point DF of 3.5 per cent – **one credit**.
- Retail units: **one credit** can be awarded where the following are achieved:
  - in sales areas – a point DF of 2 per cent over 50 per cent of the sales area
  - in common areas and offices in multi-storey retail units – 3 per cent DF over 80 per cent of the occupied spaces **or**, where used, a minimum point DF of 1.2 per cent, or 2.1 per cent for spaces with glazed roofs
  - in common areas and offices in single-storey retail units – 4 per cent DF over 80 per cent of the occupied spaces **or**, where used, a minimum point DF of 1.6 per cent or 2.8 per cent for spaces with glazed roofs.

In all of the above cases, the relevant requirements for achieving either the required uniformity ratio or the sky view and room depth criteria must be achieved for the Innovation credit to be awarded.

BUILDING-TYPE VARIATIONS: Where self-contained dwellings are assessed in multi-residential buildings using the Code for Sustainable Homes (CSH), achieving the requirements of CSH Issue Hea 1 can contribute towards the award of BREEAM credits, as long as any other occupied spaces meet the requirements of this Issue.

CONSEQUENTIAL IMPACTS ON DESIGN/TIPS: Achieving the daylighting performance standards depends to a great extent on a building's design. The depth of a building, the size and the location of windows all play crucial roles in determining daylight levels. For instance, deep-plan office buildings are very unlikely to achieve the daylight factor requirements for this credit. Some building types have not included sufficient glazing to meet these standards.

EVIDENCE TO BE PROVIDED FOR DESIGN STAGE ASSESSMENT:
- Design drawings.
- Daylight calculations covering all the necessary issues.

EVIDENCE TO BE PROVIDED FOR POST-CONSTRUCTION STAGE ASSESSMENT: As for the design stage, with calculations updated to show any changes in the as-constructed drawings.

IMPLICATION FOR SHELL-ONLY DEVELOPMENTS: None

Hea02: Indoor air quality
(Potential for natural ventilation criterion)

CREDITS AVAILABLE

1

INNOVATION CREDITS

0

The aim of this Issue criterion is to encourage a healthy internal environment by providing fresh air to a building using a natural ventilation strategy.

PREREQUISITES: None

MINIMUM STANDARDS: None

PERFORMANCE STANDARD REQUIRED: One credit can be awarded where it is demonstrated that occupied spaces within a building have been designed so that fresh air can be provided by a natural ventilation strategy, such as the following:

- Openable windows equal to 5 per cent of the gross internal area of the occupied space, defined as the geometric free ventilation area when a window is open, not the glazed area.
- Openable windows, evenly distributed, on opposite sides of rooms or floors which are between 7 and 15 m deep, to provide cross-ventilation.
- The proposed natural ventilation strategy can be shown to maintain thermal comfort conditions and ventilation rates by using ventilation design software recommended by CIBSE AM10 or the ClassVent tool for schools.
- Where a natural ventilation strategy does not rely on openable windows or the occupied space is deeper than 15 m, it must be demonstrated that an adequate cross-ventilation flow of air will be provided to maintain the required thermal comfort conditions and ventilation rates.

Plus the proposed natural ventilation strategy must be capable of providing the following two levels of easily accessible user controls offering adequate control of flow rates to the supply of fresh air:

- higher level control – to provide increased rates of ventilation to remove odours and/or prevent overheating in summer
- lower level control – to provide draught-free fresh air levels to appropriate standards in order to meet indoor air quality standards throughout the year appropriate to the occupancy load for the occupied space and any possible internal pollution levels.

An 'occupied space' is one that is occupied for 30 minutes or more by a building occupant or user. The online *Technical Manual*[6] contains a long list of spaces within buildings that can be excluded from this definition. The Assessor will determine whether any of these apply.

INNOVATION CREDITS: None

BUILDING-TYPE VARIATIONS:

- In multi-residential buildings with self-contained flats, individual bedrooms must have some form of openable windows. Although these do not need to provide the two levels of user-control described above, they do have to be occupant controlled.

→

Hea02: Indoor air quality (Potential for natural ventilation criterion) (continued)

- In industrial buildings, the above performance standards only apply to office areas, not operational areas. If the industrial building does not contain an office area, this criterion is not assessed.
- This credit is not applicable to prison buildings.

CONSEQUENTIAL IMPACTS ON DESIGN/TIPS: Buildings which are mechanically ventilated and cooled, but have the potential to be naturally ventilated, can still be awarded the credit if they can be easily modified to comply with all the above performance standards. This might be accomplished by including the appropriate number of openable windows, even if they are sealed initially to balance a mechanical ventilation system.

Buildings which are predominantly naturally ventilated but require some mechanical ventilation to boost ventilation rates during peak conditions (e.g. maximum occupancy levels and/or peak temperatures) can still be awarded the credit provided that the ventilation modelling shows that the mechanical ventilation is only required during a period that is equal to or less than 5 per cent of the annual occupied hours.

EVIDENCE TO BE PROVIDED FOR DESIGN STAGE ASSESSMENT:
- A copy of the building's specification clauses or contract requirements and drawings showing the natural ventilation requirement.
- A letter from the design team confirming details of the ventilation strategy with calculations or results from software demonstrating how the required performance will be achieved.
- Copies of any manufacturers' literature to support the potential for natural ventilation (e.g. window details confirming ventilation area).

EVIDENCE TO BE PROVIDED FOR POST-CONSTRUCTION STAGE ASSESSMENT:
Either
- As-constructed drawings, specifications, calculations, etc. confirming how the required performance standards have been achieved.

Or
- a letter from the design team or contractor confirming that the design has not changed since the design stage.

IMPLICATION FOR SHELL-ONLY DEVELOPMENTS: None

Pol03: Surface water run-off
(Surface water run-off criterion)

CREDITS AVAILABLE

2

INNOVATION CREDITS

0

The aim of this Issue criterion is to minimise the risk of localised flooding on and close to the site by avoiding, reducing and delaying the discharge of rainfall to public sewers and watercourses.

PREREQUISITES: A consultant must be appointed to carry out the necessary calculation and confirm that the performance standards described below can be achieved. This is normally the structural engineer, although a specialist hydrologist might have to be appointed if the project's structural engineer does not have this expertise.

MINIMUM STANDARDS: None

PERFORMANCE STANDARD REQUIRED: One credit can be awarded where the drainage system is designed so that:

- the site's peak rate of run-off is no greater for the developed site than it was for the pre-developed site in relation to one-year and 100-year return period events
- calculations include an allowance for climate change in accordance with best practice planning guidance – currently *Planning Policy Statement 25: Development and Flood Risk.*[17]

Where a site's impermeable paving area discharging to a watercourse or surface water drainage system decreases or remains the same from pre- to post-development, the above credit can be awarded by default. While flow calculations are not necessary, the following must be provided:

- drawings indicating pre- and post-development areas of impermeable paving
- measurements of areas of pre- and post-development impermeable paving
- a Flood Risk Assessment which identifies any opportunities for reducing surface water run-off.

If the site includes new non-adoptable highways, these must be taken into account within the calculations for a site's peak and volume run-off rates. However, the following highways can be excluded from the calculations:

- existing highways
- new adoptable highways.

One credit can be awarded, independently of the other credit, where it is shown that the site will not flood in the event of a local drainage system failure (caused by either extreme rainfall or lack of maintenance) and the following can be shown:

Either

- The post-development run-off volume, over a development's life time, is no greater than it would have been prior to development,

plus

- any additional predicted volume of run-off from the 100-year six-hour event must be prevented from escaping from the site by the use of an infiltration design or another sustainable drainage scheme (SuDS) technique.

→

Pol03: Surface water run-off (Surface water run-off criterion) (continued)

Or

- the appropriate consultant must explain why the above criteria cannot be achieved and show that the post-development peak run-off is reduced to a limiting discharge level that equals either:
  - the pre-development one-year peak flow rate **or**
  - the mean annual flow rate (Qbar) **or**
  - two litres per second per hectare.
- Calculations must include an allowance for climate change in accordance with best practice planning guidance – currently *Planning Policy Statement 25: Development and Flood Risk.*[17]

With regard to both of the above, where the building being assessed forms part of a larger development or site:

- each building can be dealt with on an individual basis, with its own dedicated catchment area that serves only that building
- where a number of buildings are being assessed, the drainage from the sub-catchment areas serving all the buildings must be considered
- the whole development or site must be assessed for compliance.

Other issues that must be considered are detailed below:

- Sites which have been derelict for five years or more require a reasonable assessment of their previous drainage network, flow rates and volumes to be made by the consultant undertaking the calculations.
- Where rainwater harvesting systems are used to reduce flood risk, BS8515: *Rainwater Harvesting Systems – Code of Practice* Annex A should be used for the calculations and the exceedance flow route capacity provided in accordance with CIRIA report C635 should ignore the beneficial effect of the rainwater harvesting system.

INNOVATION CREDITS: None

BUILDING-TYPE VARIATIONS: Where self-contained dwellings in multi-residential buildings are assessed using the Code for Sustainable Homes (CSH), and the requirements of CSH Issues Sur 1 and Sur 2[18] are met, BREEAM credits can be awarded if the whole site is compliant.

CONSEQUENTIAL IMPACTS ON DESIGN/TIPS: Guidance on how to calculate a site's peak run-off rate can be obtained from the following sources:

- the *SUDS Manual*[19]
- DEFRA/Environment Agency's *Preliminary Rainfall Runoff Management for Developments*[20]
- the Institute of Hydrology's Report 124, *Flood Estimation for Small Catchments*[21]
- the Centre for Ecology and Hydrology's *Flood Estimation Handbook.*[22]

However, the peak run-off rate and volume run-off criteria are deemed to be met if a site discharges rainwater directly to a tidal estuary or into the sea.

EVIDENCE TO BE PROVIDED FOR DESIGN STAGE ASSESSMENT: In addition to evidence from the consultant carrying out the calculations that they hold appropriate qualifications to comply with the BREEAM requirements, the consultant should provide a report including:

→

Pol03: Surface water run-off (Surface water run-off criterion) (continued)

- the type and storage volume of the drainage measures on the site
- the total area of hard surfaces
- peak and volume flow rates (in litres per second) pre- and post-development for the period return events required
- confirmation of the additional allowance for climate change designed into the drainage system
- the impact on the building of flooding from a local drainage system failure.

EVIDENCE TO BE PROVIDED FOR POST-CONSTRUCTION STAGE ASSESSMENT: Evidence is required to confirm that maintenance responsibilities have been defined for any SuDS solutions installed and:

either

- written confirmation from the developer or consultant that the solutions assessed at the design stage have been implemented

or

- where the design has changed, evidence for the design stage assessment or as-constructed details are provided.

IMPLICATION FOR SHELL-ONLY DEVELOPMENTS: None

4.3 Issues requiring the client to instruct the design team to undertake additional activities outside their normal terms of appointment

The one Issue and three parts of Issue criteria described below all require the client to instruct the design team to undertake additional activities that their normal terms of appointment are unlikely to include. It can be seen from Table 4.6 that these Issues can generally only contribute 1 or 2 per cent towards a final BREEAM score. As discussed above, while the issues address important aspects, their limited impact can make failure to achieved their performance standards less critical than in the case of credits from other Issues.

TABLE 4.6: Issues that require the client to instruct the design team to undertake additional activities outside their normal appointment terms

	Commercial buildings		Non-housing buildings							
	Offices	Retail	Industrial	Educational (schools)	Educational (higher education)	Healthcare	Prisons	Courts	Multi-residential buildings	Other buildings
Management Category										
Man04: Stakeholder participation (Consultation criterion)	1	1	1	1	1	1	1	1	1	1
Man04: Stakeholder participation (Post-occupancy evaluation/information dissemination criterion)	1	1	1	1	1	1	1	1	1	1
Weighted % value of the above credits to the final BREEAM score	1.09	1.09	1.09	1.09	1.09	1.09	1.09	1.09	1.09	1.09
Health and Wellbeing Category										
Hea01: Visual comfort (Visual arts criterion)	0	0	0	0	0	1	0	0	0	0
Weighted % value of the above credits to the final BREEAM score	0.00	0.00	0.00	0.00	0.00	0.83	0.00	0.00	0.00	0.00
Energy Category	No Issues in this category are considered in Chapter 4									
Transport Category										
Tra04: Maximum car parking capacity	2	0	2	0	2	1	0	0	2	2
Weighted % value of the above credits to the final BREEAM score	1.78	0.00	1.78	0.00	1.45	0.80	0.00	0.00	1.78	1.45
Water Category	No Issues in this category are considered in Chapter 4									
Materials Category	No Issues in this category are considered in Chapter 4									
Waste Category	No Issues in this category are considered in Chapter 4									
Land Use and Ecology Category	No Issues in this category are considered in Chapter 4									
Pollution Category	10% weighting towards BREEAM score									
Overall % value of Issues considered in Chapter 4 towards the overall BREEAM score	2.87	1.09	2.87	1.09	2.55	2.72	1.09	1.09	2.87	2.55

Man04: *Stakeholder participation (Consultation criterion)*

CREDITS AVAILABLE

1

INNOVATION CREDITS

0

The aim of this Issue criterion is to assist in delivering accessible and inclusive buildings through consultation with those people or organisations affected by the proposed building.

PREREQUISITES: The consultation process should occur during the preparation of the design brief; normally during RIBA Preparation Stage B (Design Brief).

MINIMUM STANDARDS: None

PERFORMANCE STANDARD REQUIRED: One credit can be awarded where the relevant people or organisations who will be affected by the proposed building are identified and consulted during preparation of the design brief. A Consultation Plan has to be developed outlining how and when the consultation process will happen and how the relevant people or organisations will be kept informed during the development's progress.

Relevant people or organisations include:
- actual or potential building users (if known) including facility management staff
- groups representing the community in which the development will take place
- organisations with knowledge of the proposed building type
- potential users of any shared facilities within a proposed building
- local or national heritage groups (to ensure that any historic features or buildings are protected).

The consultation process has to include the following aspects:
- impacts of the proposed building, including functionality, buildability and aesthetics
- what facilities should be provided, both within and outside the building for its occupants, visitors and users
- management and operational implications of the design
- impacts on the local community arising from a building's design and construction
- opportunities for any shared use of the building facilities and new infrastructure by the local community
- confirmation that any statutory consultation has been or will be undertaken.

During the RIBA Design Stages C–D, feedback must be given to the relevant people or organisations explaining how the consultation has influenced the design.

INNOVATION CREDITS: None

→

BUILDING-TYPE VARIATIONS: Certain people or organisations are relevant to specific building types as follows:

- For educational buildings – representatives of the Board of Governors, local education authority, etc.
- For buildings containing complex environments (e.g. laboratories) – specialist service or maintenance contractors.

Some performance standards are specific to certain building types:

- Education, healthcare, law court and major transport node buildings – an independent third-party review of the proposed development must be carried out during the preparation of the brief in RIBA Stage B and RIBA Design Stages C–D using methods such as the Design Quality Indicator[23] or the Achieving Excellence Design Evaluation Toolkit in the case of healthcare buildings.[24]
- Healthcare buildings – additionally, consultation must be undertaken between the design team and the client or senior management and staff representatives during RIBA Design Stage K (Construction to Practical Completion) using the Good Corporate Citizen model[25] and a minimum score of six achieved. There must also be a commitment from the client, facility manager or senior management to reassess the development annually using the Good Corporate Citizen model, review policies and strategies covered by the model and report back to the NHS Trust Board.

CONSEQUENTIAL IMPACTS ON DESIGN/TIPS: The level of consultation required for this Issue is greater than the usual degree of formalisation of the client's brief. If the credit for this criterion is to be awarded, it is important that the architect and other consultants agree with the client that this level of service is reflected in their terms of appointment.

EVIDENCE TO BE PROVIDED FOR DESIGN STAGE ASSESSMENT:

- A list of the people or organisations consulted.
- The Consultation Plan.
- Agendas and minutes of consultation meetings.
- Reports demonstrating how consultation feedback was subsequently acted on.
- For healthcare buildings, Good Corporate Citizen documentation and reviewing and reporting commitments.

EVIDENCE TO BE PROVIDED FOR POST-CONSTRUCTION STAGE ASSESSMENT: As for the design stage assessment, updated as necessary and, for healthcare buildings, evidence that the Good Corporate Citizen review and reporting procedures are in place.

IMPLICATION FOR SHELL-ONLY DEVELOPMENTS: None

Man04: Stakeholder participation (Post-occupancy evaluation and information dissemination criterion)

CREDITS AVAILABLE

1

INNOVATION CREDITS

0

The aim of this Issue criterion is to assist in delivering accessible and inclusive buildings by undertaking a post-occupancy evaluation (POE) to gain building performance feedback.

PREREQUISITES: None

MINIMUM STANDARDS: None

PERFORMANCE STANDARD REQUIRED: One credit can be awarded where the client commits to undertaking a POE one year after the building is completed. The POE must be carried out by an independent third party and must cover the following:

- A review of the design, procurement, construction and handover processes.
- Feedback from a wide range of building users and the facilities management team on:
  - the building's internal environmental conditions (temperature, air quality, light, noise)
  - control of these conditions
  - facilities and amenities
  - access and layout
  - other relevant issues.
- The sustainability performance of the building (energy and water consumption, performance of sustainable features and technologies, including materials, low- or zero-carbon technologies, rainwater harvesting, etc.).

The client must also make a commitment to disseminate information on the building's post-occupancy performance, to share good practice and lessons learned, on:

either
- the client or building owner's website through publicly available literature or a press release

or
- an industry sector, government or local authority sponsored website.

INNOVATION CREDITS: None

BUILDING-TYPE VARIATIONS: None

CONSEQUENTIAL IMPACTS ON DESIGN/TIPS: When buildings do not perform as planned, there are impacts on their running costs and on staff satisfaction and performance. For repeat construction clients, learning from the past can be very important. Although undertaking a POE involves costs, it can be a cost-effective way of correcting mistakes in design and commissioning of buildings in the future, resulting in improved workplace productivity.

→

Man04: Stakeholder participation (Post-occupancy evaluation and information dissemination criterion)
(continued)

Further information on POEs can be obtained from the BRE's website[26] and the Usable Building Trust.[27]

EVIDENCE TO BE PROVIDED FOR DESIGN STAGE ASSESSMENT: A signed and dated commitment from the client, or future building occupier, to undertake the POE.

EVIDENCE TO BE PROVIDED FOR POST-CONSTRUCTION STAGE ASSESSMENT: A signed and dated commitment from the client, or future building occupier, to undertake the POE.

IMPLICATION FOR SHELL-ONLY DEVELOPMENTS: The client can demonstrate compliance, and be awarded the full credit, by making the POE part of a tenancy lease or by developer and tenant collaboration, but the client or developer must be involved in the POE exercise.

Hea01: Visual comfort (*Visual arts* criterion)

CREDITS AVAILABLE

1

INNOVATION CREDITS

0

The aim of this Issue criterion is to assist in providing a best practice visual environment and comfort for building users through implementing an art strategy in healthcare buildings only.

PREREQUISITES: All fluorescent and compact fluorescent lamps must be fitted with high-frequency ballasts.

MINIMUM STANDARDS: For any BREEAM rating, all fluorescent and compact fluorescent lamps must be fitted with high-frequency ballasts.

PERFORMANCE STANDARD REQUIRED: One credit can be awarded where:
Either
- an art coordinator is appointed to the development, who:
    - holds a relevant qualification in an arts-related subject
    - has at least two years' experience relating to the application of arts in a social context
    - is solely dedicated to the project or is working on similar projects.
Or
- an art policy or strategy is prepared and endorsed at senior management level during RIBA Stage B (Design Brief), which addresses the following issues:
    - enhancing the healthcare environment
    - building relationships with the local community, patients and their families

→

- relieving the anxiety of both patients and their families through interventions in treatment and recovery areas
- inclusion of living plants
- generating creative opportunities for staff through training.

INNOVATION CREDITS: None

BUILDING-TYPE VARIATIONS: This Issue criterion only applies to healthcare buildings.

CONSEQUENTIAL IMPACTS ON DESIGN/TIPS: It is not necessary for the project being assessed to have an art coordinator allocated to it exclusively. The art coordinator can work on several projects, or with several establishments run by the same Health Trust. This might reduce the cost of achieving this credit as the art coordinator's fees can be spread across a number of projects.

EVIDENCE TO BE PROVIDED FOR DESIGN STAGE ASSESSMENT: Copies of correspondence from the design team or Health Trust confirming the appointment of the art coordinator or a copy of the Trust's arts policy and strategy document.

EVIDENCE TO BE PROVIDED FOR POST-CONSTRUCTION STAGE ASSESSMENT:
Either
- Documentation demonstrating the work of the appointed art coordinator and confirmation of their qualifications and experience
Or
- a copy of the Trust's arts policy and strategy document.

IMPLICATION FOR SHELL-ONLY DEVELOPMENTS: None

Tra04: Maximum car parking capacity

CREDITS AVAILABLE

1 or 2
(depending on building type)

INNOVATION CREDITS

0

The aim of this Issue criterion is to encourage the use of non-car travel by restricting the number of car parking spaces on a site.

PREREQUISITES: None

→

MINIMUM STANDARDS: None

PERFORMANCE STANDARD REQUIRED: One credit can be awarded for the following building types, where the number of parking spaces is not greater than the figure indicated:
- Public (non-housing) buildings – healthcare hospital buildings (acute, specialist, teaching,
  mental health) – one parking space per:
  - four members of staff
  plus
  - one parking space per four beds
  plus
  - two parking spaces per consulting, examination, treatment or therapy room and accident
    and emergency cubicle.
- Public (non-housing) buildings – GP surgeries, health centres and community hospitals: one
  parking space per:
  - two medical staff
  plus
  - one parking space per three non-medical staff
  plus
  - two parking spaces per consulting, examination, treatment or therapy room and accident
    and emergency cubicle.

Up to two credits can be awarded for the following building types, depending on the number of
building users and the Accessibility Index (AI), as indicated in Table 4.7 (overleaf):
- Commercial buildings – office and industrial buildings.
- Multi-residential buildings – student residences, key worker accommodation, sheltered hous-
  ing, care homes and supported housing for the disabled.
- Public (non-housing) buildings – further and higher education buildings.
- Other buildings – transport type 1 and 2 buildings and MOD buildings (where building users
  are living-out personnel).

The following types of car parking spaces are excluded from the calculation to determine credits
in relation to this Issue:
- disabled
- mother/parent and child
- motorbike
- car-share spaces (the building occupier will have to confirm that they have an enforceable
  car-share policy).

Unless the design team can provide evidence of the number of building users, the default occupancy rates given in Table 7-1 in the online *Technical Manual*[6] should be used to calculate the
number of building users. Building users, depending on building type, are defined as:
- staff – those who work in a building
- students – those who access a building for study during an academic term or day
- residents – those who live in a building permanently or for a short period of time.

→

TABLE 4.7: *Tra04: Maximum car parking capacity* – credit allocation, © BRE Global Ltd 2011

Building type	Building's Accessibility Index			Number of credits
	<4	≥4 – <8	≥8	
	Maximum car parking capacity = 1 space per number of building users (X), where X is:			
Commercial buildings – offices and industrial	3	4	5	1
Multi-residential buildings – student residences and key worker accommodation	4	5	6	2
Multi-residential buildings – sheltered housing, care homes and supported	4	5	6	1
housing for the disabled	5	6	7	2
Public (non-housing) buildings – further and higher education buildings	15	20	25	1
	20	25	30	2
Other buildings – transport types 1 and 2	3	4	5	1
	4	5	6	2
Other buildings – MOD buildings (where building users are living-out personnel)	2	3	4	1
	3	4	5	2

Note: 'Other buildings, transport type 1' is a building predominantly occupied by staff with occasional business-related
    visitors/users (check with BREEAM Assessor).
    'Other buildings, transport type 2' is a building occupied by a number of core staff with a large number of
    consistently frequent visitors/users, either resident or non-resident (check with BREEAM Assessor).

Where the assessed building is part of a wider development and parking is not designated to individual buildings, compliance is assessed:
either
- on the basis of the car parking capacity of the whole development
or
- on the basis of the car parking allocated on a pro-rata basis to each building type.

INNOVATION CREDITS: None

BUILDING-TYPE VARIATIONS: This Issue is not assessed for the following building types:
- commercial buildings – retail
- public (non-housing) buildings – pre-schools, schools, sixth-form colleges, prison buildings, courts
- other buildings – buildings specifically required to be located rurally (e.g. National Park visitor centre) occupied by a core number of staff with a large number of consistently frequent visitors or users, either resident or non-resident, and transport hubs.

→

CONSEQUENTIAL IMPACTS ON DESIGN/TIPS: The architect must clarify the client's car parking requirement as early as possible in the design process. This often exceeds the performance standard for this Issue for commercial reasons.

EVIDENCE TO BE PROVIDED FOR DESIGN STAGE ASSESSMENT:
- Drawings or specification clauses or contract documentation confirming numbers and types of car parking spaces.
- Correspondence from the design team or client confirming the number of building users.
- Confirmation of the building's AI as calculated for *Tra01: Public transport accessibility*.
- For healthcare buildings, correspondence from the design team or client confirming:
  - the number of patient and residential beds

  plus
  - the number of consulting, examination, treatment, therapy and accident and emergency rooms.

EVIDENCE TO BE PROVIDED FOR POST-CONSTRUCTION STAGE ASSESSMENT:
- The Assessor's site inspection report, photographic evidence and as-constructed drawings confirming the number and type of parking spaces provided.
- Correspondence from the design team, client or building occupier confirming the number of building users or a physical check by the Assessor of the number of building users, if practicable.

IMPLICATION FOR SHELL-ONLY DEVELOPMENTS: None

4.4 Issues which are building-type specific

There are three Issues and one Issue criterion within the Energy and Health and Wellbeing Categories described below which are building-type specific and/or specific as the result of the inclusion of certain types of facilities, such as laboratories. It can be seen from Table 4.8 that the contribution of these Issues is variable as they impact on some building types and not on others. The potential impact on higher education buildings or other buildings with laboratories and cold storage systems can be as high as a 6 per cent contribution to the final BREEAM score.

TABLE 4.8: Issues that are building-type specific

	Commercial buildings			Non-housing buildings						
	Offices	Retail	Industrial	Educational (schools)	Educational (higher education)	Healthcare	Prisons	Courts	Multi-residential buildings	Other buildings
Management Category	No Issues in this category are considered in Chapter 4									
Health and Wellbeing Category										
Hea02: Indoor air quality (*Laboratory fume cupboards* criterion)	0	0	0	1	2	2	0	0	0	2
Weighted % value of the above credits to the final BREEAM score	0.00	0.00	0.00	0.88	0.88	0.83	0.00	0.00	0.00	0.94
Energy Category										
Ene05: Energy-efficient cold storage	0	2	2	0	2	2	0	0	0	2
Ene07: Energy-efficient laboratory systems	0	0	0	1	5	0	0	0	0	5
Ene08: Energy-efficient equipment	2	2	2	2	2	2	2	2	2	2
Weighted % value of the above credits to the final BREEAM score	1.41	3.17	3.17	2.04	5.43	3.17	1.46	1.46	1.41	5.43
Transport Category	No Issues in this category are considered in Chapter 4									
Water Category	No Issues in this category are considered in Chapter 4									
Materials Category	No Issues in this category are considered in Chapter 4									
Waste Category	No Issues in this category are considered in Chapter 4									
Land Use and Ecology Category	No Issues in this category are considered in Chapter 4									
Pollution Category	No Issues in this category are considered in Chapter 4									
Overall % value of Issues considered in Chapter 4 towards the overall BREEAM score	1.41	2.53	2.53	2.92	6.65	4.20	1.46	1.46	1.41	6.76

Hea02: Indoor air quality
(Laboratory fume cupboards criterion)

CREDITS AVAILABLE

1 or 2

INNOVATION CREDITS

0

The aim of this Issue criterion is to encourage a healthy internal environment by the specification of appropriate ventilation of laboratory fume cupboards and containment areas.

PREREQUISITES: None

MINIMUM STANDARDS: None

PERFORMANCE STANDARD REQUIRED: One credit can be awarded for buildings containing fume cupboards which are manufactured and installed to comply with:
either
- BS EN 14175: Part 2 (2003) for general purpose fume cupboards
- BS7989 (2001) for re-circulatory filtration fume cupboards
- BS EN 12469 (2000) for microbiological safety cabinets

or
- for schools, sixth-form colleges and further education buildings with laboratories and fume cupboards for subjects up to A-level standard to Building Bulletin 88[28]
- where ducted fume cupboards are used, the discharge velocity from the extract fan stack must be ≥10 m/s to BS EN 14175: Part 2 (2003).

One credit can be awarded for buildings with Containment Level 2 and 3 laboratories where the following are provided:
- Ventilation systems constructed to best practice guidance in the Advisory Committee on Dangerous Pathogens' *Management, Design and Operation of Microbiological Containment Laboratories: Approved Code of Practice.*[29]
- Filters must be located outside these areas for ease of cleaning and replacement.
- An emergency button in each Containment Level 2 and 3 laboratory.
- Confirmation that individual fume cupboard locations and stack heights are in accordance with HMIP *Technical Guidance Note (Dispersion) D1.*[30]

INNOVATION CREDITS: None

BUILDING-TYPE VARIATIONS: This Issue criterion only applies to building types containing the laboratories and fume cupboards described above. Where a building does not contain fume cupboards, or Containment Level 2 and 3 laboratories, this Issue criterion will not be assessed.

CONSEQUENTIAL IMPACTS ON DESIGN/TIPS: Confirming that the performance standards have been achieved in relation to this Issue criterion is likely to be the responsibility of a specialist within the service engineer consultancy.

→

EVIDENCE TO BE PROVIDED FOR DESIGN STAGE ASSESSMENT: Copies of contract specification clauses, drawings confirming the design for the fume cupboards and/or Containment Level 2 and 3 laboratories are required.

EVIDENCE TO BE PROVIDED FOR POST-CONSTRUCTION STAGE ASSESSMENT: In addition to the Assessor's site inspection report and photographs:
- as-constructed drawings or specification confirming the installation of fume cupboards and Containment Level 2 and 3 laboratories as proposed at the design stage
- manufacturers' or suppliers' literature or letters confirming that fume cupboards have been manufactured and installed in accordance with the required performance standards.

IMPLICATION FOR SHELL-ONLY DEVELOPMENTS: None

Ene05: Energy-efficient cold storage

CREDITS AVAILABLE

2

INNOVATION CREDITS

1

The aim of this Issue criterion is to encourage the use of energy-efficient cold storage refrigeration systems to reduce operational greenhouse gas emissions.

PREREQUISITES: None

MINIMUM STANDARDS: None

PERFORMANCE STANDARD REQUIRED: The **first credit** can be awarded where the components and controls of cold storage refrigeration systems have been designed, installed and commissioned to:
- comply with the Code of Conduct for Reducing Carbon Emissions in the Retail Sector[31]
- use only cold storage refrigeration systems and components on the Enhanced Capital Allowances Energy Technology Products List[9]
- comply with the performance standards set out for *Man01: Sustainable procurement (Construction and handover criterion)*.

The **second credit** can be awarded where, in addition to the above, the cold storage refrigeration systems must meet the following standards:
- For retail buildings: emit fewer indirect greenhouse gas emissions (CO_{2e}) than a *baseline supermarket* by using the CO_{2e} saving technologies described in the Carbon Trust's *Refrigeration Road Map*.[32]

→

- For non-retail buildings: emit less CO_{2e} than an appropriate *alternative baseline system* with the same duty, service conditions and ancillary equipment. The design team must supply details of the alternative baseline system and confirm that the technologies included are typical of the building type.

Indirect greenhouse gas emissions must be calculated as described for total equivalent warming impact in Annex B of BS EN 378: *Part 1 – Refrigeration Systems and Heat Pumps and Environmental Requirements*. Additional guidance on undertaking these calculations can be found in *Guideline Methods of Calculation TEWI*.[33]

INNOVATION CREDITS: One Innovation credit can be awarded where, in addition to meeting the above performance standards, the refrigeration system installed is:

- described in the Future Technologies section of the Carbon Trust's *Refrigeration Road Map*[32]
- one that will achieve a saving in CO_{2e} emissions when compared with current technologies.

BUILDING-TYPE VARIATIONS: No additional variations besides those described above.

CONSEQUENTIAL IMPACTS ON DESIGN/TIPS: While the Carbon Trust's *Refrigeration Road Map*[32] was developed for use in the retail sector, many of the technologies it describes can be used in non-retail situations.

EVIDENCE TO BE PROVIDED FOR DESIGN STAGE ASSESSMENT: For the **first credit**:

- Contract specification clauses or a letter from the design specialist confirming that the specification of the cold storage refrigeration systems and components meet the required performance standards.
- Confirmation that the proposed cold storage refrigeration systems and components are on the Enhanced Capital Allowances Energy Technology Products List.[9]
- Evidence to demonstrate compliance with the performance standards of *Man01: Sustainable procurement* (*Construction and Handover* criterion).

For the **second** and the **Innovation credit**, in addition to the above, evidence must be provided:

- to confirm the savings in CO_{2e} emissions for the specified technology and how these savings will be achieved, including justification of assumptions and methods used for the calculations
- to show that the calculations have been carried out by an appropriately qualified professional.

EVIDENCE TO BE PROVIDED FOR POST-CONSTRUCTION STAGE ASSESSMENT: For the **first credit**:

- as provided at the design stage, updated to show any design changes.

For the **second** and the **Innovation credit**:

- as provided at the design stage, updated to show any design changes

plus

- confirmation of the installed technology.

IMPLICATION FOR SHELL-ONLY DEVELOPMENTS: Where the tenant will install the cold storage refrigeration systems, one of the Options 1, 2 or 3 (described in Chapter 2, section 2.11) can be used to assess compliance with the required performance standards.

Ene07: Energy-efficient laboratory systems

CREDITS AVAILABLE

1, 3 or 5

INNOVATION CREDITS

0

The aim of this Issue criterion is to minimise the CO_2 emissions from operational energy in laboratories, which can consume four times the energy of a typical office.

PREREQUISITES: None

MINIMUM STANDARDS: None

PERFORMANCE STANDARD REQUIRED: One credit can be awarded for schools, sixth-form colleges and further education buildings in the following circumstances:

- Where re-circulatory filter fume cupboards are used, in the majority of cases, instead of ducted fume cupboards. (The credit can still be awarded where ducted fume cupboards are specified if their use is required by the building's brief. This will occur in situations where laboratories require full extraction systems on health and safety grounds, due to the type of experiments being undertaken. Usually these will be laboratories undertaking research and development work, such as further education buildings.)
- Where the specification of fume cupboards in schools, sixth-form colleges and further education buildings teaching A-level subjects complies with Building Bulletin 88 and BS7989 (2001) in the case of re-circulatory fume cupboards and BS EN 14175: Part 2 (2003) for ducted fume cupboards.

One credit can be awarded for other building types with laboratories which address the following points:

- The performance standards set out for *Hea02: Indoor air quality* (*Laboratory fume cupboards and containment areas* criterion) are met.
- Average design air flow rates in fume cupboards need be no greater than 0.16 m³/second per linear metre of sash opening to fume cupboard.
- Measurement of volume flow rates in the exhaust ducts as they leave the laboratory boundary takes into account any reduction in (inward) fume cupboard leakage.
- Any reduction in air flow does not compromise the health and safety of laboratory occupants.

Where the area of the following laboratory plant or systems exceed the following figures, then additional credits can be awarded:

either

- **up to two additional credits** can be awarded if the laboratory area accounts for at least 10 per cent of the building's floor area

or

- **up to four additional credits** can be awarded if the area of the laboratories accounts for at least 25 per cent of the building area.

These additional credits are only awarded where best energy practices, from the list on page 207, are included and it can be demonstrated that:

- they will reduce the laboratory's total energy consumption by 2 per cent or more

→

- the health and safety of laboratory occupants are not compromised.

Only whole credits can be awarded for the following best energy practices, so generally two of the practices listed below must be included for at least one credit to be awarded:

- **One credit** if the specific fan power for various laboratory systems is equal to or better than the following:
    - for general supply air handing units with heating and cooling – 1.5 watts/litre per second
    - for general extract systems – 1.2 watts/litre per second
    - for local, ducted extract ventilations – 1.0 watts/litre per second
    - for containment area extract systems without High-Efficiency Particulate Air (HEPA) filtration – 1.5 watts/litre per second
    - for containment area extract systems with HEPA filtration – 2.5 watts/litre per second
    - for fume cupboard extract systems – 1.5 watts/litre per second.
- Specifying fume cupboards, in further education buildings, with an average design air flow rate greater than 0.12 m³/second per linear metre of sash opening – **half a credit**.
- Minimise room air change rates and overall ventilation flows by grouping together or isolating activities and equipment with high filtration/ventilation requirements – **half a credit**.
- Specifying heat recovery from exhaust air, while avoiding cross-contamination, or use of refrigerant or water cooling systems – **half a credit**.
- Specifying cooling recovery from exhaust air heat exchangers, while avoiding cross-contamination, or use of refrigerant or water cooling systems – **half a credit**.
- Grouping areas with cooling loads to take advantage of supply efficiencies and thermal transfer – **half a credit**.
- Specifying free cooling coils in chillers or dry air coolers for specific activities – **half a credit**.
- Matching supply with demand by using modularity, variable speed drives and pumps, etc. – **half a credit**.
- Specifying particle monitoring linked to air flow controls – **half a credit**.
- Achieving a high level of diversity in central plant laboratory duct sizing – **half a credit**.
- Reducing air change rates by matching ventilation air flows to environmental needs and demands of containment – **half a credit**.

INNOVATION CREDITS: None

BUILDING-TYPE VARIATIONS: No additional variations besides those described above.

CONSEQUENTIAL IMPACTS ON DESIGN/TIPS: Teaching facilities and other laboratories or workshops with a limited number of fume cupboards and containment provisions, or no energy-intensive equipment, where energy consumption is no more than 50 per cent higher than the typical office benchmark (as set out in CIBSE Technical Memorandum TM 46) can be excluded. When calculating laboratory areas the following should also be excluded:

- support offices
- meeting rooms
- storage
- ancillary and other support areas with low service requirements.

→

EVIDENCE TO BE PROVIDED FOR DESIGN STAGE ASSESSMENT: For schools, sixth-form colleges and further education buildings:

- copies of drawings and contract specification clauses

and/or

- copies of suppliers' or manufacturers' literature confirming compliance with the above performance standards.

For other building types, including higher education buildings:

- evidence to demonstrate compliance with the performance standards for *Hea02: Indoor air quality* (*Laboratory fume cupboards and containment areas* criterion)
- confirmation from the design team of how the above performance standards have been achieved

plus

- the modelling or calculations and manufacturers' literature confirming compliance.

EVIDENCE TO BE PROVIDED FOR POST-CONSTRUCTION STAGE ASSESSMENT: For schools, sixth-form colleges and further education buildings:

- copies of as-constructed drawings and specification clauses

and/or

- copies of suppliers' or manufacturers' literature confirming that installed systems comply with the above performance standards.

For other building types, including higher education buildings:

- as-constructed evidence to demonstrate installed compliance with the performance standards for *Hea02: Indoor air quality* (*Laboratory fume cupboards and containment areas* criterion)
- a commissioning report on the installed systems demonstrating that stipulated design performance and air flows have been achieved.

IMPLICATION FOR SHELL-ONLY DEVELOPMENTS: None

Ene08: Energy-efficient equipment

CREDITS AVAILABLE

2

INNOVATION CREDITS

0

The aim of this Issue criterion is to encourage the procurement of energy-efficient equipment to provide optimum performance and operational unregulated energy savings.

PREREQUISITES: None

→

MINIMUM STANDARDS: None

PERFORMANCE STANDARD REQUIRED: Two credits can be awarded where any of the functions or equipment described below:
- are present in the completed building
- could be responsible for a *significant majority* of the unregulated energy used within the completed building
- comply with the specified detailed compliance performance standards.

The range of qualifying functions or equipment includes the following:
- Small power, plug-in equipment, including computers and their monitors, scanners, photocopiers, printers, etc. which qualify for:
  - the Enhanced Capital Allowances Scheme[9]
  - award of an Energy Star[34]
  - a Government Buying Standard[35] in terms of its procurement
  - green tick standard from Buying Solutions.[36]
- Swimming pools which are installed with approved covers and where the air temperature of the pool area is only 1°C above the water temperature.
- Communal laundry areas that use heat recovery from waste water and greywater in washing processes and in which the equipment qualifies for the Enhanced Capital Allowance Scheme.[9]
- Data centres (e.g. server rooms and communications equipment including cooling equipment) designed to meet the Best Practices standard of the EU Code of Conduct on Data Centres[37] **plus** with temperature set points that are not less than 24°C (measured at the location of the equipment racks).
- IT-intensive operating areas (areas where more than one computer per 5 m^2 is provided; for example, training suites, design studios and IT areas) that use natural ventilation and cooling strategies, with forced ventilation only activated when internal temperatures exceed 20°C and active cooling if internal temperatures exceed 24°C, **plus** automatic power-down when equipment is not in use.
- In residential areas, appliances including washing machines, fridges and freezers, tumble dryers and dishwashers that are recommended by the Energy Saving Trust.[38]
- For healthcare equipment, where the procurement of large-scale equipment and sets (50 plus) of electrical equipment is determined by life-cycle costing as detailed in EnCO$_2$de Chapter 3.0.[39] **Plus**, for each piece of equipment, at least two 'fitness for purpose' options (i.e. functional criteria that the piece of equipment is required to meet) demonstrating better performance are analysed. The analysis considers direct running costs, indirect running costs (including administration costs), cost of disposal, spending to save, recyclability, improved manageability, energy performance, reduced harmful emissions to the atmosphere and improved services, comfort and productivity.
- Kitchen and catering facilities which can demonstrate that at least one energy measure outlined in Sections 8, 9, 11, 12, 13, 14 and 15 in *CIBSE Guide TM50*[40] has been incorporated.

The above must also meet the detailed compliance performance standards provided in the online *Technical Manual*.[6]

→

INNOVATION CREDITS: None

BUILDING-TYPE VARIATIONS: None

CONSEQUENTIAL IMPACTS ON DESIGN/TIPS: It is likely that the service engineer, in conjunction with the client or building occupier will have to check whether those functions or equipment will be present and whether they will meet the compliance criteria. This Issue is complicated by the fact that there is no authoritative definition of what is meant by a 'significant majority' of the unregulated energy. It is simply left to the judgement of the design team and the Assessor.

EVIDENCE TO BE PROVIDED FOR DESIGN STAGE ASSESSMENT:
- Contract specification clauses, design drawings and energy calculations.
- Manufacturers' product details.
- Evidence to show compliance with any of the Schemes required by the performance standards.

With respect to healthcare equipment:
- a life-cycle analysis report is required, detailing how this has informed the procurement of the equipment
- evidence confirming the 'fit for purpose' exercise and subsequent option selection.

EVIDENCE TO BE PROVIDED FOR POST-CONSTRUCTION STAGE ASSESSMENT:
- Manufacturers' product details.
- Evidence to confirm that installed equipment complies with the performance standards required.

With respect to healthcare equipment, as for the design stage, updated to show the as-installed status.

BUILDING-TYPE VARIATIONS: None

IMPLICATION FOR SHELL-ONLY DEVELOPMENTS: If all or any of the above equipment or plant is to be provided as part of the fit-out works, one of the Options 1, 2 or 3 (described in Chapter 2, section 2.11) can be used to assess compliance with the required performance standards.

References

1   Building Bulletin 98: *Briefing framework for secondary school projects* and Building Bulletin 99: *Briefing framework for primary school projects*, see: www.education.gov.uk/schools/adminandfinance/schoolscapital/ buildingsanddesign/a0010896/area-guidelines-for-schools-building-bulletin-82

2   British Board of Agrément certificates can be found at: www.bbacerts.co.uk/default.aspx

3   For the European Regulation on Classification, Labelling and Packaging of Substances and Mixtures, see: http://ec.europa.eu/environment/chemicals/ghs/index_en.htm

4   For information on UK Chemicals (Hazard Information and Packing for Supply) Regulations 2009, see: www.hse.gov.uk/chip/

5   For the Decorative Paint Directive 2004/42/CE, see: http://eur-lex.europa.eu/LexUriServ/LexUriServ.do?uri=OJ:L:2004:143:0087:0096:EN:PDF

6   BREEAM *New Construction: Non-Domestic Buildings – Technical Manual*, see: www.breeam.org/BREEAM2011SchemeDocument/

7   Standard Assessment Procedure can be viewed at: www.bre.co.uk/sap2009/page.jsp?id=1642

8   *Metric Handbook – Planning and Design Date*, 3rd edition (2008), edited by David Littlefield, Architectural Press, Oxford

9   For the Enhanced Capital Allowance Scheme, see: www.eca.gov.uk

10 BRE *Green Guide to Specification*, at: www.bre.co.uk/greenguide/podpage.jsp?id=2126. This can be accessed by anybody if they first register, by selecting:

    • a building type (e.g. commercial which includes office, retail and industrial buildings)

    • a main building element (e.g. external wall construction)

    • an individual element type that forms part of the chosen main building element (e.g. rendered or fairfaced blockwork cavity wall) and possibly another sub-element layer

    • a generic building element description with a Green Guide rating from A+ to E, which links to a detailed breakdown of its environmental impacts (including a 60-year $kgCO_2$ equivalent figure which is required for calculating how many points can be achieved).

    However, this can sometimes seem to be a long-winded process before the descriptions of the building elements are eventually reached.

11 For details on the UK Government's Timber Procurement Policy go to the Central Point of Expertise for Timber Procurement website, at: www.cpet.org.uk/uk-government-timber-procurement-policy/the-uk-government-policy/

12 For the Convention on International Trade in Endangered Species (CITES) of Wild Fauna and Flora appendices, see: www.cites.org/eng/app/index.shtml

13 For information on BRE Global's BES60001 certification scheme, see: www.greenbooklive.com/search/scheme.jsp?id=153

14 AggRegain, website run by WRAP, see: http://aggregain.wrap.org.uk/

15 The Institute of Refrigeration's Carbon Dioxide as a Refrigerant Code of Practice can be obtained from: www.ior.org.uk/ior_publication.php?pubid=ELEXMV2GAI

16 The Institute of Refrigeration's Ammonia Refrigeration Systems Code of Practice can be obtained at: www.ior.org.uk/ior_publication.php?pubid=STEXMVZ5AJ

17 For *Planning Policy Statement 25: Development and Flood Risk*, see: www.planningportal.gov.uk/planning/planningpolicyandlegislation/currentenglishpolicy/ppgpps/pps25

18 *Code for Sustainable Homes – Technical Guide* (November 2010), Department for Communities and Local Government, available at: www.communities.gov.uk/planningandbuilding/sustainability/codesustainablehomes/

19 *SUDS Manual* (C697), Construction Industry Research and Information Association (CIRIA): www.ciria.org.uk/suds/publications.htm

20 *Preliminary Rainfall Runoff Management for Developments* – R&D Technical Report W5-074/A/TR/1: Revision D (2005), Department for Environment, Farming and Rural Affairs and the Environment Agency: http://archive.defra.gov.uk/environment/flooding/documents/research/sc030219.pdf

21 Report No. 124, *Flood Estimation for Small Catchments* (1994), DCW Marshall and AC Bayliss, Institute of Hydrology: www.ceh.ac.uk/products/publications/documents/IH124FLOODESTIMATIONSMALLCATCHMENTS.PDF

22 *Flood Estimation Handbook* (2008), Centre for Ecology and Hydrology: www.hydrosolutions.co.uk/products.asp?categoryID=4668

23 The Design Quality Indicator method can be seen at: www.dqi.org.uk/website/default.aspa

24 The Achieving Excellence Design Evaluation Toolkit for Healthcare Building can be seen at: www.dh.gov.uk/en/Publicationsandstatistics/Publications/PublicationsPolicyAndGuidance/DH_082089

25 The Good Corporate Citizen assessment test method can be seen at: www.corporatecitizen.nhs.uk/

26 For information on post-occupancy evaluations, see: www.bre.co.uk/page.jsp?id=1793

27 Useful information on feedback techniques can be found on the Usable Building Trust's website at: www.usablebuildings.co.uk/

28 For Building Bulletin 88 – 'Fume cupboards in schools', see: www.education.gov.uk/publications/standard/publicationDetail/Page1/0112710271

29 The Advisory Committee on Dangerous Pathogens' *Management, Design and Operation of Microbiological Containment Laboratories: Approved Code of Practice*, see: http://books.hse.gov.uk/hse/public/saleproduct.jsf?catalogueCode=9780717620340

30 *Guidelines on Discharge Stack Heights for Polluting Emissions*, Her Majesty's Inspectorate of Pollution (now part of the Environment Agency) Technical Guidance Note (Dispersion) D1 (1993), ISBN 0 11 752794 7 (currently out of print)

31 Code of Conduct for Reducing Carbon Emissions in the Retail Sector (2011), Carbon Trust, British Refrigeration Association and Institute of Refrigeration, see: www.ior.org.uk/ior_general.php?r=OUK8BA622271

32 *Refrigeration Road Map – An Action Plan for the Retail Sector* (CTG021) (2010), The Carbon Trust, available at: www.carbontrust.co.uk/Publications/pages/publicationdetail.aspx?id=CTG021

33 *Guideline Methods of Calculation TEWI – Issue 2*, British Refrigeration Association, can be seen on the Federation of Environmental Trade Associations (FETA) website, at: www.feta.co.uk/bra/index.htm

34 For the Energy Star labelling scheme, see: www.energystar.gov/index.cfm?c=products.pr_find_es_products

35 For the Government Buying Standards, see: http://sd.defra.gov.uk/advice/public/buying

36 For the Buying Solutions website, see: www.buyingsolutions.gov.uk/aboutus/sustainability/sustainable-solutions/quickwins

37 For the EU Code of Conduct on Data Centres, see: http://re.jrc.ec.europa.eu/energyefficiency/html/standby_initiative_data%20centers.htm

38 For the Energy Saving Trust, see: www.energysavingtrust.org.uk/Home-improvements-and-products/Home-appliances

39 For the *Health Technical Memorable 07-02: EnCO2de, Making Energy Work in Healthcare*, Department of Health, see: www.dh.gov.uk/en/Publicationsandstatistics/Publications/PublicationsPolicyAndGuidance/DH_4131671

40 *CIBSE TM50: Energy Efficiency in Commercial Kitchens*, CIBSE: www.cibse.org/index.cfm?go=publications.view&item=450

chapter five

The cost of BREEAM

This chapter explores both the actual cost of an Assessment and the possible extra burdens it imposes on development costs. While there are inevitably costs involved, these do not have to be excessive and can offer good value for money.

5.1 The cost of undertaking an Assessment

As with most professional services, there are no fixed or standard fee scales for Assessors. Fees are determined by market competition so it is not possible to give even a ballpark rate for any job. Clients or their agent (often the architect) can ask a number of Assessors to quote for the type of Assessment needed (see Chapter 1 for contact details). A number of clients are now partnering with a number of Assessors to establish fixed fees for Assessments. Assessors will need some basic information on which to base their quotations, such as:

- the type, size and location of the building or development
- whether single or multiple buildings are to be assessed
- the time scale for the construction of the building or development to be assessed.

A typical scope of activities in an Assessor's quotation will include:

1. registering the project with BRE – which incurs a fee paid to BRE
2. attending and conducting a pre-assessment meeting – issuing minutes and/or a report, confirming what information is to be provided to achieve the agreed BREEAM target and identifying who will provide it
3. preparing a draft BREEAM Assessment Report to be issued to the client and design team
4. completing the design stage assessment – following receipt of any outstanding information requested in the draft assessment
5. submitting the draft assessment to BRE for checking prior to issue of the Interim BREEAM Certificate – for which BRE will charge a fee, payable on submission
6. forwarding the Interim BREEAM Certificate to the client
7. undertaking a site visit and attending a meeting, to assess the status of the completed works in order to determine what information is required to complete the post-construction stage assessment
8. preparing a draft Post-Construction Stage Assessment Report to be issued to the client, design team and principal contractor with recommendations on any additional information required to maintain the BREEAM rating achieved in the design stage assessment

9   completing the post-construction stage assessment – on receipt of the outstanding information

10   submitting the Assessment to BRE for checking so that they can issue the Final BREEAM Certificate – BRE will charge a fee for this, payable on submission

11   forwarding the Final BREEAM Certificate to the client.

Extra costs must be adequately set out in the quotation. For example, if printed copies of the completed Design Stage Assessment and Post-Construction Stage Assessment Reports are required, the costs should be included in a quotation. Other extra costs include BRE's certification fees and overheads, including BRE's annual licence registration fees.

Similarly, the quotation should include provisional costs, such as hourly rates for Assessors and the cost of site visits. Differences in quotations from Assessors will, among other things, reflect the charging rate of the Assessor and the efficiency of an organisation in undertaking and writing up the Assessments.

Undertaking only a post-construction stage assessment might achieve some small savings in an Assessor's costs but, as explained in Chapter 1, this is a very short-sighted approach to adopt. The small economic gain will not compensate for failing to achieve the BREEAM rating possible if the normal route of undertaking design stage and post-construction stage assessments is followed. It should also be noted that the BRE fees will be the same in either case.

While it is certainly true that a BREEAM Assessment for very large projects will cost more than for smaller projects, a similar fee can cover a fairly wide range of project values. This, unfortunately, has tended to mean that the proportion of the cost incurred by a BREEAM Assessment increases proportionally as a project's value decreases. The time required by the Assessor to check the information provided and to compile the Assessment might not vary significantly between projects of different sizes, since a £10 million project may have a similar level of complexity to a project half its value in terms of BREEAM Assessment criteria. An Assessor's fee may vary from as little as 0.001 per cent up to 1 per cent of a project's value. This has discouraged some clients from submitting very small projects for Assessment. It appears that BRE have recognised this problem and are currently developing a more cost-effective process for applying BREEAM 2011 to small buildings.

BRE's certification fees are payable when the Assessor registers the Assessment with BRE and when they submit both the design stage assessment and the post-construction stage assessment. There is also a separate range of fees covering registration and certification of BREEAM International Assessments.

As explained in Chapter 2, there are two ways in which Innovation credits can be awarded, either by:

• meeting the exemplary level of performance standards of certain Issues, as indicated in Table 2.3, or

• making an application to BRE Global to have a particular building feature, system or process recognised as being innovative.

This second approach will carry an additional cost, as BRE charges a flat rate fee for each Innovation credit application, currently £1,000 per application payable on submission. Should BRE refuse the Innovation credit application, the decision can be appealed, but this will incur an additional fee. Currently, this stands at £250 per application, which will be refunded should the appeal be successful.

The cost of an application for an Innovation credit must be added to the cost of providing the innovative solution when considering whether it is a cost-effective way of achieving an additional credit and the extra 1 per cent it will contribute to the Assessment's score. It might be more cost-effective to improve a building's performance standard in other ways and gain the additional credit from another Issue. As explained in Chapter 2, due to the weighting given to different categories some credits can be worth more than 1 per cent to the final BREEAM score.

5.2 The extra cost required to achieve a BREEAM Excellent rating

Not surprisingly, clients will want to know the cost of targeting a high BREEAM rating. While anecdotal views abound that it must cost more to achieve, say, a BREEAM Excellent rating, what actual evidence is there to support this belief?

One of the stated objectives of BREEAM is that it should be a driver to improve environmental standards in building design and construction. The standards set by BREEAM should always exceed those required by current Regulations. Figure 5.1 compares the number of buildings designed and constructed to levels of environmental performance set against a regulatory benchmark. Logically, any building which achieves a BREEAM rating would be placed to the right of the regulatory minimum benchmark in Figure 5.1. Buildings achieving BREEAM Excellent or Outstanding ratings will be further to the right again and at end of the graph are those buildings achieving exemplar sustainable standards. Cost consultants normally base their development cost projections on a building which just achieves compliance with the statutory regulations, unless requested to do otherwise. So, does it follow that a building that has to achieve an Excellent rating will cost more and, if so, how much more?

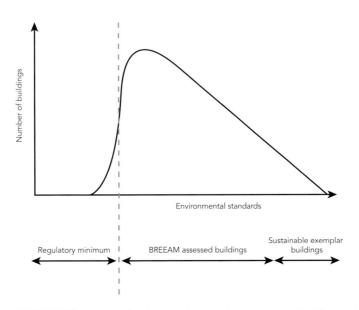

FIGURE 5.1: Comparison of environmental standards and numbers of buildings designed

There have been two major research studies which have tried to assess the cost implications of achieving various BREEAM ratings. The first of these was published by Cyril Sweett and the BRE in 2005. *Putting a Price on Sustainability*[1] looked at real cost data and identified a range of increases to capital costs that might be expected for various BREEAM ratings. It also identified additional costs associated with each incremental improvement in performance when moving up the scale of BREEAM ratings and the type of initiatives that had to be included in a project from its concept stage. In addition, they examined three separate site location scenarios, which were:

- **poor location sites** – where no location credits would be achieved
- **typical location sites** – where a selection of credits would be achieved for a brownfield site with some access to local public transport and amenities
- **good location sites** – where all the location credits were achievable.

Putting a Price on Sustainability[1] studied four building types – a house, a naturally ventilated office, an air conditioned office and a PFI healthcare centre. Although the results of the study are of interest, it should be remembered that the two offices were assessed using BREEAM Offices 2004, the healthcare centre using a BREEAM bespoke assessment and the house using EcoHomes 2003. Its principal conclusion, however, is still of interest:

major performance improvements can be achieved cheaply and even at no cost at all.[1]

The study of the Office Schemes showed the impact of a site's location on possible additional costs arising from an Assessment. Even on a poor location site, a BREEAM Good rating was achievable, for both naturally ventilated and air-conditioned offices, at either a minor reduction or increase in the capital costs (see Figure 5.2). To achieve a BREEAM Very Good rating on a poor location site will involve an increase in capital costs as follows:

- naturally ventilated offices – plus 2 per cent
- air-conditioned offices – plus 5.7 per cent.

On a typical location site, achieving a BREEAM Very Good rating results in a minor reduction in costs for naturally ventilated offices and a minor increase for air-conditioned offices. However, to achieve a BREEAM Excellent rating on typical location sites there were increased costs for both:

- naturally ventilated offices – plus 3.4 per cent
- air-conditioned offices – plus 7 per cent.

On good location sites, achieving a BREEAM Excellent rating reduced these costs as follows:

- naturally ventilated offices – plus 2.5 per cent
- air-conditioned offices – plus 3.3 per cent.

These figures reflect a perceived wisdom within the construction industry, that there is a cost premium to construct a BREEAM Excellent building. Experience also suggests that, over time, this premium reduces, after the introduction of a new BREEAM Scheme, as general design and construction standards improve and move closer to the level required for a BREEAM Excellent rating. When a new BREEAM Scheme is introduced, the performance standard required to achieve each

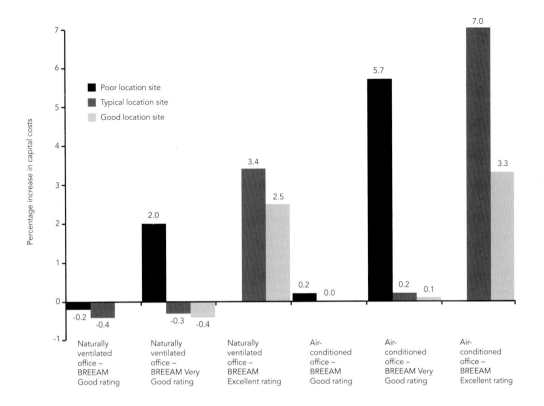

FIGURE 5.2: Comparing increases in capital costs for various BREEAM Offices 2004 ratings on poor location, typical location and good location sites

SOURCE: Figures taken from *Putting a Price on Sustainability,*[1] © BRE Global Ltd 2005

BREEAM rating is improved. So it is likely that the introduction of BREEAM 2011 will result in a premium being payable for BREEAM Excellent buildings. As mentioned in Chapter 1, however, there is now evidence to suggest that a BREEAM Excellent office can attract a 22–27 per cent premium on its rent.[2] This will offset the additional capital costs required to achieve the improved performance standards, if viewed in the longer term.

Subsequent to the Cyril Sweett study, Anna Surgenot (BREEAM Centre Sustainability Group) and Ian Buttress (Faithful and Gould) published *Putting a Price on Sustainable Schools* in 2008,[3] which studied a primary school and a secondary school. The study investigated the additional costs incurred in achieving a BREEAM Good, Very Good or Excellent ratings for:

- poor location sites – greenfield sites with poor transport links where no location credits would be achieved in an Assessment
- good location sites – brownfield sites with good transport links where a selection of location-based credits would be achieved in a BREEAM Assessment.

It was assumed that a good location site:

- had been previously developed
- was contaminated but had been treated
- had a transport node (with a frequent service) within 800 m
- was of no ecological value and the construction of the school did not have a negative impact on the ecological value of the site.

While *Putting a Price on Sustainable Schools*[3] concluded that BREEAM school ratings could be achieved at 'little extra cost, and even at no extra cost', reaching higher sustainability standards of performance did incur additional costs. This ranged from as little as one-fifth of one per cent for a secondary school on a good location site, to nearly 10 per cent in the case of a primary school on a poor location site. Unlike the above example of increased rents for offices, increased costs for state schools will be borne by public funding. This is why, during the Building Schools for the Future programme, the BREEAM target was only a Very Good rating.

Figure 5.3 indicates that the additional cost of achieving a Good rating and a Very Good rating for schools on good location sites is minimal (ranging between an increase of 0.2 per cent and 1.8 per cent). Additional costs are lower for secondary schools, which tend to be larger, than primary

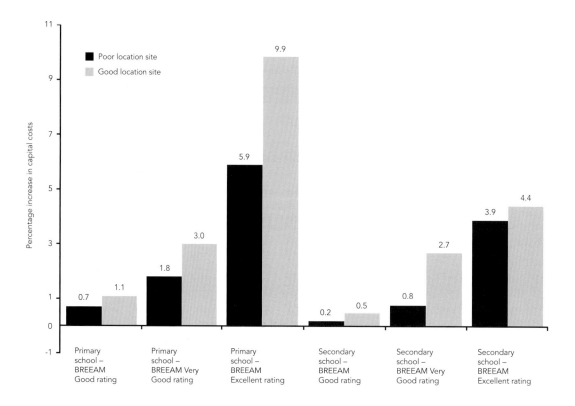

FIGURE 5.3: Comparing increases in capital costs for various BREEAM School ratings on poor location and good location sites

SOURCE: Figures taken from *Putting a Price on Sustainable Schools*,[3] © BRE Global Ltd 2008

schools, which are smaller, as the result of economies of scale. Even on poor location sites the additional cost of achieving a Very Good rating is no more than 3 per cent. The additional costs for achieving a BREEAM Excellent rating are higher, however, ranging between 3.9 per cent and 5.9 per cent (for secondary and primary schools respectively) for good location sites. This increases to 4.4 per cent and 9.9 per cent for poor location sites. The scale of the additional capital costs for the schools on good location sites is not dissimilar to that seen with offices, as discussed above. One of the conclusions drawn in *Putting a Price on Sustainable Schools*,[3] however, was that careful consideration of the design and specification at an early stage of a project helps to minimise any additional costs. This reinforces the recommendations described in Chapter 2 on how the requirements for credits can be achieved at the earliest possible stage.

Although these research papers are now over six and three years old respectively, they reach the following similar conclusions:

- location and site condition can have a major impact on costs
- effective management of the design and procurement process is critical in ensuring that low-cost options are identified and achieved
- costs can rapidly increase once all low-cost options have been implemented
- to minimise costs, sustainability must be considered at the earliest possible stage.

5.3 The cost impact of a site's location

The clear message is that it costs more to achieve a high BREEAM score for a poor location site. This is important, as around one-tenth of a potential score is dependent on a site's location.

Figure 5.2 shows that in achieving a BREEAM Very Good rating for both naturally ventilated and air-conditioned offices the difference in costs can be an increase of between 2.4 per cent and 5.6 per cent in relation to poor location sites, where no site location credits are achievable, and good location sites, where all site location credits can be achieved. While *Putting a Price on Sustainability*[1] does not cost the impact of achieving a BREEAM Excellent rating on poor location sites, it does indicate that the additional capital costs between developing a typical location site and a good location site is between 0.9 and 3.7 per cent. The increase in costs appears to be considerably lower for naturally ventilated offices than for air-conditioned offices. This might suggest that a move towards natural ventilation strategies for offices is a more cost-effective way of achieving a BREEAM Excellent rating. It should also not be forgotten that evidence suggests that BREEAM Excellent offices may command higher rents.

Figure 5.3 shows a similar story for schools, even if the scale of variation is different. For schools achieving a BREEAM Very Good rating, the additional capital costs for developing on poor location sites compared to good location sites are between 1.2 per cent and 1.9 per cent. For schools wanting to achieve a BREEAM Excellent rating, the additional capital cost is between 4 and 5.5 per cent.

5.4 Which credits cost more?

While the data in *Putting a Price on Sustainability*[1] and *Putting a Price on Sustainable Schools*[3] are now relatively old, they still offer insights into the cost of achieving one set of credits as opposed to another.

5.5 Principal contractor operating in an environmentally friendly manner to the benefit of the BREEAM Assessment

The research behind the two publications considered the additional capital costs of achieving performance standards similar to those required to award the credits from the following Issues.

- Man01: Sustainable procurement (*Construction and handover* and *Aftercare* criteria)
- Man02: Responsible construction practices
- Man03: Construction site impacts.

These Issues affect the Tender Specification and effectively require the principal contractor to operate in an environmentally friendly manner to the benefit of a BREEAM Assessment.

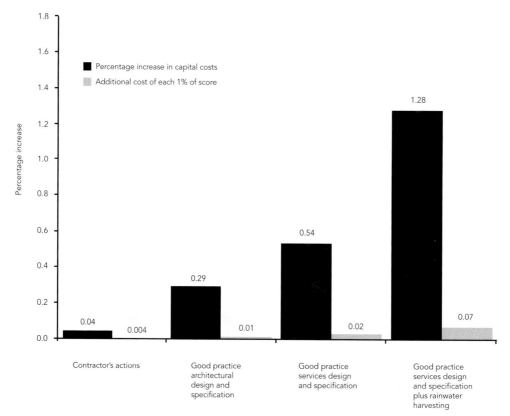

FIGURE 5.4: Increase in capital costs for quick win BREEAM Issues

SOURCE: Figures taken from *Putting a Price on Sustainability,*[1] © BRE Global Ltd 2005, and *Putting a Price on Sustainable Schools,*[3] © BRE Global Ltd 2008

The potential additional cost of these credits came to less than one-tenth of 1 per cent, as indicated in Figure 5.4. This seems to be a very cost-effective way of scoring around 6 per cent of an Assessment's score. While the associated costs of credit *Wst01: Construction waste management* were not considered by the studies, as they were not a BREEAM requirement at that time, many contractors are already actively reducing their site construction waste and increasing recycling and should, therefore, be able to meet the performance criteria required by BREEAM. This situation is being driven, among other reasons, by the need to avoid escalating landfill tax costs and some of these credits should be achievable without any overall additional costs.

5.6 Good practice architectural design and specification

The architect is normally responsible for just under half of those Issues, considered in Chapter 3, whose performance standards are easier to achieve by adopting good practice design and specifications. Of these, about 60 per cent, or those Issues whose standards are nearest, were costed in the research papers. The additional capital cost that is incurred from adopting all their requirements (with the minor exception of providing internal blinds) was under one-third of 1 per cent, as indicated in Figure 5.4. Another eighth-tenths of one-percent could be added from *Hea01: Visual comfort* (*Glare control and view out* criterion), arising from the cost of providing internal blinds. Of the remaining 70 per cent of Issues considered in Chapter 3, it could be argued that only two would normally attract additional capital costs. These are:

- *Hea06: Safety and security* (*Safe access* criterion) – if an additional access road is required
- *Mat02: Hard landscape and boundary protection* – if there is an additional cost in using recycled aggregates to ensure that the hardstanding areas achieve a Green Guide A or A+ rating.

Taking advantage of quick win good practice solutions to the architectural design and specification suggested in Chapter 3 will add around 10 per cent to a final BREEAM score at an additional cost of less than one-third of 1 per cent. This is a very cost-effective means of gaining credits.

5.7 Good practice services design and specification

The services engineer is normally responsible for just over half of those Issues considered in Chapter 3 whose performance standards are easier to achieve by adopting good practice design and specifications. Of these, around 75 per cent, or those Issues whose standards are nearest, were costed in the above research papers. The additional capital cost incurred in achieving the performance requirements of these Issues is just over half of 1 per cent (Figure 5.4). Of the remaining Issues not costed, only the following two Issues could incur additional costs:

- *Ene06: Energy-efficient transport systems*
- *Ene07: Energy-efficient laboratory systems.*

Again, it appears that adopting a good practice approach to the services design and specification is a cost-effective way of achieving just over 10 per cent of an Assessment's final score. In addition,

Putting a Price on Sustainability[1] considered that the reduction of water consumption by the specification of water-efficient sanitary ware was cost neutral. Also, the use of rainwater harvesting to reduce water consumption still further was found to incur an additional cost of between 0.3 and 0.9 per cent.

5.8 Reducing CO_2 emissions

Putting a Price on Sustainable Schools[3] also provides a potentially interesting insight into which low- and zero-carbon energy options may be the most cost-effective in generating additional credits from the following Issues:

- *Ene01: Reduction of CO_2 emissions* – through the reduction of energy demand and the use of low- or zero-carbon energy generation to increase a building's Energy Performance Ratio for New Construction (see Chapter 4 for details of how this is calculated)
- *Ene04: Low- and zero-carbon technologies* – through the reduction of CO_2 emissions from a building's regulated energy (see Chapter 4).

It shows that the additional cost in terms of fees of developing a renewable energy feasibility study, a prerequisite for gaining any BREEAM credits under *Ene04: Low- and zero-carbon technologies*, is extremely cost effective. It was, in fact, less than three-hundredths of 1 per cent.

Putting a Price on Sustainable Schools[3] investigated the following range of low- and zero-carbon energy options which might be used to reduce a building's CO_2 emissions and so gain additional credits against *Ene1: Reduction of CO_2 emissions*:

- ground source heat pumps for heating
- solar thermal panels for hot water
- photovoltaic panels for generating electricity
- biomass boiler for heating and hot water
- wind turbine for generating electricity.

The study provides a figure illustrating the amount by which each of the options reduces levels of carbon emissions (in $kgCO_2/m^2$ per annum) along with an additional capital cost figure in £/m². The information provided has been used to generate the graph in Figure 5.5. This shows that while the greatest reduction in CO_2 emissions (on a $kgCO_2/m^2$ per annum basis) usually came from the installation of photovoltaic panels to generate electricity, these panels were also the most expensive option and resulted in the greatest percentage increase in capital costs. The use of a biomass boiler to help to meet the heating and hot water demand, although a close second in terms of $kgCO_2/m^2$ per annum saved, was the second lowest in terms of additional costs.

The most useful aspect of Figure 5.5 lies in the possibility of extending the analysis to create a value representing the percentage increase in capital costs for each $kgCO_2/m^2$ per annum saved. This shows, again, that the most expensive option is the use of photovoltaic panels, followed by ground source heat pumps, solar thermal, wind turbines and finally (the least expensive) biomass boilers. While wind turbines seem to run biomass boilers a close second in terms of additional costs for each $kgCO_2/m^2$ per annum saved, there will be many instances where a site is simply not suitable

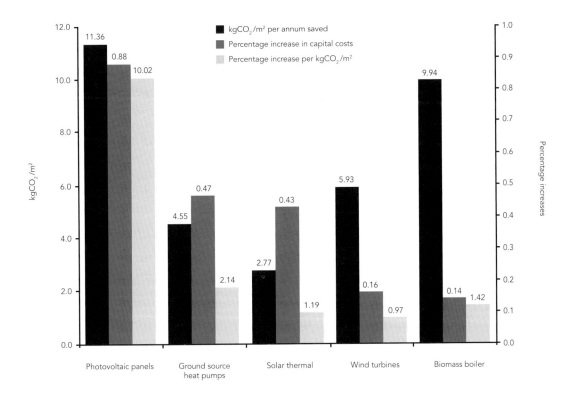

FIGURE 5.5: Increase in capital costs for low- and zero-carbon technologies
SOURCE: Figures taken from *Putting a Price on Sustainability*,[1] © BRE Global Ltd 2005, and
Putting a Price on Sustainable Schools,[3] © BRE Global Ltd 2008

for a medium to large wind turbine (reasons include the proximity of adjoining residential areas or the potential for wind turbulence from surrounding buildings). Even the use of a biomass boiler has to be considered in terms of the future availability of biomass fuel from local, sustainable sources, as well as the availability of storage space for the biomass fuel and its delivery. Judging from this analysis, the best options might finally be the use of the mid-range cost options of ground source heating and solar thermal panels.

Putting a Price on Sustainability[1] offers only a limited insight into cost-effective ways of reducing CO_2 emissions. The study of the air-conditioned office looks at the additional cost of reducing CO_2 emissions by using 100 m^2 of photovoltaic panels and 100 m^2 of solar thermal panels. The 100 m^2 of photovoltaic panels are likely to generate only 12,800 kWh during a typical year, which equates to a reduction in energy demand of approximately 1.27 kWh/m^2 per annum. This means that around 0.7 kgCO_2/m^2 per annum will be saved. The 100 m^2 of solar thermal panels will save around 0.6 kgCO_2/m^2 per annum, assuming around 50 per cent of the annual hot water demand of the office will be provided. This means that the photovoltaic panels and solar thermal panels save 1.3 kgCO_2/m^2 per annum for an additional capital cost of 1.77 per cent. This equates to an increase in capital costs of 1.36 per cent for each saved kgCO_2/m^2 per annum, reflecting the current expense of installing photovoltaic panels. This is similar to the findings in *Putting a Price on Sustainable Schools*.[3] Figure 5.5 suggests that using a combination of photovoltaic and solar thermal panels would result in a combined additional cost of 1.31 per cent for each saved $kgCO_2/m^2$ per annum, which is not necessarily the cheapest option.

The above figures do not take into account any potential income from the generation of electricity from photovoltaic panels through the government's Feed-in Tariff Scheme[4] or for the generation of heat through the proposed Renewable Heat Incentive.[5] This income can be used to offset the increase in capital costs of providing these technologies, significantly shortening their payback periods, depending on the terms of the schemes at the time of development.

5.9 Summary of cost impact of certain credits

The importance of developing a site that is in a good location in BREEAM terms is vital, with the potential to contribute around 10 per cent to a final score.

Also, targeting the BREEAM Issues described as 'quick wins' in Chapter 3 is a highly cost-effective way of achieving a large number of BREEAM credits. These Issues all fall into three main categories:

- actions by the main contractor
- taking a good practice approach towards the architectural design and specifications
- taking a good practice approach towards the building services design and specifications.

However, the additional costs of achieving credits relating to *Ene01: Reduction of CO$_2$ emissions* and *Ene04: Low- and zero-carbon technologies* are likely to be much more significant, depending on which approach to low- and zero-carbon energy generation is adopted.

It appears that around 35 per cent of a final BREEAM score might be achievable by targeting the quick wins on good location sites for an additional capital cost of just over 1.5 per cent. This equates to an additional cost of just six-tenths of 1 per cent for each additional 1 per cent added towards the value of a final BREEAM score (Figure 5.4). Obviously, it pays to be wary of gross generalisations, but this appears to be a cost-effective way of achieving around 60 per cent of the score needed for a Very Good rating and 50 per cent of the score needed for an Excellent rating. It also highlights the importance of recognising which quick wins can be achieved on a project at the earliest possible stage of the design process, allowing the design team time to identify those Issues in which the remaining credits can be targeted in the most cost-effective way.

References

1   Cyril Sweett and BRE Centre for Sustainable Construction (2005) *Putting a Price on Sustainability*, BRE Trust, Watford

2   Andrea Chegut, Piet Eichholtz and Nils Kok (July 2011) (Maastricht University) *The Value of green buildings: New Evidence from the United Kingdom.* Available at: www.sirp.se/l/getfile.ashx?cid=280784&cc=3&refid=34

3   Anna Surgenor and Ian Buttress (2008) *Putting a Price on Sustainable Schools*, BRE Trust, Watford

4   For details of the Government's Feed-in Tariff Scheme, see:
    http://www.ofgem.gov.uk/Sustainability/Environment/fits/Pages/fits.aspx

5   For details of the Government's Renewable Heat Incentive, see:
    http://www.ofgem.gov.uk/e-serve/RHI/Pages/RHI.aspx

Index